Keynes and the Quest for a Moral Science

Keynes and the Quest for a Moral Science

A Study of Economics and Alchemy

Wayne Parsons

Professor of Public Policy
Queen Mary, University of London

Edward Elgar
Cheltenham, UK • Northampton, MA, USA

Published by
Edward Elgar Publishing Limited
The Lypiatts
15 Lansdown Road
Cheltenham
Glos GL50 2JA
UK

Edward Elgar Publishing, Inc.
William Pratt House
9 Dewey Court
Northampton
Massachusetts 01060
USA

Paperback edition 2010

A catalogue record for this book
is available from the British Library

Library of Congress Cataloguing in Publication Data
Parsons, D. W.
        Keynes and the quest for a moral science: a study of economics
    and alchemy / Wayne Parsons
        Includes bibliographical references and index.
        1. Keynes, John Maynard, 1883–1946.   2. Keynesian economics.
    3. Economics—Moral and ethical aspects.   I. Title.
    HB103.K47P37 1997
    330.15'6—dc21   96–49722
                                                                              CIP

ISBN   978 1 85898 373 8 (cased)
        978 1 84980 291 8 (paperback)

Typeset by Manton Typesetters, 5–7 Eastfield Road, Louth, Lincolnshire LN11 7AJ, UK
Printed and bound in Great Britain by Marston Book Services Limited, Oxford

For my mother and father and
the possibilities for *their* grandchildren.

Nature is so keen and subtle in her operations that she cannot be dealt with except by a sublime and accurate mode of treatment. She brings nothing to the light that is at once perfect in itself, but leaves it to be perfected by man. This method of perfection is called Alchemy. So, whatever is poured forth from the bosom of Nature, he who adapts it to that purpose for which it is destined is an Alchemist.

Paracelsus (1493–1541)

The future will be what we choose to make it. If we approach it with cringing and timidity, we shall get what we deserve. If we march on with confidence and vigour the facts will respond.

Keynes (1883–1946)

In the history of human thinking the most fruitful developments frequently take place at those points where two different lines of thought meet ... hence if they actually meet, that is, if they are at least so much related to each other that a real interaction can take place, then one may hope that new and interesting developments may follow.

Heisenberg (1901–1976)

Contents

Preface and acknowledgements

If you are called to write a book, you will not fail to do so, even if it is delayed for sixty or seventy years, or even longer. If you carry it within you and turn it over in your mind you need not rush at it at once. It will not always remain within, it will have to come out ... Wait: the hour will strike. (Paracelsus, 1988: 115–6)

The precise use of language comes at a late stage in the development of one's thoughts. You can think accurately and effectively long before you can, so to speak, photograph your thoughts. (Keynes, in Rymes, 1989: 102)

Our conscious representations are sometimes ordered *before* they have become conscious to us. (von Franz, 1990: 308)

Keynes once wrote that his *General Theory of Employment Interest and Money* was the product of a struggle to escape, and without wishing to draw the slightest comparison between this book and the *General Theory*, it is important to preface the arguments which follow with the observation that they are also the outcome of a long struggle to escape, both from Keynesian economics and the economics of the 'new right' which supplanted it in the 1980s. Rather unusually for my generation I came to Keynes via Marshall, rather than through Samuelson or Lipsey and this fact has, I think, largely shaped and coloured how I first saw and how I continue to see his work and its theoretical and practical significance. Let me explain. On being told that I was to study economics in the sixth form I dutifully trotted off to my local library to find out more about it. The only book that was available which offered any guidance was Alfred Marshall's *Principles of Economics*. On finishing the *Principles* and having taken his advice to read J.S. Mill's *Principles of Political Economy*, together with some Ruskin and Malthus, I was utterly determined to become an economist. I was hungry to know more and at the back of the 1947 edition of the *Principles* were a few pages advertising other books published by Macmillan. Of the names mentioned there was one I vaguely recognized from history classes: 'The late Lord Keynes'. I went on to read the *Essays in Persuasion*, 'How to Pay for the War', *Essays in Biography* and *The Economic Consequences of the Peace* and eventually my researches that summer led me to buying (for the enormous sum of twenty five shillings!!) Harrod's biography and tracking down Keynes's talk on 'Art and the State' to the reading room of the splendid old central library in

Cardiff. By that time the course had begun and I waited eagerly to find out what the *General Theory* was really all about. When I did eventually come to the *General Theory* I read it through the lens of these other books. So, having read 'How to Pay for the War', and 'The Economic Possibilities for Our Grandchildren', and other writings in the context of Marshall, Mill, Ruskin and Malthus I could never see Keynes as a kind of technocrat or inflationist nor as the father of growth mania and deficit spending – which were some of the images hung around his neck in the 1970s – neither could I appreciate the 'normal science' which portrayed Keynes's economics as 'revolutionary' as to my mind the *General Theory* was always a book which had to be read as the natural successor to Malthus, Ruskin, Mill and Marshall, rather than as anything to do with modern economic textbooks. And yet at the same time, I found Keynes's way of thinking about economics in an uncertain world as revolutionary as Einstein's theory of relativity and the ideas of quantum physics. Needless to say such thoughts as these when voiced in class did not exactly endear me to my economics teachers (one in particular) who had most probably never read the *General Theory* in the first place and who were totally incapable of understanding the connection between economics, physics, ethics and aesthetics, much less the role of Lydia Lopokova and Bloomsbury. Above all, I think that my teachers were most perplexed to understand my interest in the relationship between money, Freud and potty training even though it was (as I insisted) all in the 'Auri Sacra Fames' section of the *Treatise on Money*! However, at least my teachers introduced me to Shackle's work on uncertainty and Joan Robinson's writings which was some compensation for the all the normal science of Keynesian mechanics which had to be learnt and reproduced for examination purposes. From the very beginning of my study of economics, therefore, I was struggling to escape from the confines of the Keynesianism I encountered in textbooks and in political and economic rhetoric. This book is a belated attempt to make good that youthful escape and finally justify spending all my hard earned pocket money on Harrod's life of Keynes.

Economics, sadly, never lived up to what I had read in those great books during the summer holidays. As I worked my way through Lipsey and Samuelson (*et al.*) I could not help feeling that Mill, Marshall and Keynes had practically nothing to do with modern positivist economics: there was little vision, morals, psychology, politics or sociology or commonsense and an excessive amount of rather unnecessary mathematics. The maths in particular was very perplexing given the arguments of Marshall and Keynes as to its uses and abuses. I well recall my undergraduate decision to concentrate on political science rather than economics: it was after I read Keynes's review of Tinbergen in the *Economic Journal* for 1939. It confirmed my worst fears about the mumbo-jumbo of modern economics. I count that discovery as being one of the most fortunate pieces of academic serendipity. Economics, it turned out, was just *another* kind of hydrolic engineering, physics or chemistry: it was a lost cause. Although I have never forgotten my first summer kiss with economics, and the doors that it opened into areas of literature and knowledge which have enriched my life ever since, in due course I became disenchanted with its deterministic ethos, repelled by the mechanicism of the normal science as presented in the leading textbooks, totally immune to the charms of Marxism and Benthamism in their various forms and deeply sympathetic to the work of what Keynes termed 'cranks' and the more 'unorthodox' economists such as Boulding, Galbraith, Kohr and Schumacher. Since my days as an undergraduate and postgraduate student of political science what I have found most difficult to understand was why my view of Keynes – which was formed from actually reading the works of Keynes rather than of 'Keynesians' – was so far removed from what economists preached and politicians practiced. I never really had any sense that I had lived through a 'Keynesian era', so much as one which was overwhelmingly concerned with 'economic growth' and driven by the very Benthamite 'worm' (sic) which Keynes had thought the main enemy of human progress. A large part of the blame for this may be traced back to the revolution in economics and public policy which was proclaimed in the name of Keynes. By the end of the 1970s Keynes (*qua* the monstrous creation of modern economics) was declared dead, and the revolution a ghastly mistake. For over a decade and more those of us who believed in Keynes's view that market mechanisms left to themselves would not work for the benefit of society as a whole, nor to promoting a fairer and more creative and productive economy, had, in Britain and elsewhere, to stand on the sidelines as the main body of the political agenda was shaped by those who laid the blame for the failures of the post-war era upon the works of that infamous homosexual and corruptor of young minds, John Maynard Keynes. The tide had turned and it was difficult to see what could be said or what action could be taken to stop the resurgence of the perverse and dismal doctrines which Keynes had done so much to discredit. I seem to recall that my lessons and lectures in economics were once replete with instances and illustrations drawn from Daniel Defoe's *Robinson Crusoe*. In recent years this picture of Robinson Crusoe has come to form a picture in my mind of the present state of my own, and no doubt many others' political economy. Out there in the bay is the wreck of the HMS Keynes, brought to its sad plight by the stormy events of the 1970s and 1980s and the assaults of pirates from Chicago and the port of Liverpool. We few, we happy few, who still regard Keynes's economics as a far more satisfactory basis for public policy than any other framework, stand on the shore gazing wistfully at the wreck and wondering what to do. For Thatcher's children there seem to be no problems. One of their number once suggested to me, for example, that all one could really do is treat HMS Keynes rather like the Mary Rose and preserve it as a museum piece in the history of thought, rather than as a viable craft to use for modern day voyages.

Happily, there have been number of important attempts to re-formulate or re-fit Keynesian economics so as to make it more seaworthy. My aim in writing this book is not to reiterate the economic arguments of these scholars but to offer another perspective on Keynes in the hope that social scientists and those involved in policy making and agenda setting will seek out his writings and come to a fuller understanding of his immense importance as a social theorist and philosopher. As a student of public policy I believe that the study of Keynes still has much to offer those of us concerned with the relationship of the social sciences to the policy process. Not being a professional economist I have no desire to engage in the theoretical and technical reconstruction which is necessary if Keynesianism is to play a more pre-eminent role in influencing the policy agenda. This book maybe read as a modest attempt by a political scientist to swim out to the wreck and like a latter day Robinson Crusoe retrieve those tools and intellectual equipment which may prove most useful to constructing a new agenda for both the theory and practice of public policy. In so doing the author is convinced that the framing of a new policy agenda requires that we appreciate the urgent need to reintegrate economics with other academic disciplines – especially politics, psychology, sociology and philosophy. The emphasis which we find in Marshall and Keynes on economics as a 'moral science' is, I believe, well suited to this task of re-fashioning the relationship between different forms of policy inquiry and the practice of policy making. In this regard Keynes's writings have never been so relevant as they are today. With the Keynesianism of the past (thankfully) dead and buried, we can now proceed to explore his work as a whole and think about what practical implications flow from the process of re-evaluating the ideas of one of the most significant and most maligned social scientists of the twentieth century. Indeed, if the social sciences are to regain their influence in respect of what Dewey (1927) once termed the 'public and its problems', the moral and psychological dimensions which Marshall and Keynes had thought so central to understanding society must become a far more vital feature of its responsibility to help clarify the ends and means of public policy. With the Keynesianism of the past out of the way we are now free to understand his radical vision of a different kind of society occupying the 'extreme left of celestial space and imagination' (IX: 309) and open to the possibilities of human energies and enterprise. And with the wealth of Keynesian scholarship now available, which facilitates a more contextual understanding of Keynes, we can at last see his life and work in an organic way, rather than through the atomistic viewpoints of economic theorizing.

In the 1980s I wrote a number of pieces which explored the political and epistemological aspects of Keynes's ideas (Parsons, 1983, 1985). One area of Keynes which had commanded my attention since my earliest encounter with his work were his ideas on Newton and alchemy, and the relationship between Keynes's revolution and those of Newton and Einstein in physics which was stimulated by reading Keynes and Bohr in the Royal Society's collection of papers to celebrate the 300th anniversary of Newton's birth (Royal Society, 1947) and Pigou's bad tempered review of the *General Theory* (Pigou, 1936). But the Keynes/Einstein issue was finally brought into focus for me by reading Friedman and Donley's fascinating study of Einstein in 1985 (Friedman and Donley, 1985). The result of this was a working paper on 'Newton the Man and Keynes the Economist'. One of the problems with this paper was that it rather tamely excluded both the insights of Carl Jung on alchemy, and my thoughts on Keynes and Einstein even though they formed an important background to the analysis. In this book I have decided to bring Jungian perspectives to the fore so as to give a more central position to alchemy as a metaphor through which to examine Keynes's economics. It may seem strange that a book about making Keynes more relevant to the late twentieth century and the twenty-first century should choose to employ a metaphor drawn from the most ancient of times – alchemy. I lay no claim to originality in making the connection between economics and alchemy: John Ruskin (Ruskin, 1907: 1) and Keynes himself drew the comparison. More recently David Hendry has employed the metaphor to consider the nature of, and prospects for, the black art of econometrics. Econometricians, he claims, have found their philosophers' stone: 'it is called regression analysis' (Hendry, 1993: 14). Of course, as he points out, we cannot actually call it so: who after all would want to apply to the London School of Economics and Political Alchemy? However, the idea of social science as a form of alchemy is highly appropriate for both exploring Keynes and the policy orientated disciplines: far from marking a step back alchemy points a way forward to a quantum approach which I believe is inherent in the *General Theory*. In my own mind this train of thought began to form after the Bronowski series for the BBC on *The Ascent of Man* (1973) wherein he observed that nuclear power was in a sense the fulfilment of the alchemist's dream. This notion in turn reminded me of the interpretation of relativity and quantum physics to be found in Russell's *ABC of Relativity* and *An Outline of Philosophy* and also in James Jeans's *Physics and Philosophy* which I thought were very suggestive of some of the ideas and language we find in Keynes. Later Friedman and Donley's book published in the mid-1980s completed the circuit by showing how relativity and quantum mechanics impacted on the arts in the 1920s and 1930s, and thus returned me back to Bohr, Pigou's review, Russell and Jeans, and Bloomsbury.

To put the normative underpinning of this book in simple terms it is that the social sciences ought to reinvent themselves so that they abandon their modernist claims to be a 'scientific' study of society in favour of a *premodern* approach which is more like that of true alchemy: that is, the policy sciences should be viewed as investigations into problems which seek to bring about defined or desired end states (or 'solutions') and clarify values, rather than offer a quasi 'scientific' explanation of social, economic or political phenomena. Social science as alchemy believes that thinking about problems in the 'real' and uncertain world can change and transform them. *In observing and analysing the social scientist participates in realising the possibilities of things.* In a quantum sense beliefs about reality alter reality. Economics, therefore, uses words to both 'investigate reality' *and* 'play upon sentiment' (Robinson, 1969: 63) just as in the same way the alchemist both investigated and transmuted. As we shall see, the true alchemist was not simply conducting experiments and observations – like a modern scientist – he was also seeking to bring about a transmutation in both himself and in the materials which were the object of his scientific and spiritual endeavours. I argue that Keynes was far more of an alchemist than a 'scientist' and that the roots of many of the dilemmas which face the social sciences today are to be found in the complex intellectual inheritance of Isaac Newton which was uncovered by Keynes himself. In considering the role of the social sciences in the 1990s we can go no further without going back to the dawn of the age of reason and the contradictory and ambiguous contribution of its great founding figure – Isaac Newton.

Keynes was one of the most perceptive students of Newton's work and in this book I want to use his insight into Newton's method and psychology to provide a window into Keynes's economics and also to shed some light on the future of the social sciences as a form of knowledge *of* and *for* the policy process (Lasswell, 1951). I consider Keynes to be part of a distinct branch of 'Newtonian economics': the main stem of which leads to a highly mechanistic view of the world. This group, of what we might term 'rude mechanicals', were lumped together by Keynes into the category of 'classical economics' whose deterministic *laissez-faire* principles derived from a profoundly mechanical (Cartesian) view of the laws of the economic universe: natural laws could be known, but should not be interfered with. What we term the economic alchemists were those – such as Keynes – who shared Newton's concern with transforming, completing and perfecting nature's handiwork by reconciling contradictory forces. Keynes's vision of the moral sciences rejected the crude mechanical view of analysing blind laws, in favour of a social science which actively seeks to shape and reform the world. Keynes's economics is more like Newton's alchemy than his 'science': it is fundamentally post-Newtonian, but not necessarily incommensurate with 'classical' economics. The *General Theory* has more in common with the physics of relativity and quantum mechanics than the clockwork universe of Ricardo and Bentham. His economics invites us to embrace a vision of social science which is active in empowering mankind to live better in an uncertain and insecure world. One of the worst things that could happen to civilization for Keynes would be to allow the crude mechanicals and technicians to run the economy as if it *were* a Newtonian – or rather Descartian – machine. Alas, however, the heirs of Jeremy Bentham may yet have had the last laugh. In writing this book the author intends not to go gently into that last goodnight of a Newtonian sleep. We can rail against the darkness! But there may be some cause for optimism in the fact that economics no longer enjoys the kind of position it had in the 1960s as the premier policy science. As economics has become ever more technical and mathematical and its track record in modelling has got worse, its influence on thinking about economic policy problems has waned. The present author is not at all sure that economics is capable of saving itself without a little help from its friends and a radical reorientation of the discipline so as to make it less like pseudo science and more like the kind of moral science advanced by Keynes. Free from the shackles of positivism and the visitations of Tinbergen's ghost economics could once again interact with ethics, philosophy, psychology and political science rather than remain in a state of not so splendid intellectual isolation.

The book is subtitled as an examination of Keynes's *quest* for a moral science and by this we wish to convey the idea that his life and work follows the classical pattern of the quest myth: the search for something which is lost and must be recovered (Raphael, 1965: 116). The grail for Keynes was the recovery of a lost moral science. On his journey our hero has to slay many monsters and overcome several evils: for Keynes the chief serpents are Ricardo and Bentham and their intellectual progeny. He enters the den of the 'lethargic monster' called '*laissez-faire*' (IX: 287) and strikes an apparently fatal blow. Our hero embodies the struggle against contradictions and opposites and thus in these pages plays the part of a liberator who sets out to vanquish the malevolent mechanicals and shows how to to confront the 'dark forces' of uncertainty and ignorance (as he describes them in the *General Theory*). The image we wish to convey is of Keynes as a twentieth century Faust battling with the contradictions in the microcosm of his own personality and the paradoxes of the economic macrocosm and whose life and work sought to find a harmony in the opposites of his self and society. We see Keynes as less of a post-modern figure than someone whose vision encompassed the age of magic and the age of Freud and quantum physics and whose life's work it was to seek a science which could transform capitalism by a devising a new way of thinking and feeling. In short, our hero is an alchemist.

An essay of this kind has necessarily to be dependent upon a large number of bigger books. Recent Keynesian scholarship has done so much to widen our view of Keynes and I am enormously indebted to the works of Skidelsky, Moggridge, O'Donnell, Carabelli, Hession, Fitzgibbons, Mini and others in helping me to think out my own ideas and confirm some of my earlier intuitions. In particular, I am indebted to Hession's book which was so useful on the issue of androgeneity (an important theme in alchemy and in the life of Keynes) and Mini's study of Keynes and Bloomsbury which discusses the relation of Keynes to aesthetics and the work of Virginia Woolf, Lytton Strachey and the rest. Shelia Dow's history of macroeconomic thought, which came out in 1985, was especially useful in suggesting the distinction between Descartian/Euclidean economics and 'Babylonian economics' at a time when I was thinking about Newtonian and Quantum physics: it became clear to me through reading her work that economic alchemy is a stream of thought which has its source in the rivers of Babylon. Over the years I have also benefited from correspondence with, and the work of, Lord Skidelsky who has done such a tremendous amount to stimulate and advance the study of Keynes. Any serious student should acquaint themselves with the work of Skidelsky and other recent scholars if they are to move beyond the 'textbook' Keynes. And I remain ever thankful to my colleagues in the department of economics at QMW, Professors Bernard Corry and Alan Coddington and Professor Sir Trevor Smith in my own department for provoking and encouraging me early on in my career to think through many of the ideas about Keynes which are presented (at long last) in this book and in previous publications. Finally, I should like to express my gratitude to my students at the Universities of London and Maryland for the classes and lectures which helped in no small way to shape the book.

In an earlier (and much longer) draft of this book I endeavoured to engage in more of a dialogue with recent scholarship on Keynes and Post-Keynesian economics, but I have decided that a critical survey of the rapidly growing literature was really another project entirely and so I have simply tried to say what I want to say, and allow (in Keynes's sense) his words to mix with the thoughts and feelings of the reader. I have consequently refrained from citing too many commentaries on Keynes in the text so as to make a full use of what Keynes himself wrote, rather than what has been written about his life and ideas. The references are cited by volume number (except for the *General Theory of Employment Interest and Money* and the *Treatise on Probability* where we use the abbreviation 'GT' and 'TP' respectively) from the collected writings as published by the Royal Economic Society, Macmillan and Cambridge Univeristy Press. I gratefully acknowledge their permission to quote from the thirty volumes which contain the great bulk of his writings which were penned or published from 1913 onwards. As far as alchemy is concerned, all scholars in the field must readily acknowledge the fascinating and illuminating work of Betty Jo Teeter Dobbs on Newton's alchemy, and the writings of Jung and other analytical psychologists, especially Jolande Jacoby, and more recently Nathan Schwartz-Salant. The books by Holmyard, Gilchrist and Haeffner and Ronald Gray's *Goethe The Alchemist* have also proved invaluable and readers interested in the hermetic arts will profit from consulting their work. Edward Edinger's essay on *Faust* was also a great help in enabling me to clarify my ideas, as did Stuart Atkin's suberb translation of *Faust* which I have used in the text. Writing this book has also been sustained and informed by the insights of Sir Michael Tippett's music (especially *Child of our Time*, *The Mask of Time*, *Midsummer Marriage* and *Icebreak*) which deals with a central leitmotif of this present volume: the problem of opposites. If Tippett's music failed to get me thinking there was always the poetry of Alfred Marshall's favourite alchemist, Goethe, set to the music of Schumann, followed by a loud and prolonged burst of *Der Ring des Nibelungen* or Mahler's Eighth! When the music fell silent the chorus of 'Where is this Keynes book then?' from Edward Elgar had a certain motivational effect – even if it lacked Wagner's inspirational quality.

As ever, my wife Mary and our sons John and Ben who cheerfully tolerate my musical excesses, moods and mess, have been my strength and my joy.

Vollendet das ewige Werk!

1. A Bloomsbury Faust

Two souls, alas! reside within my breast. (Goethe, 1994: 1112)

Faust's sin was that he identified with the thing to be transformed. (Jung, 1968: 497)

God created iron, but not that which is to be made of it. He enjoined fire, and Vulcan, who is lord of fire, to do the rest. From this it follows that iron must be cleansed of its dross before it can be forged. To release the remedy from the dross is the task of Vulcan ... Nothing has been created as *ultima materia* – in its final stage. Everything is at first created in its *prima materia*, its original stuff; whereupon Vulcan comes, and by the art of alchemy develops it into its final substance. For alchemy means: to carry to its end something that has not yet been completed. (Paracelsus, 1988: 93; 141)

Androgeny is ... the ultimate goal of the alchemist's search. All the disciplines grouped under the general heading of hermeticism ... suppose that the human being, once he is rid of his innermost darkness and lack of understanding, realises that he is bisexual. ... From this point of view, the hermaphrodite symbolises bisexuality controlled, refined and harmoniously integrated. (Nataf, 1994: 11)

Throughout the work ... we are confronted in varying degrees with the polarity between knowledge of the kind obtained through intellectual processes (the knowledge of scientists) and that obtained from deep inner sensibilities (the knowledge of creative artists). Sometimes in their divinations of the future, these different sources of knowledge coincide and complement each other. (Tippet, on *The Mask of Time*, 1995: 246).

John Maynard Keynes was born in Cambridge in 1883. He was the son of John Neville and Florence Ada Keynes. His father was a university don and administrator and his mother became Cambridge's first woman mayor. He was educated at Eton and King's College Cambridge. He entered the Civil Service in 1906 and worked in the India Office for three years. During this time, he was to work on a fellowship dissertation on probability (*A Treatise on Probability*), which was subsequently published after the First World War. He was successful in obtaining his fellowship in 1909 and returned to Cambridge as Alfred Marshall's protégé. In the next few years Keynes became an economist of some repute and an acknowledged expert on Indian monetary reform. He published a book on *Indian Currency and Finance* (1913) and was a member of the Royal Commission on Indian Finance and Currency. On the commencement of the First World War Keynes was brought into the Treasury and by the end of the war his preeminence as the leading economist of his generation was such that he was appointed as the principal Treasury representative at the Peace Conference of 1919. The experience of the conference led Keynes to resign his appointment and publish a damning indictment of the procedings and its outcomes in *The Economic Consequences of the Peace* (1919). This book established Keynes as a major international figure in post-war economic debates. From then on Keynes was a tireless campaigner for economic reform and a new approach to economic policy making. He was a prolific journalist and when Britain returned to the gold standard in 1923 his *Tract on Monetary Reform* was to mark him out as a formidable critic of ruling conventional wisdom. There followed two major theoretical works which set out the economic arguments for managing the economy: *A Treatise on Money* (1930) and *The General Theory of Employment Interest and Money* (1936). Despite failing health in the years following the *General Theory*, Keynes continued to be active in promoting his ideas and played an important role in British economic policy making during the second world war. He died in 1946, leaving a wife, Lydia, and a large collection of published and unpublished work.

Such is the *curriculum vitae* of life which had so many dimensions and facets. He was a philosopher, an economist, a civil servant, a journalist, a man who was interested in the arts of life as well as the arts of policy. He was a man of Whitehall and a man of Bloomsbury. He was an art collector, and a bibliophile, and someone who moved between so many different worlds that the term 'economist' hardly captures the breadth of his contribution to the history of his times. Keynes's economics was devised in a period of the twentieth century when old certainties were everywhere giving way to new uncertainties. In science, the work of Einstein, Planck, Bohr, Heisenberg, *et al.* was transforming perceptions of space and time. In art Picasso and Cézanne were challenging notions of representation, light, movement and geometry. In politics, the old stable European order collapsed in the Great War to end all wars; liberal democratic capitalism was no longer the only model of social organization; and Marxism offered another way of thinking about the human condition in an age in which God was dead or dying. Technological developments were providing new ways of communicating and travelling. In literature, poets and novelists such as James Joyce, T.S. Eliot, William Faulkner and Virginia Woolf were experimenting with new forms and ways of writing. Lytton Strachey had revolutionized the art of biography with the publication of *Eminent Victorians*. In music, Schoenberg, Webern and Stravinsky were shocking audiences with their harmonies and discords. In the world of ballet, Diaghilev was revolutionizing dance, stage design and costume and inspiring artists, choreographers and musicians. In psychology, Sigmund Freud had revolutionized the way in which people thought about the mind and human sexuality and sub-conscious instincts. It is in this intellectual and cultural setting that the economics of J.M. Keynes belongs: he had met both Einstein and Planck; was a collector of impressionist paintings; he was a close friend of Virginia Woolf, Lytton Strachey and James Strachey, the English translator and editor of the works of Freud; he was a participant in the Versailles peace settlement; and, of course, a lover of the ballet and the husband of one of Diaghilev's most famous ballerinas. In art and science, aesthetics, and ethics, what was solid had turned into air: God had come to play dice and the old geometries, moralities, faiths and religions were of little help. As artists of all kinds were 'seeking to find a more truthful, more expressive way of treating the realities of human existence' (Griffiths, 1985: 422), and scientists were exploring a world in which Newton and Euclid were no longer adequate as explanations of the universe as once they were, Keynes set himself the task to construct an economics more suited to the realities of a world that had been changed utterly by the First World War, as it had been by Einstein, Freud and Marx and which was a long way removed from the self-assurance and confidence of Victorian England.

Keynes was a skilled biographer and some of his finest compositions are to be found in his biographical essays (Volume X, of the collected writings). In this book we will use one of his last biographical essays, 'Newton the Man', which explores the significance of Newton's alchemy, as an instrument with which to investigate his ideas and method. This is not to say that Keynes was writing a kind of parallel biography in his essay on Newton, even though the parallels are quite striking, but to suggest that we can use his thoughts on one revolution in science – the Newtonian revolution – to examine the Keynesian revolution in economics. Keynes used economics as an 'engine' to power his ideas, rather than as a means for 'discovering concrete truth' (X: 199). Economics was therefore a means of persuasion, rather than of discovery, just as in the same way in which, as Keynes points out, Newton used scientific discourse as a way of demonstrating, rather than discovering truth. For Keynes theories had to mix with the real world, and be shaped and re-formed in the minds and actions of others. Economic theories were like 'eggs' in that they were expressions of potentialities which had to live and breathe rather than exist in some kind of intellectual stone. Ideas were children of the mind that went out into the world and possessed a life quite independent of their progenitors. As Mini notes, Keynes was very fond of the analogy of mental products as 'eggs' and he uses it in a variety of contexts (Mini, 1994: 166; see also Hill and Keynes (eds) 1989: 234, 327 *et passim*). In a review of Wells's *Clissold*, for example, Keynes refers to the book as being a 'great big meaty egg', and in keeping with this favourite metaphor great economists were pictured as 'rare birds' and 'soaring eagles'! The egg seems to represent for

Keynes (as it did for the alchemists) a symbol of potentiality and transformation. Creativity, for Keynes, had androgenous characteristics: it involved the
capacity of individuals to combine apparently opposite gifts.

> The study of economics does not seem to require any specialised gifts of an
> unsually high order. Is it not, intellectually regarded, a very easy subject com-
> pared with other branches of philosophy and pre science? Yet good or even
> competent economists are the rarest of birds. An easy subject, at which very few
> excel! The paradox finds its explanantion, perhaps, in that the master-economist
> must possess a rare *combination* of gifts. (X: 173)

Marshall's 'double' and 'divided' nature and his 'many sidedness', for example, were important aspects of his greatness as a 'soaring eagle' (also the
alchemical symbol of light) in the world of economics. For Keynes therefore
economics involved the reconciliation of opposites within the (microcosm) of
the mind of 'rare birds', and the reconciliation of opposing forces with the
economic macrocosm. The *economist* had to be an artist, an historian, a
mathematician, politician, and philosopher, who was near the earth but able
to remain aloof. The *economy* had to equally combine and unify contradictory forces – such as the state and the market, capitalism and socialism – if
the full creativity of human enterprise and imagination were to be realised. I
want to suggest in this book that Keynes was practicing alchemy, rather than
Newtonian science. If it seems rather fanciful to suggest that we can think of
Keynes as an economic adept, it is well to remember that, as Carabelli notes,
he 'did not consider magical thought as unreasonable. On the contrary … he
judged its inductive and analogical reasoning perfectly legitimate' (Carabelli,
1988: 108). Keynes was of the view that, as Skidelsky puts it: 'the distinctions
between magic, science and art were less interesting than the similarities'
(Skidelsky, 1992: 414).

Keynes, therefore, has to be re-read in terms of someone who was reverting
to what Fitzgibbons describes as a 'pre-enlightenment system of thought',
(Fitzgibbons: 1991, 132). The irony is, as Fitzgibbons notes, that he has for so
long been portrayed as precisely the opposite: 'a positivist who promoted the
political and scientific neutrality of economics' (Fitzgibbons, 1991: 132). The
Keynes we wish to explore may well have given birth to a positivistic, technocratic economics, but Keynes's economics has much deeper pre-modern roots.
Indeed, the image which comes to mind is drawn from the fairy stories which
he loved in his childhood or his description of Lloyd George as an 'extraordinary figure' who was a 'visitor to our age from the hag-ridden magic and
enchanted woods of Celtic antiquity' and whose mission it was to free the 'soul
of man' from the 'spirits of the earth' (X: 23–4). Keynes wanted to set free the
soul of capitalism from the spirits of *laissez-faire* political economy. His mission was to to show how to restore economic equilibrium and bring the state

and the market into a new relationship. Like the practitioners of the hermetic arts this harmony for Keynes could only come about in the uniting of opposites. The image of Keynes we wish to paint, accordingly, is not the Keynes we find in textbooks, but of a Faust in Bloomsbury or a Mephistopheles in Whitehall seeking the goal of the alchemist's art: the harmonious conjunction of opposites, and an 'organic unity through time' (X: 436).

The life and work of Keynes embodied much of the tension which is to be found in the archetypal quest for integration and wholeness described in Goethe's great alchemical poetic drama, *Faust*. Keynes's economics is struggling with the problems of opposites: good and evil; scholarship and the striving for practical influence and power over the real world. The Faust legend provides a window onto the complex relationship between Keynes the man and Keynes the economist. If this sounds a rather extravagant claim to make, it is well to keep in mind that this comparison was also made by Oswald Falk – Keynes's closest business associate and friend: 'He described Newton as Copernicus and Faustus in one, and doubtless he thought he resembled them both' (cited in Skidelsky, 1992: 23). As readers of this book may be rather unfamiliar with the details of Goethe's epic (or its musical representations and interpretations) it may be helpful at this point to briefly sketch some of the main features of the story upon which we wish to draw.

God makes a wager with the devil – Mephistopheles – to see if he can tempt one Dr Faust. In so doing the Lord proclaims that he does not hate the 'spirits of negation' as they are a necessary force for human growth and progress. Mephistopheles is, as he later tells Faust, a force which, whilst 'always willing evil, always produces good'. We first encounter the doctor in his study depressed and frustrated at his inability to discover the 'seminal forces' that 'binds the universe together'. He is bored with the academic life and wishes to experience the real world. Unlike his manservant Wagner, Faust is no longer content with the joys of the written word. Faust wrestles with his conflicting desires:

Two souls, alas! reside within my breast,
and each is eager for a separation:
in the throes of coarse desire, one grips
the earth with all its senses;
the other struggles from the dust
to rise to high ancestral spirits. (Goethe, 1994: 1111–17)

Mephistopheles soon appears and makes him an offer he can't refuse. Faust wishes to:

plunge into the torrents of time,
into the whirl of eventful existence!

> There, as chance, wills,
> let pain and pleasure
> success and frustration, alternate;
> unceasing activity alone reveals our worth. (Goethe, 1994: 1752–59)

Faust dedicates himself to the pursuit of knowledge through searching out the contradictions and polarities of life. His pledge is that he will return to Hell with Faust if ever he rests contented on this journey. His first adventure into the world of extremes involves a love affair with a young girl (Margarete) who dies and whose soul is taken up to heaven at the end of part one.

In the second part of the drama we move from the contradictions and torments of sexual love to the problems of economics, and the love of money. In a plot which follows a familiar alchemical pattern (Jung, 1968: 327–39; Edinger, 1990: 46–7): a sick King/Kingdom needs the help of a 'philosopher', who desends to bring about the *coniunctio* (the union of opposites) to heal the King. Faust and Mephistopheles arrive in a Kingdom which is falling apart and in which society 'strives for fragmentation'. Mephistopheles diagnoses the sickness as a monetary phenomena and argues that the solution lies in the gold buried under ground. The devil shows the way to possess the philosophers' stone by introducing them to the idea of paper money secured on the reserves of gold 'stored underground'.

> Of course you can't just pick it off the floor,
> but Wisdom's skill is getting what's most deeply hidden ...
> and if you ask who will extract it, I reply:
> a man that nature has endowed with mighty intellect. (Goethe, 1994: 4890–95)

The Emperor and his court are delighted with the resulting economic up-turn which flows from Mephistopheles's alchemy and as a reward for solving the economic depression Faust is given a job in the Treasury!!

We next meet the Emperor at the close of Faust's journey. Alas, the Emperor has come to believe that 'the whole world could be had for money' and the consequence was war. By now Faust has experienced the contradictions of the world, has met with success and failure and has come to an understanding of what he really wants to do: tame and control the elemental forces of the sea.

> The surging sea creeps into every corner,
> barren itself and spreading barrenness ...
> Imbued with strength, wave after wave holds power
> but then withdraws, and nothing's been accomplished –
> a sight to drive me to despair,
> this aimless strength of elemental forces!
> This has inspired me to venture to new heights,

to wage war here against these forces and subdue them.
It can be done! (Goethe, 1994: 10 215–222)

Mephistopheles tells him that he must seize the opportunity of war to get his wish. Faust helps the Emperor win his war in return for a stretch of coastline.

In the closing sequence of the drama Faust wishes that he could have a clear uninterrupted view of his lands, but two kind old people (Baucis and Philemon) need to be re-housed first. Unfortunately, in endeavouring to move the couple, they are killed. Finally Faust is visited by four old grey women: want, debt, distress and care. As Faust is a wealthy man he is only troubled by the latter lady. Care (Sorge) tells him that she has brought many men down and into darkness and despair. Under her sway her victims worry and think only of the future and consequently 'get nothing done' and are unable to decide. She it is who blinds mankind and as her parting gift she blinds Faust. Confronted by the power of Sorge to frustrate human creativity Faust discovers a light in his inner being. Faced with the utter reality of human uncertainty and the capacity of Sorge to stifle and distort he discovers the energy and will to begin his task of controlling the sea by constructing 'rigid bands' and draining a stagnant and contaminated marsh.

> If I can furnish space for millions to live – not safe, I know, but free to work
> in green and fertile fields, with man and beast
> soon happy on the new-made soil…
> the tide may bluster to its brim,
> but where it gnaws, attempting to rush in by force,
> communal effort will be quick to close the breach.
> To this idea I am committed wholly,
> it is the final wisdom we can reach:
> he, only, merits freedom and existence
> who wins them every day anew…
> If only I might see that people's teeming life,
> share their autonomy on encumbered soil;
> then, to the moment, I could say: tarry awhile, you are so fair –
> the traces of my days on earth
> will survive into eternity! (Goethe, 1994: 11, 563–84)

In contemplation of this great work of human progress Faust dies and his soul his taken to heaven by the *Mater Gloriosa* in the company of his beloved Margarete.

Keynes's economics is essentially Faustian in that it is rooted in the belief that the spirit of negation has to be acknowledged and used. Capitalism is a system which obtains the good through evil and immoral forces. They cannot be abolished, but understood, canalized and transmuted. The problem formulated by Faust and Keynes is one of how man can wrestle with and overcome and integrate the opposite and contradictory forces within himself and in the world: the ego and its shadow; good and evil; science and art; male and female; intuition and analysis; facts and feelings; left brain and right brain; capitalism and socialism; individualism and collectivism; knowledge and ignorance; certainty and uncertainty. Keynes has, in common with Dr Faustus, a divided nature. Two souls resided in his breast: the soul of a Cambridge Apostle and a member of Bloomsbury which desired the academic and aesthetic heights of another world; and the soul of the City of Mammon and Whitehall which desired to embrace the real world and make money and policy. Keynes embodied the philosopher and aesthete and the technocrat and manager; the desire for love and culture and the urge for power and influence; he was the friend of pacifists and a part of a government at war. Methodologically he fused his capacity for logical thought, with a profound belief in the role of intuition in human knowledge. He was a homosexual who eventually found a woman (Lydia) to give his life a stability throughout a busy and demanding life. Lydia was the most unlikely of companions for a man of Bloomsbury and Whitehall, and yet in this marriage of opposites Keynes was to find happiness and love. He was not content to be an academic, like his father, nor remain in the safe insulated world of Cambridge and Bloomsbury, Keynes wants it all: he wishes to plunge into a world of contradiction. After the First World War he is immersed in the depths of a sick and ailing civilization. He is unable to exercise the kind of influence to bring about a harmonious resolution of conflict and leaves the Palace of Versailles to journey on and find other means to achieve his goal of transforming opinion, whilst at the same time transforming himself. Like Mephistopheles, Keynes sees the solution to the sick Kingdom in the realm of gold and paper money and spends the next two decades attempting to influence events by working on the orthodoxy which holds public policy in its thrall. The system, he proclaims is 'not self-adjusting and without purposive direction, it is incapable of translating our actual poverty into potential plenty' (XIII: 491). Money, he argues, contains the possibilities of wealth, peace and life, but if misunderstood and worshipped it can turn to poverty, war and death. Human insecurity, worry and care for the future can blind creativity and enterprise and choke the will to decide and act. Then comes the war and the services of the old man are required by the Empire. He seizes the opportunity and labours hard and long to bring the elemental forces of a monetary economy under control so that individual freedom can be preserved and extended and the capacity of the community to combat and divert the ebbs and flows and storms of the economic cycle can be increased and care and insecurity lessened. This work is not completed and he dies at a moment of triumph and failure. Cambridge, his beloved Alma Mater, claims his soul, but his ashes are cast into the winds and claimed by Mother Earth. The age of magic and magicians is gone and the age of the econometricians has begun!

The main influences shaping Keynes's approach to the art and science of economics may be considered to be three men of Cambridge: Moore, Marshall and Malthus. To this trinity we may add the ideas of a man from Dublin, Edmund Burke, whose political philosophy was, perhaps, closest to his own views on reform and the dangers of abstract rationalism and revolution and much else (Helburn, 1991). In his undergraduate essay on Burke written in 1904 we find an early and significant demonstration of Keynes's desire to combine apparent opposites: an attempt to marry Burkean conservatism with the possibilities of rational liberal individualism. On the one hand, his essay shows his sympathy for avoiding risks, and pragmatic expediency in which the state acted to preserve individual freedom, rather than advance an abstract theory. On the other, Keynes is unhappy with Burke's 'timidity' and his attitude towards truth and reason as sources of radical change. In this essay we find the essential arguments for the need to find a 'middle way' which are to be put forward later on in his 'The End of Laissez-Faire', published in 1926. Of the four it was without doubt G.E. Moore whose ideas were to be the most signficant influence on Keynes's early intellectual development. Marshall was largely responsible for Keynes's shift from philosophy to economics, and it was Malthus who Keynes regarded as the first of the Cambridge economists and the father of the line of thought from which he claimed intellectual descent.

Understanding Keynes's economics must begin with Moore's *Principia Ethica*, published in 1903. Although Keynes was to modify his Moorism over the years it remained at the core of his way of thinking. From the encounter with Moore he was to go on and write his *Treatise on Probability* which is now recognized as being absolutely essential to the study of Keynes, rather than an early work of philosophy which has a passing relevance to his later theory and practice. This creates a difficulty for the non-philosopher because the *Principia* and the *Treatise* are not easy works to comprehend without a background in ethics and probability. No doubt it was because of this that the philosophical underpinnings of Keynes were so badly neglected by 'Keynesians'. However, an appreciation of Keynes in the whole is really not possible without his early beliefs and interests. In this chapter we cannot hope to do little more than urge the reader to get to grips with more detailed accounts and ultimately to actually read the *Treatise on Probability*. Furthermore, so many of Keynes's early writings which provide great insight into his later thinking were not published in the Collected Writings. The availability of these youthful essays to a wider audience will in time do much to re-position Keynes's place in the history of ideas.

Moore's book came as a revelation to Keynes and his fellow Apostles. Moore argued that the foundation of morality must be understood in neo-platonist terms. That is to say, what can be held to be good cannot be reduced to what is 'useful' or that which we desire. What was good, is good (Moore, 1903: 6). A moral life was one in which we comprehend 'the good' and endeavour to increase the amount of good – truth, beauty and friendship – in the world. Ah, but the problem is: how can we know if the outcomes of our actions will result in good? The answer Moore gave upset the young Keynes: when in doubt follow the conventional rules which are held to promote good. For Moore it was all a matter of probability: if we follow the rules it is more probable that good will result. Rules should be followed because we are uncertain about consequences and in such cases rule following, rather than rule breaking, yields a higher probability that good will be increased. This is what Keynes took to task in his *Treatise on Probability* which occupied much of his time during a formative period of his life. Keynes argued that, although he accepted the objective and intuitive nature of the good, he could not accept that we had to follow rules and conventions so as to increase the probability that good will follow. Moore's argument, it appeared to Keynes, turned on the notion that, in making decisions about right conduct, we ought to rely on consideration of the 'relative probability' of different actions resulting in good effects. It was an argument predicated on the *relative frequency* of rules producing good effects.

> It seems then, that with regard to any rule which is *generally* useful, we may assert that it ought *always* to be observed, not on the ground that in *every* particular case it will be useful, but on the ground that in *any* particular case the probability of its being so is greater than that our being likely to decide rightly that we have before is an instance of its disutility. In short, though we may be sure that there are cases where the rule should be broken, we can never know which these cases are, and ought, therefore, never to break it. (Moore, 1903: 162–3)

During the time Keynes took to respond to this argument Keynes changed from being a student of philosophy, ethics and mathematics, into an economist and international figure of some repute. The *Treatise on Probability* consequently forms, as it were, a bridge from the world of Cambridge, Bloomsbury and Moore into the world of Marshall, Whitehall, and Versailles. But it also is a text which shows Keynes as a Janus-like figure facing the world of rational calculation, and the world of magic. Many of the ideas which he sets out in this book are to find their expression and application in the books, articles and pamphlets for which he was to became famous, but it is only when we have read the treatise that we can understand the methodology which underpinned his attempts at persuasion.

Moore had argued that we should aim to maximize the universal good by following general social rules since in so doing we will *probably* do more good than harm. Keynes takes issue with this idea that probabilistic frequency is a satisfactory basis upon which to argue that we ought to follow conventions in seeking to increase the good. If we can only make decisions based on the kind of certainty which Moore proposes, then we are destined to remain prisoners of our ignorance, and chained to conventional wisdom. As was the case in his analysis of Burke, he wanted to have his cake and eat it: although he was inspired by Moore's philosophy which pointed the way to truth, beauty and friendship as manifest goods, he could not accept the proposition that in order to maximize the universal good we had to be timid, defeated by ignorance, and dependent on calculations as to the magnitude of probabilities. Keynes needed to free himself from the restraints of Moore's prescription to follow those rules of conduct which are deemed to be more likely to lead to the greater good. The *Treatise on Probability* takes a very broad view of its subject: it is concerned with knowledge, intuition, and uncertainty. Human cognition, it posits, cannot be reduced to the kind of mechanical approach which has long been favoured by students of probability. An underlying theme of the treatise is a critique of Laplace's belief in Newtonian mechanical determinism. For Laplace the mathematics of probability demonstrated that, as he famously observed to Napoleon, the hand of God was not necessary to keep the universe working – ' Je n'ai pas besion cet hypothèse'. Thus by attacking the Laplacian theory of probability Keynes was implicitly challenging the hypothesis that the universe could be understood in purely mechanical or mathematical terms. Laplace's mathematics was, as he was to argue later in respect of classical economics, seeking to 'prove too much' (TP: 92). Mathematicians had sought to extrapolate from the mathematics of games calculations of risk and probability into the arena of *complex* human problems which were full of uncertainty and where calculation was limited and statistical frequencies existed which were of an entirely different nature to that which existed in games of chance. Laplace's law of succession had its 'proper limits' (TP: 370) and mathematical approaches to probability are in reality 'special cases' (TP: 374) and not to be applied in a general sense. Reality is more heterogeneous and complicated than the mathematics of a game will suggest: the game analogy therefore is not helpful, but on the contrary, it is highly misleading. Man stands in a different relationship to the real world than he does to the odds of pulling out a black ball from an urn, or selecting a number in roulette. Laplace's Newtonian mechanics goes too far in claiming to be a way of thinking about probability in those situations and events where nature is more *organic* than *atomistic*. Keynes argues that probability relationships are not always measurable, many relationships are incomparable, and that the world is infinitely more complex than true and false, certain and impossible: between the extremes of knowledge and impossibility are degrees of belief which involve human intuition as well as scientific knowledge. Human beings had to come to terms with the limitations of their knowledge in a world wherein opinions and beliefs must, perforce, serve as guides when calculation fails or proves inadequate. Keynes's aim in the treatise is to show how knowledge acquired through probability, although formed by intuitive reasoning rather than certain knowledge, can constitute a sound basis on which to make decisions. Keynes refutes the view that knowledge can be conclusive or certain: human knowledge, he maintains, depends on circumstances and is relative to the 'constitution of the human mind'. Knowledge will vary from man to man, and in accordance with differences in the intuitive powers of individuals and not *all* probabilities are capable of measurement or comparison (TP: 18–19). In contrast to Bentham, who once suggested a 'barometer of probability' on which witnesses in a court of law could mark their degree of certainty (TP: 21), Keynes argues that mathematical conceptions of probability are not helpful in situations where orders of magnitude cannot be established and whose material is not homogenous. However, because numerical probability is so very limited, it does not mean that we are 'adrift in the unknown' (TP: 35). In the twilight world in which there are degrees of rational belief probability can still serve as a guide. But, says Keynes, although probability can be our guide we have to think very differently about certainty and uncertainty than in terms of the framework propagated by mathematicians and Benthamites. For Keynes probability is concerned with *propositions* which are rational, but not conclusive, that is to say we have to take into account the psychological and cognitive context of human reasoning and *argument* in conditions of limited knowledge and uncertainty. In particular Keynes focuses on the limits of induction and empiricism and the way in which science has confused what is *rational* from what is *true*. We may well arrive at truth by apparently irrational means and an excessive belief in rationality and the 'alchemy of logic' (PT: 89) may lead us to an entirely false sense of truth and certainty. As an instance of this confusion between truth and rationality engendered by induction and empiricism Keynes argues that many have ridiculed the 'supposed irrationality of barbarous and primitive peoples' (PT: 273). Quoting from Frazer's *The Golden Bough* Keynes notes that:

> Reflection and enquiry should satisfy us that to our predecessors we are indebted for much of what we thought most our own, and that their errors were not wilful extravagances or the ravings of insanity, but simply hypotheses, justifiable as such at the time when they were propounded, but which a fuller experience has proved to be inadequate ... Therefore, in reviewing the opinions and practices of ruder ages and races we shall do well to look with leniency upon their errors as inevitable slips in the search for truth. (Frazer, 1995: 261; cited PT: 273)

Why is it, Keynes asks, do we assume that the analogies of rational scientifc method lead to truth, and regard those of primitive beliefs and superstitions as little more than 'ravings of insanity'?

is it certain that Newton and Huyghens were only reasonable when their theories were true, and that their mistakes were fruits of a disordered fancy? Or that the savages, from whom we have inherited the most fundamental inductions of our knowledge, were always superstitious when they believed what we know to be preposterous? (PT: 274)

Keynes suggests that we should not reject the analogies of the past just because they do not conform to the accepted frameworks of scientific explanation. When we read these comments in the context of Frazer's *The Golden Bough* Keynes's state of mind becomes more apparent. Sir James Frazer (1854–1941) – another man of Trinity, Cambridge – published his celebrated study of magic and religion between 1890 and 1915 in twelve volumes. Following its great success he published a one volume abridgement in 1922. The passage which Keynes cites is contained in a section of *The Golden Bough* concerned with 'our debt to the savage'. Frazer argues that we should not be dismissive of the contribution of the magicians of the past to the growth of human knowledge. 'Crude' and 'false' as it was magic provided 'practical guidance of a life system'. The flaw in magical thinking and practice was not in its 'reasoning, but in its premises', so to:

stigmatise these premises as ridiculous because we can easily detect their falseness, would be ungrateful as well as unphilosophical. We stand upon the foundation reared by the generations that have gone before ... For when all is said and done our resemblances to the savage are still more numerous than our differences from him; and what we have in common with him, and deliberately retain as true and useful, we owe to our savage forefathers who slowly acquired by experience and transmitted to us by inheritance those seemingly fundamental ideas which we are apt to regard as original and intuitive. (Frazer, 1995: 261)

Frazer argues that we can understand the development of human thought as moving through magical, religious and scientfic ways of thinking and consequently the line between rationality and irrationality is not so well defined as modern man is wont to suppose. Frazer was fascinated by the close relationship between magic and science and the place of magical and scientific elites in society and how the former group paved the way for the latter.

the analogy between the magical and scientific conceptions of the world is close. In both of them the succession of events is assumed to be perfectly regular and certain, being determined by immutable laws, the operation of which can be forseen and calculated precisely; the elements of caprice, of chance, and of accident are banished from the course of nature. Both of them open up a seemingly boundless vista of possibilities to him that knows the causes of things and can touch the secret springs that set in motion the vast and intricate mechanism of the world. Hence the strong attraction which magic and science alike have exercised on the human mind; hence the powerful stimulus that both have exercised on the pusuit of knowledge. (Frazer, 1995: 48)

Magic for Frazer is thus 'next of kin to science', but religion differs from both magic and science in holding to the belief that there are higher powers over man which rule the world and which have to be won over and conciliated. Magic and science, on the other hand, posit that the course of nature is determined 'not by the passions or caprice of personal beings, but by the operation of immutable laws acting mechanically'. However, magic, whilst acknowledging that the world is governed by 'immutable laws', believes that forces 'can be turned to account by any one who knows how to manipulate them by the appropriate ceremonies and spells' (Frazer, 1995: 51). Magic thus forms a deep 'mental stratum' which crops up in modern day Europe as in the Australian wilderness, or in ancient Egypt (Frazer, 1995: 55). In time we find that as:

> the conception of the elemental forces as personal agents is giving way to the recognition of natural law; then magic, based as it implicitly is on the idea of a necessary and invariable sequence of cause and effect, independence of personal will, reappears from the obscurity and discredit into which it had fallen, and by investigating the causal sequences in nature, directly prepares the way for science. Alchemy leads up to chemistry. (Frazer, 1995: 91)

We must not doubt, therefore, the intelligence of earlier and more primitive cultures: their magical methods of reasoning were no less sound than that of the scientist. The modern standing of scientific expertise is in direct line of succession from the 'public magicians' and 'magician kings' of the past whose skills were used for the benefit of the community as a whole to cure disease, control the weather, or forecast the future (Frazer, 1995: 60). With this kind of argument Keynes would have found much with which to agree. However, Keynes did not see the line of demarcation between magic and science as quite so well defined as Frazer. Keynes had a definitely anti-empiricist view of causality: experience, for Keynes, was an inadequate guide to reality, and in this regard he would have sided with the alchemists in believing in the crucial role of intuition in human knowledge. As he argues in the treatise, experience is not our sole guide into the reality of things: in practice we rely on more than 'positive knowledge and direct data experience' (TP: 94). Keynes also took a far more magical attitude towards knowledge: like the alchemists, and contrary to the beliefs of the chemists, he saw human beings as *participants* in constructing reality: knowledge had a transformative power.

On the page following his discussion of Frazer, Keynes again makes use of a writer whose concerns were far removed from probability in order to make his argument about rationality and truth clearer. He observes that 'animism' may well contain a commonsense truth even though it does not adhere to an inductive and empirical methodology. In a footnote refering us to Hudson's

Far Away and Long Ago he enlarges upon this idea. W.H. Hudson (1841–1922) was born not far from Buenos Aires in 1841 and came to London in 1874 where he made a living writing about natural history and his experiences in South America. By the time of the publication of *Far Away and Long Ago* in 1918 he was acknowledged by many to be one of the finest writers of his generation. John Galsworthy, for example, in his foreword to the book, proclaims him as a great writer and naturalist and significantly in a passage which Keynes must have warmed to, he observes that Hudson was wholly opposed to the influence of the 'pale mechanicians' of the age. The passage cited by Keynes occurs in chapter seventeen, 'A boy's animism', wherein the author recounts his feelings on remembering a youthful encounter with a black serpent. This prompts him to reflect on 'animism':

> or that sense of something in nature which to the enlightened or civilised man is not there, and in the civilised man's child, if it be admitted that he has it at all, is but the faint survival of a phase of the primitive mind. And by animism I do not mean the theory of a soul in nature, but the tendency or impulse or instinct, in which all myth originates, to *animate* all things; the projection of ourselves into nature; the sense and apprehension of an intelligence like our own, but more powerful in all visible things. It persists and lives in many of us, I imagine, more than we know. ... It is my belief that the animistic instinct, if a mental faculty can be so called, exists and persists in many persons. (Hudson,1918: 224–5, 233; cited TP: 275)

Keynes must have read Hudson and thought that this notion of animism captured perfectly what he was trying to say in the very academic language of the main text. Keynes comments that:

> This 'tendency or impulse or instinct', refined by reason and enlarged by experience, may be required, in the shape of an intuitive *à priori* probability, if some of those universal conclusions of common sense, which the most sceptical do not kick away, are to be supported with rational foundations. (TP: 275)

Later on this theme of the role of human instincts is to be expressed in explicitly Freudian terms, and we find clear echoes of Hudson in a famous passage of the *General Theory* wherein he talks about 'animal spirits'. In these passages on Frazer and Hudson we find the Keynes who will become fascinated with Newton's alchemy, and come to believe the possibility that the secret of making gold had been discovered! Here too we encounter the Keynes who was quite prepared to believe that 'cranks' in the past had uncovered some fundamental economic truths which the 'pale mechanicians' of political economy had overlooked. This is the Keynes who had (by 1918, if not some time before) become aware that deep impulses and instincts were vital forces in human behaviour. But above all in these few pages we encounter Keynes with one foot in the age of magic and another in the age of science. As he muses on the *The Golden Bough* we find Keynes wholly rejecting the prevailing notion of science as a Newtonian mechanical enterprise. By the time of the publication of the treatise he had already rejected the chemistry of economics and had begun to explore its alchemical uses in transmuting opinions and values. The Keynes who had published *The Economic Consequences of the Peace* a few years before the treatise had come to realize that opinions, beliefs, and feelings were the *prima materia* which could be used to change the world and release human potentialities and possibilities.

The treatise maintains that the exaggerated sense of certainty propagated by modern science had given rise to ideas about causation, uniformity in the natural world, and its atomistic organization which must be refuted.

> The kind of fundamental assumption about the character of material laws, on which scientists appear commonly to act, seems to me to be much less simple than the bare principles of uniformity. They appear to assume something much more like what mathematicians call the superposition of small effects, or as I prefer to call it ... the *atomic* character of natural law. The system of the material universe must consist, if this kind of assumption is warranted, of bodies which we may term ... *legal atoms*, such that each of them exercises its own separate, independent, and invariable effect, a change of the total state being compounded of a number of separate changes each of which is solely due to a separate portion of the preceeding state. ... Each atom can, according to this theory, be treated as a separate cause and does not enter into different organic combinations in each of which it is regulated by different laws. (TP: 276–7)

Keynes argues that the supposed atomic character of natural law is inadequate for understanding causality as there may well be 'quite different laws of wholes of different degrees of complexity, and laws of connection between complexes which could not be stated in terms of individual parts' (TP: 277). In which case:

> natural law would be organic and not, as is generally supposed, atomic. If every configuration of the universe were subject to a separate and independent law, or if very small differences between bodies – in their shape or size, for instance – led to their obeying quite different laws, prediction would be impossible and the inductive method useless. (TP: 277)

Science may therefore presume too much about the relation of atomic parts to the way in which *complex wholes* actually work. Yet, upon this atomistic hypothesis statistical inference – with its 'mask of alchemy' (TP: 367) – can mislead us into thinking that 'because statistics are numerous, the observed frequency is therefore stable' (TP: 368). However, says Keynes, this assumption of a stable atomistic set of relationships is a very big presumption: closer observation of statistical inferences indicate that 'stable frequencies are not very common and cannot be assumed lightly' (TP: 368). Nature *does* exhibit regularity, stability, cause and effect and atomism, but Keynes's argument is that to assume that this framework is *adequate* for those events, situations, and conditions where there is no regularity, little stability, lack of discernable cause and effects and where we have to understand things in the whole is questionable. A little later on in the treatise Keynes emphasizes this point about the instability of the social universe.

> In social and physical statistics the ultimate alternatives are not as a rule so perfectly fixed, nor the selection from them so purely random, as in the ideal game of chance ... Generally speaking, for large classes of social statistics we have a more or less stable population including different kinds of persons, in certain proportions, and on the other hand sets of environments, and the manner of allotting the environments to the persons vary in a random manner from year to year ... In all such cases as these, however, prediction beyond what has been observed is clearly open to sources of error which can be neglected in considering, for example, games of chance; – our so-called 'permanent' causes are always changing a little and are liable at any moment to radical alteration. (TP: 458)

Keynes, therefore, does not rule out the existence of 'supernormal' (sic) stability in nature, but argues that we have to be aware that human beings face a world in which there is 'subnormal' stability, and in which frequencies are oftentimes 'chaotic' (TP: 460). He argues that a mathematical way of thinking is a dubious basis for analysing human behaviour and is highly unsatisfactory as a guide for action in a real world where, however poor and incomplete it is, human knowledge *does* exists. Significantly, before he gets to the section of the book where he tackles Moore, Keynes points out that there are distinct realms of subjective and objective probability and chance. Objective chance is that which we find in an urn containing the infamous black and white balls. However, the world of human beings is not like that of urns full of balls since in the practice of human decision making we confront events in which 'the mind of the subject' is involved (TP: 311). That is to say, when we make a judgment about an event in the real world we have knowledge and beliefs which enter into the situation. Causality and chance in the world of men are therefore wholly different to that which exists in the mathematician's urn. The probability with which Keynes is concerned is that which pertains in the realm of human action and which is dependent on knowledge, ignorance and mind. This is a realm where things happen 'which we have no reason to expect' and where, although we may be in the twilight, we are not entirely blind (TP: 311). For Keynes this is the crux of the matter: *we are not blind*. Life is not a game of blind man's buff, since we have a capacity for reason and forming beliefs and opinions. We can never be certain, as in the probable outcomes of 'blind chance', but we can arrive at a degree of belief which gives us confidence to act. There is consequently as Keynes states:

> no *logical* difference between the problem of establishing a law of telepathy and that of establishing the law of gravitation. There is at present a *practical* difference on account of the much narrower scope of our knowledge, in the case of telepathy, of cognate matters. We can, therefore, be much less certain; but there is no reason why we should necessarily remain less certain after more evidence has been accumulated. (TP: 332)

This argument also holds for the existence of non-human spirits, the ether and the consciousness of dogs and trees!

It is at this point where Keynes has made the case against the view of humans as inhabiting a world of blind chance that he finally takes Moore's *Principia Ethica* to task for arguing that we cannot know or forsee the consequences of our actions, and therefore we ought to follow customs, convention and rules as they will probably lead to more good. Moore's argument, says Keynes, rests on the notion that we can only 'know for certain what will happen generally ... before we can assert a probability' (TP: 342). However, this is manifestly at odds with the theory of probability which is advanced by Keynes: it does not follow that because we do not have any certain knowledge of the future that we have to rely on conventional or established views of what to do so as to increase the amount of goodness. Keynes's point is that our ignorance of the future is not the main problem, but the relation of parts to wholes. If we suppose that goodness is organic (like physical laws) then in making decisions we ought to consider the probability of our actions in part increasing the good in the whole. In the whole probabilities cannot, in many cases, be calculated: degrees of goodness are not numerically measurable or arthimetically additive, neither are degrees of probability numerically measurable.

> Thus even if we know the degree of advantage which might be obtained from each of a series of alternative courses of actions and know also the probability in each case of obtaining the advantage in question, it is not always possible by a mere process of arithmetic to determine which of the alternatives ought to be chosen. If, therefore, the question of right action is under all circumstances a determinate problem, it must be in virtue of an intuitive judgment directed to the situation as whole, and not in virtue of an arithmetical deduction derived from a series of separate judgments directed to the individual alternatives treated in isolation. (TP: 345)

Another problem with the notion that we can rely on mathematical calculation and expectation in making decisions is the question of the 'weight of argument', that is to say, the weight of information, or knowledge, which is relevant to a given proposition. The weight of argument is an important idea in Keynes's philosophy – it is, for example, to form a key component of chapter twelve of the *General Theory*. Weight, he argues, comprises the sum of favourable and unfavourable evidence for a proposition and like probability, it cannot be measured (TP: 77). As the amount of relevant evidence increases so does the weight of argument, but the magnitude of probability may increase or diminish depending on the balance of favourable and unfavourable evidence. (See page 182 for a diagrammatic representation of this idea.) Increasing weight of evidence does not give us certainty, but it does give us a sense of confidence in our belief, and thereby a more substantial basis for action (TP: 77). Thus if two probabilities are equal in degree, we should rationally choose a course of action which is based on the greater body of knowledge (TP: 345). Even so, as he argues earlier on in chapter six of the treatise, there are limits to the information search. There must come a point when it is 'no longer worth while to spend trouble, before acting, in the acquistion of further information' (TP: 83). At this point intuitive judgment comes into play, rather than pure calculation: we make a decision based on the beliefs which we hold as to the probabilites of different outcomes.

Finally, Keynes raises the problem of risk: 'other things being equal, that course of action is preferable, which involve least risk and the results of which we have the most complete knowledge' (TP: 347). It is rational for human beings to be somewhat cautious and choose a course of action which has the lowest risk, and the greatest probability of obtaining the greatest good. Small or incremental change in which risks are lower, and the weight of evidence higher is rationally preferable to big or revolutionary change in which the risks of achieving good is high, and the weight of evidence is low. 'A high weight and the absence of risk increase *pro tanto* the desirability of the action to which they refer, but we cannot measure the amount of the increase' (TP: 348). This (Burkean) observation about risk which maintains that we cannot measure the desirability of a course of action is central to Keynes's argument for a moral science. Mathematics is of use in human decision making, but there are many complex areas of human endeavour where arithmetic, statistics and algebra are of little use, and may often serve to distort our understanding and perceptions. Indeed, we may be unable to act as we become preoccupied with getting more and more information and knowledge so as to increase our sense of certainty and confidence. As he later observed (in 1937) of the need for better economic data, being 'well informed makes the process of arriving at decisions much more complicated and difficult' (XXI: 409). Mathematical thinking, therefore, is of *limited* use in dealing with the problems of human beings.

The hope, which sustained many investigations in the course of the nineteenth century, of gradually bringing the moral sciences under the sway of mathematical reasoning, steadily recedes ... The old assumptions, that all quantity is numerical and that all quantitative characteristics are additive, can no longer be sustained. Mathematical reasoning now appears as an aid in its symbolic rather than in its numerical character. (TP: 349)

Probability can serve as a guide for modern man, as magic had served him in the past, but only when we realize that it is not simply to do with *mechanical* logic, mathematical frequency, and numerical data. Because mankind has a capacity for intuitive judgment – weighing evidence and assessing risk – we can still make decisions on the basis of beliefs which do not have *absolute* certainty, but a *degree* of certainty. The fact that we are ignorant about the future does not mean that we are unable to make rational judgments in order to penetrate 'into the real world' (TP: 56). Probability, however, cannot tell us what conclusions are true, nor can it provide us with certainty of success. Nevertheless, we can go forward in rational confidence free from the conservatism of Moore's *Principia*: in the twilight of probability we may be myopic, but we are not blind to possibility (TP: 356).

In his conclusion Keynes leaves us with two big ifs. Firstly, the practical usefulness of statistical inference can only exist *if*, as modern science claims: 'the universe of phenomena does in fact present those peculiar characteristics of atomism and limited variety' (TP: 468). And secondly: '*If* the contemporary doctrines of biology and physics remain tenable, we may have a remarkable, if undeserved, justification of some of the methods of the traditional calculus of probabilities' (TP: 468). However, by the time Keynes was writing, scientific knowledge had already moved some way in questioning many of the dominant scientific paradigms. Bernhard Riemann, for example, had developed a non-Euclidean geometry showing the limited validity of Euclid's axioms on curved surfaces; Poincaré, with whose work Keynes was very familiar, had already demonstrated that the universe may well be far more chaotic, random, unpredictable and complex than the clockwork model of the universe supposed; the metaphysics of evolution was being radically challenged in the work of Henri Bergson, Samuel Alexander and Alfred Whitehead. The deterministic Newtonian world view was everywhere under attack. By the time of the publication of the treatise the work of Einstein, Planck, and Bohr had shown that these ifs were no longer sustainable assumptions for a *general* theory of nature. The weight of relevant evidence was pointing inexorably towards the conclusion that these were revolutionary times. In the May of 1919, for example, the crucial experiment by Eddington had verified Einstein's explanation of gravitation. The world had entered an age of uncertainty, chance and probability, and for Keynes it was also an age of great possibilities which could be realized when once we abandoned a belief in analytical certainty, and mechanistic ways of thinking. By 1921 the old certainties of the natural and social universe had collapsed: physics was being turned upside down; politics and economics was in a state of chaos; and Europe apparently on the edge of an abyss. Keynes can only leave us with these two big ifs which suggest that, in the aftermath of the First World War, and the revolutions in scientific thought, mankind would have to find new ways of thinking. These ways of thinking he concludes might have more in common with the age of magic than the age of science:

> Professors of probability have been often and justly derided for arguing as if nature were an urn containing black and white balls in fixed proportions. Quetelet once declared in so many words – 'l'urne que nous interrogeons, c'est la nature'. But again in the history of science the methods of astrology may prove useful to the astronomer; it may turn out to be true – reversing Quetelet's expression – that 'La nature que nous interrogeons c'est une urne'. (TP: 468)

This idea of astrological methods being of use to the astronomer is a fitting description of Keynes's quest for a moral science to serve as a guide in a world in which religion was dying and for whom god was dead. This left only magic and science: alchemy and chemistry. As was apparent in *The Economic Consequences of the Peace*, Keynes wanted to analyse and explain the world, but he also wanted to change it. This comes out in his essay on Edgeworth where he returns to one of the central arguments of the treatise.

> Mathematical Psychics has not, as a science or study, fulfilled its early promise. In the 'seventies and 'eighties of the last century it was reasonable, I think, to suppose that it held great prospects. When the young Edgeworth chose it, he may have looked to find secrets as wonderful as those the physicists have found since those days. But ... this has not happened, but quite the opposite. The atomic hypothesis which has worked spendidly in physics breaks down in psychics. We are faced at every turn with the problems of organic unity, of discreteness, of discontinuity – the whole is not equal to the sum of its parts, comparisons of quantity fail us, small changes produce large effects, the assumptions of a uniform and homogenous continuum are not satisfied. Thus the results of Mathematical Psychics turn out to be derivative, not fundamental, indexes, not measurements, first approximations at the best; and fallible indexes, dubious approximations at that, with much doubt added to what, if anything they are indexes or approximations of. (X: 262)

But it was not only Edgeworth who had skated on thin ice and felt his foundations slip away (X: 262–3). The Keynes who penned this biographical essay had come to realize that the Great War had changed everything: it was not just the certainties of mathematics which had vanished. From a young man who had also hoped to sit aloft in a Cambridge 'heron's nest', Keynes in the 1920s had come to realize the importance of a concern 'with the earth' (X: 266). By the time of the publication of the treatise Keynes had long accepted that it was not the best vehicle for what he wanted to say about knowledge in the real world. This point was conceded by Keynes to Ramsey when he argued that degrees of belief (or the *a priori* probabilities) were 'part of our human outfit, perhaps given to us by natural selection, analogous to our perceptions and our memories rather than to formal logic' (X: 338–9). This comment is one of the few instances of Keynes reconsidering the issues which had dominated his mind for so very long. His admission in 1931 that. Ramsey had been right (in 1922) and that he was happier with a biological explanation rather than one couched in terms of probability and logic is perhaps indicative of how far he had come to accepting the importance of natural selection in human evolution – something which was a central idea contained in Marshall's *Principles* (see Marshall, 1947: 248, 270). It was also an argument which closely accorded with Keynes's views on eugenics and population which comes to the fore in his discussions on Malthus. In 1923, for example, he writes:

A point may be reached when ... blind instruments of selection do harm rather than good, and must be replaced by deliberate reason. It is many generations since men as individuals began to substitute moral and rational motive as their spring of action in place of blind instinct. (XVII: 453)

Keynes, in recognizing the validity of Ramsey's arguments in 1931, is only admitting to a change, *less in his way of thinking, than in his way of persuading,* that had taken place a decade earlier when he had found the theories of Marshall and Malthus increasingly more *agreeable* and relevant for dealing with the real world and its problems.

Several years after his observation on Ramsey, Keynes gave a fuller account of his change of mind in his essay 'My Early Beliefs' (1938). This essay has been the subject of much argument as to what he 'really' meant but what he says is simply that the beliefs that he held as a young man were subject to development and modification. The essay was occasioned by observations made by David Garnett regarding the views of D.H. Lawrence on the attitudes and beliefs of Keynes's Cambridge set, including Garnett, Duncan Grant, and Francis Birrell. Lawrence thought that the whole crowd were just a bunch of self-obsessed people living their lives like beetles, with not a care for anyone else, and without a scrap of 'reverence'. This recollection of the encounter with Lawrence before the First World War prompted Keynes to write his first 'philosophical' thoughts since he had finished his *Treatise on Probability.* Keynes reflected that there was a good deal of truth in Lawrence's criticism of his early beliefs and uses it as a point of departure on a tour through his mental or spiritual development. As a young man he had discovered a religion: how had that religion fared?

Keynes tells us that Moore's *Principa Ethica* had the most overwhelming impact on his mind. It opened up a 'new heaven and a new earth' (X: 435). This new religion made them fear nothing and gave them a dispensation to disregard conventional morality. In this new religion all that mattered were 'states of mind', and the contemplation of love, beauty, and truth. It was a religion which cared little about the real world of 'wealth, power, popularity or success' (X: 437). Moore gave him the basis of a rationalism which had no need of the Victorian morality which they all despised, but a method of relentlessly pursuing the truth. They were essentially withdrawn from the world and enjoyed a 'supreme self-confidence' and contempt for the unconverted. This is the kind of smug, arrogant beetle-like behaviour which so incensed Lawrence. Keynes, however, does not reject it entirely. He argues that it remains a truer and sweeter religion than other religions – such as on offer from Marx or Freud. He proclaims that he has held fast to the 'fundamental intuitions' of the *Principia Ethica*, but in practice they proved inadequate as a guide to making his way in the real world.

> they are much too few and too narrow to fit actual experience which provides a richer and more various content. That they furnish a justification of experience wholly independent of outside events had become an added comfort, even though one cannot live today secure in the undisturbed individualism which was the extraordinary achievement of early Edwardian days, not for our little lot, but for everyone else too. (X: 444)

Moore's sweet unwordly religion was a 'comfort', but it was of little use in dealing with the real world outside Bloomsbury and Cambridge. Economics was less of a comfort, but of more practical use. However, in one very important respect, Moore's book did provide a vitally important perspective on the outside world which was to stand Keynes in good stead: an 'escape' from the Benthamite tradition which had for so long dominated practical affairs. Moore had identified the main problem: Benthamite calculation. Keynes's period as a Moorean monk had shown him the dangers posed by Bentham and his followers. Years on, and with the benefit of practical experience of the real world of power, wealth, politics and ambition, Keynes had come to realize the truth of Moore's gospel for it was none other than Jeremy Bentham who was:

> the worm which has been gnawing at the insides of modern civilisation and is reponsible for its moral decay. We used to regard the Christians as the enemy, because they appeared as the representatives of tradition, convention and hocus-pocus. In truth it was the Benthamite calculus, based on the over-valuation of the economic criterion which was destroying the popular ideal. (X: 445–6)

One of the most important lessons which Keynes had learnt from Moore was how pernicious were Benthamite doctrines which grossly overvalued calculation and the economic problem. The lesson served to 'immunize' him and his fellows from other reductionist philosophies – not least that of Marxism. However, on the minus side, Moorism led to a failure to understand the importance of rules, and of what Lawrence had termed 'reverence'. Their denial of conventional morality – about which Keynes is somewhat ambiguous, as he says that he himself remains an 'immoralist' – is he thinks far less important than the mistake which underpinned their repudiation of the need to obey general rules: their failure to understand human nature. This error had clearly become so apparent to Keynes as a result of his experience as chronicled in *The Economic Consequences of the Peace*. Thus although Keynes continued to adhere to the sweet unworldly side of Moore's religion – a belief in the primacy of truth, beauty and human relations – he came to realize that what Moore and his fellow apostles had totally got wrong was the *reasonableness* of human nature. They had actually fallen into the same hole which Bentham made it his task to dig ever deeper – the belief in human rationality as the engine of human progress. This was the fault line under the temple of Moore, which the First World War was to fracture so completely. It exposed their lack of reality, and the superficiality of their judgment and feelings:

> In short, we repudiated all versions of the doctrine of original sin, of there being insane and irrational springs of wickedness in most men. We were not aware that civilization was a thin and precarious crust erected by the personality and the will of a very few, and only maintained by rules and conventions skilfully put across and guilefully preserved. (X: 447)

In holding such little regard for 'traditional wisdom or the constraints of custom' they showed a lack of 'reverence ... for everything and everyone' (X: 448–9). Keynes admits to having profoundly misunderstood human nature: he had been 'pre-Freudian' and confessed to still having a strong belief in rationality. He even pokes fun at it by noting that he is still 'silly' enough to busy himself writing letters to *The Times* and frequently giving way to his 'impulse to protest'. At heart, therefore, although having modified his beliefs to take account of the irrational aspects of human thought and behaviour, Keynes admits to having retained his early Moorean belief in a Platonic realm of ideas: 'I behave as if there really existed some authority or standard to which I can successfully appeal if I shout loud enough – perhaps it is some hereditary vestige of a belief in the efficacy of prayer' (X: 448).

If we read these remarks in the light of his introduction to his *Essays in Persuasion*, then it is evident that Keynes considers his work as an economist to have grown out of his early faith. He remained in the Church of Moore, but (as the author of the *Treatise of Probability*) as a dissenting voice. In his concluding paragraphs Keynes rightly dates the demise of his pure Moorean religion: the war had done for it, as Lawrence had predicted.

And as the years wore on towards 1914, the thinness and the superficiality, as well as the falsity, of our view of man's heart became, as it now seems to me, more obvious; and there was too, some falling away in the purity of the original doctrine. (X: 449)

Keynes, however, had not entirely lost his faith. He realized that if the kind of values and civilization which he had come to believe in – those of Moore – were to survive then he had to 'make contact with the eddies and currents underneath' (X: 450) the storms unloosed by the war. Despite the charm, intelligence, affection, and unworldliness of their pre-war existence, it was, for him, no longer possible to skim on the surface of a world when the crust of rational civilization was being torn asunder by the erruption of passions which he and his fellows had failed to comprehend until 1914. The war made him an economist.

In recent years a growing debate has emerged as to the relationship of Keynes's early philosophical ideas and his work as an economist. However, there is a danger that the debate surrounding Keynes the philosopher actually clouds the issue of what he 'really meant', rather than making matters clearer. Broadly these various interpretations can be placed on a continuum of 'change' and 'continuity'. That is, some argue, Keynes's philosophical position remained largely unchanged, whilst on the other hand there are those who maintain that he changed his mind in a number of important respects. It is not the object of this book to get involved in this debate, but to argue that we must keep in mind that Keynes did make one big change: in the period before the First World War when he had completed the *Treatise on Probability* and accepted the appointment as a teacher of economics he abandoned philosophy as a way of life and became an economist to earn his living. This is not to say that Keynes lost his interest in philosophy, or that the issues raised in his study of probability ceased to be important, or that he lost his Moorean faith, but that he found that economics was a better vehicle for what he had to say and what he wanted to be. Economics enabled him to do good and make money and influence people. Marshall's economics provided him with the methods of thought and a way of life which could advance those early values and beliefs. Keynes was to depart from Marshall's economics in a number of important respects – as he was from Moore's ethics. However, in so many respects Keynes's economics echoes Marshall's ideas and *Principles* even though he chose to criticize aspects of his theories. (As was also the case with Moore.) Keynes had grown up in the shadow of Marshall. This familiarity means that we do not find Keynes responding to reading Marshall's *Principles* with the kind of undergraduate sense of revelation which accompanied *Principia Ethica.* Keynes does not go around announcing 'Wow, have I read a book, or what!?' His journey towards economics was not by way of a Pauline (or Moorean) conversion, so much as finding economics increasingly more satisfactory as both a way of thinking and as a way of life. The way of life came first, and the way of thinking came second. Keynes became an economist first – due to the persistence of Marshall and the sheer boredom of the India Office – and then began to think and express ideas through economics. Economics was an escape route from the world of Whitehall back to the cosy world of Cambridge. At first there are no signs that this adoption of economics as a career marked a departure from his Moorean faith, but as his interest in economics deepened his philosophical concerns were transfused into a new body of knowledge and a new life of activity in the real world. Thus Keynes's intellectual development conformed to Marshall's great dictum (*Natura non facit saltum*): he did not move in leaps, but changed and evolved his thought over time and as a result of experience. Keynes found in Marshall's *Principles* ideas with which he could agree and which confirmed many of the conclusions which he had come to via the study of ethics and probability. As he found economics more *agreeable*, so the preoccupations which had dominated his life (1905–9) up to his failure to get a fellowship first time around (Moore and probability) began to recede from the forefront to the back of his mind. Reading Marshall from the perspective of an apostle of the *Principia*, and the author of a treatise on probability, it is apparent why he found himself agreeing with so much of the *Principles of Economics*. A number of ideas contained in the *Principles* may be mentioned to illustrate points of agreement between Keynes's own beliefs, both early and late. (Page references are to the eighth (1920) edition, published in 1947.)

- Economics was not an exact science, because it deals with the 'subtle and changing forces of human nature' (14, 31). It uses common sense (38) and ordinary language (51). Mathematics should not predominate in economic analysis.
- It is concerned with studying the manifestation of mental states (16), and is interested in the role of habit, custom and impulse in human behaviour (20, 723, 728).
- Many human motives cannot be reduced to self interest (24), and there are severe limitations to measuring human motivations (26).
- Money and the money motive is an important measure of human conduct and motivation (14, 15, 27, 33, 38).
- The practical motive of economics is the question of how to act so as to 'increase the good and diminish the evil influences of economic freedom' (41) and to 'gain practical knowledge for its own sake, and to obtain guidance in the practical conduct of life' (42). This requires the use of perception, imagination and reason – but most of all imagination (43).
- There is a hierarchy of wants. Economic progress involved developing

creative human activites rather than the indulgence of 'sensuous craving'. 'Leisure is used less and less as an opportunity for mere stagnation'. Thus: 'although it is man's wants in the earliest stages of his
development that give rise to his activities, yet afterwards each new
step upwards is to be regarded as the development of new activities
giving rise to new wants, rather than of wants giving rise to new
activities' (89).

- Time was the source of the 'greatest difficulties' in economics (109,
  112).
- Human progress can come about through improvement in the human
  population and must be gradual (248). Marshall believed in applying
  the theory of natural selection to economic problems and was hopeful
  that Eugenics would be able to increase man's capacity to control over
  natural developments (248).
- The need to control 'malignant forms of speculation' (719).
- The dangers of overstating the economic evils. It is necessary to 'look at
  the whole of the economic, to say nothing of the moral and other aspects
  of a practical problem before attempting to deal with it at all' (722).
- Ideas are important.

Ideas, whether those of art or science, or those embodied in practical appliances,
are the most 'real' of gifts that each generation receives from its predecessors. The
world's material wealth would quickly be replaced if it were destroyed, but the
ideas by which it was made were retained. If however the ideas were lost, but not
the material wealth, that would dwindle and the world would go back to poverty.
And most of our knowledge of mere facts could quickly be recovered if it were
lost, but the constructive ideas of thought remained; while if the ideas perished,
the world would enter again on the Dark Ages. (780)

In these issues, as in many others, Keynes found much with which to agree in
Marshall's *Principles*. During the war he noted, for example, that: 'Marshall
always used to insist that it was through ethics he arrived at political economy
and I would claim myself in this, as in other respects to be a pupil of his'
(cited in O'Donnell, 1989: 165). In his essay on Marshall Keynes makes
great play with the fact that Marshall came to economics through ethics (X:
171), something which is directly parallel to Keynes's own journey, and also
that he had a 'double nature' in being a preacher and scientist (X: 173). This
duality is, of course, only too apparent in the life of the author of *Essays in
Persuasion*. Marshall, he argues, wanted to get involved in the 'vast laboratory of the world', as did Keynes, except that Marshall's laboratory was made
from the business and working classes (X: 187), whereas Keynes's laboratory
was formed out of public opinion, bankers, investors, civil servants, and
politicians. In his essay on Marshall he makes it clear that where he departs

from Marshall's approach to economics is with regard to Marshall's morality and his intellectual cautiousness. Keynes became an economist *because* of Marshall, and spent the early years teaching Marshall's economics with little dissent from the great man's theories. Thus the young Keynes at the India Office and later as an economics don may be viewed as a man of two books the *Principia* and the *Principles*: he was an apostle of Moore and a pupil of Marshall. However, by the time of the First World War and its tragic aftermath Keynes had evidently found a third man: Malthus.

Thomas Malthus (1766–1834) was a clergyman who is most famous for his *Essay on the Principle of Population as it Affects the Future Improvement of Society* (1798), and later *An Investigation of the Cause of the Present High Price of Provisions* (1800), and the *Principles of Political Economy* (1820). Keynes's thoughts on these (and other) writings evolved over a number of years and was expressed in published form in the essay he prepared for *Essays in Biography* (1933) and in the same year he was writing the *General Theory* in a piece for the *Economic Journal* (1935). This latter essay was subsequently added to form the work now included in Volume 10 of the collected writings. By the time of the 1935 essay Keynes had come to see Malthus as he was later to portray Newton – a victim of his popularizers who took what they wanted from his writings whilst failing to understand his philosophy as a whole. The intuitive alchemist, Newton, fathered a mechanical view of the universe and of scientific method, whilst the intuitive clergyman, Malthus, fathered a host of children who used his ideas (later mixed with Darwinism) to defend the *status quo* as well as Karl Marx who was dedicated to overthrowing capitalism (X: 105). There are two parts to Newton's work (science and alchemy) and similarly Malthus is also composed of two 'divided parts' which, when put together, reveal the whole. There is the part of Malthus which was a 'moral scientist' and historian – as revealed in the *Essay on Population* – and the part which was the economist as found in his *An Investigation of the Cause of the Present High Price of Provisions*, *The Principles*, and his correspondence with Ricardo. In the *General Theory* he makes use of both parts, but is mainly concerned to show how Malthus's concept of 'effective demand' is the vital missing link in modern economics. Keynes's view (in both his essay on Malthus and in the *General Theory*) is that: 'If only Malthus, instead of Ricardo, had been the parent stem from which nineteenth century economics proceeded, what a much wiser and richer place the world would be to-day!' (X: 100–101). Malthus was the 'first of the Cambridge economists' (X:107) and in linking his own ideas with those of Malthus he is manifestly laying claim to be the direct intellectual heir of Malthusian moral science.

Malthus's influence on Keynes was manifested early on in his speech on population to the Oxford Political Philosophy and Science Club in 1914. He had begun to read economics seriously from 1905 onwards and by this time he had become familiar with his writings. Malthusian economics is a major theme of *The Economic Consequences of the Peace* (1919) and a key issue in his contributions to the *Manchester Guardian Commercial* suppplements on reconstruction (1922) (XVII: 440–46; 453–4) and his interest in Malthus was to deepen over the following decades. He wrote a masterly essay on Malthus in 1922 (and later revised it in 1933) and the *General Theory* and other works are replete with references to the first of the Cambridge economists. Keynes saw himself writing in the Cambridge tradition of economics as a 'moral science'. Malthus was one of the fathers of this tradition and Keynes, the protégé of Marshall, claims himself as heir to this tradition by his assertion that economics was a moral science (XIV: 297, 300; X, 301). Keynes argued that the greatest disaster which befell economics was that it took a wrong turn by adopting Ricardian abstraction, rather than Malthusian moral science. The influence of Malthus on Keynes may be seen in three periods in his life. First, before the First World War, with Keynes's use of Malthus's analysis of population growth. Second, in the 1930s when Keynes was preparing the *General Theory* he was to be taken by Malthus's concept of 'effective demand'. And finally, after the *General Theory*, when in several observations, Keynes came closest to defining what he believed was the true nature of economics as a 'moral science'. The essay on Malthus which was published in *Essays in Biography* (1933) shows Keynes drawing together the various strands of Malthus's thought which came to shape his own thinking and which he used to support his theory. Keynes saw his task in the *General Theory* as setting people back onto the right Malthusian road away from the mental cul-de-sac built by Ricardo and his followers. If Moore provided the framework for his philosophy, it is Malthus to whom Keynes felt closest in the seeking to re-invent a moral science for policy making in the twentieth century. It is important therefore that we make clear what Malthus's idea of moral science encompassed since it is apparent that, by the late 1930s, Keynes's notion of economics had developed into a form of modern Malthusianism. We shall be exploring this theme in subsequent chapters, but at this point it may be useful to point out the main aspects of Keynes's Malthusianism.

- His belief that human history was greatly influenced by human instincts, the most important of which is our sexuality.
- Whereas Malthus believed that the exercise of rational 'moral restraint' was the primary means by which human instincts could be diverted to provide the motive force for good, Keynes came to believe that the state had to accept the responsibility of regulating and restraining economic forces so as to create the conditions in which the good society could come about.

- Like Malthus Keynes believed that it was possible to so order the world that human reason could take the upper hand in human behaviour.
- Economics was a moral science which could provide the tools for human improvement.
- Economics was not like the natural sciences. As Malthus argued, in words that are echoed in Keynes's critique of the Ricardian revolution and Tinbergen's economics:

We should fall into a serious error if we were to suppose that any propositions, the practical results of which depend on the agency of so variable a being as man, and upon the qualities so variable a compound as the soil, can ever admit of the same kinds of proof, or lead to the same certain conclusions, as those which relate to figure and number. There are indeed in political economy great general principles, to which exceptions are of the most rare occurrence, and prominent land-marks which may almost always be depended upon as safe guides; but even these, when examined, will be found to resemble in most particulars the great general rules in morals and politics founded upon the known passions and propensities of human nature: and whether we avert to the qualities of man, or of the earth he is destined to cultivate, we shall be compelled to acknowledge, that the science of political economy bears a nearer resemblance to the science of morals and politics than to that of mathematics. (Malthus, 1968: 1)

What followed from this for Keynes, as for Malthus, was that economics should not be excessively abstract (as Marshall also insisted), but rooted in the experience of the real world. Economic progress was inextricably linked with moral and mental progress. Unlike Moore or Marshall, Keynes (like Malthus) remained true to his religion. He did not abandon the *Principia Ethica* or the *Principles* as they had the Bible. Despite his modifications to Moore's ideas he remained a practising member of the church which he had embraced on first opening Moore's great book. And, although he broke with Marshall's economics he did not dissent from his general approach. In becoming an economist Keynes did not change his philosophy, he made what would be termed today a smart career move. He realized that as an economist he could attain the kind of public attention and practical influence which a philosopher could never hope to attain. Parson Malthus preached, and Keynes saw his mission as persuasion. Moore, Malthus and Marshall were all men of belief and the young Keynes was also a man in search of a new religion. The parallel between the age of Newton and the age of Keynes is instructive on this point. As Dobbs notes in her seminal work on Newton's alchemy, the growth in the interest in subject during the seventeenth century was amongst those, like Newton, who were turning away from theological convention as being irrelevant and devisive. Alchemy thus came to serve a religious function for the adepts at a time when Christianity was failing to provide the clear guide which they required (Dobbs, 1975: 80). I think that we can envisage Keynes in a similar mood of dissatisfaction in the decade or so before the First World War: religion was finished, Moore was a new beginning, but it was somewhat inadequate as a guide to action. Keynes found in economics a new alchemy which showed how knowledge could transform and empower. Like Malthus, therefore, Keynes began as a philosopher, became a man of events and facts and thence spread his wings as an economic theorist (X: 107). And, rather like Newton, he begins with the sober chemistry of probability and gives it up for the possibilities of economic alchemy (Westfall, 1994: 112–16).

The change of direction in Keynes is well marked out. In his book on *Indian Currency Reform* (1913) we find the emerging economist seeking to offer analysis and prescription and it is here we find the first sign of a new-found fascination which is to dominate his thoughts in the years to come: money and gold. Six years later Keynes's transformation into an economist is complete with his brilliant and devasting critique of a consummate human folly, the Treaty of Versailles. *The Economic Consequences of the Peace* (1919) shows us the many facets of Keynes's thought which are developed in later writings, especially his twin concerns: money and the Malthusian devil. But we also find echoes of *Principia Ethica*; his ideas on uncertainty, ignorance and probability which had been formulated in the *Treatise on Probability*; and sentiments which could have been composed by Edmund Burke. It is a book written by a man with a mounting passion to bring about a decrease in human stupidity and an increase in 'intelligent' reasoning published at a time when it looked as if civilization was on the edge of a deep and dark precipice. Keynes, the follower of Moore, held out a beacon of light pointing towards the imperative of seeking goodness and truth in human affairs. Keynes the economist draws on Malthus to warn of the dangers of an excessive growth of population and the lack of resources and upon his own expertise and intuition on the central role which money plays in shaping events. The Keynes who wrote this great book is no longer a 'water spider' (X: 450) skimming the surface of a smooth Cambridge pond. Keynes by this time had waded through some of the murkiest waters in history. He emerged from Paris to face a world that no longer had the certainties of Harvey Road and Victorian England. Philosophy and probability were far from forgot, but after the First World War Keynes had come to realize that economics was destined to be the method and tool of future human progress.

The alchemist begins with his experiments by acting upon crude 'prime material'. Adepts of the so called 'Royal Art' might begin with 'base matter', such as lead, excreta, or urine and subject the substances to what is expressed in the maxim *'Solve et coagula'*, that is 'dissolve and combine'. Dissolving meant to refine, destroy and break down the substances and is followed by a process of combining the dead and putreyfing matter into a new, reborn and purifed substance. In psychological terms it may be viewed as a process in which old ideas, attitudes, beliefs and illusions are destroyed and subjected to the heat of doubt, questioning, and despair, from which contradictory and conflicting elements a new 'perfected' life is formed. Keynes's prime material, upon which he was to work all his life in order to bring about the transmutation of capitalism, was that curious, elusive and mercurial substance known as public opinion. Appropriately enough, *The Economic Consequences of the Peace* is dedicated 'to the formation of the general opinion of the future' (II: 189). Great events, he thought, flow like a tide in human affairs, and in *The Economic Consequences of the Peace* Keynes proclaims a faith in the possibility that these currents can be shaped and directed by 'setting in motion those forces of instruction and imagination which change opinion' (II: 188). To do this he urges us to use the following maxim of dissolving and combining political *prima materia*: 'The assertion of truth, the unveiling of illusion, the dissipation of hate, the enlargement and instruction of men's hearts and minds' (II: 188). This theme of changing opinion is developed in *A Revision of the Treaty* (1922). The modern statesman is depicted as a creature of public opinion who, to suit himself, will excuse decisions (such as the Versailles Treaty) by appealing to the pressure of public opinion and the demands of the mob.

> He may judge rightly that this is the best of which a democracy is capable – to be jockeyed, humbugged, cajoled along the right road. A preference for truth or for sincerity *as a method* may be a predjudice based on some aesthetic or personal standard, inconsistent in politics, with practical good. (III: 2)

Keynes, however, is not content with such a democracy, and he characterizes the modern dilemma as a struggle less between 'true and false' as between 'outside' and 'inside' opinion. Those on the 'inside' draw upon a limited range of opinion and either pay too much, or too little attention to outside opinion. Too much, because they are ready to do anything in order to concede to it, and yet too little because they think it is fickle and facile. However this disregard for opinion is dangerous since:

> what is said before the world is, still, of deeper consequence than the subterranean breathings and well-informed whisperings, knowledge of which allows inside opinion to feel superior to outside opinion, even at the moment of bowing to it. (III: 3)

Public opinion for Keynes was the very stuff of which possibilities could be made. It was, he argues, like Rousseau's General Will, a 'mysterious entity' that could be formed and shaped by men of ideas.

Public opinion held that Hans Andersen's Emperor wore a fine suit; and in the United States especially, public opinion changes sometimes, as it were, *en bloc*. If, indeed, public opinion were an unalterable thing, it would be a waste of time to discuss public affairs. And though it may be the chief business of newsmen and politicians to ascertain its momentary features, a writer ought to be concerned, rather, with what public opinion should be. (III: 125)

Keynes saw his mission as persuading opinion – both on the inside and outside – by the method of *'Solve et coagula'* he had set out in the *The Economic Consequences of the Peace* so as to break the 'charms' of political ruling opinion. In the 1920s Keynes was an active journalist and laboured hard to 'influence the course of events in time' (IX: xxii). Following the success of the *The Economic Consequences of the Peace* Keynes was invited to edit a supplement on reconstruction for the *Manchester Guardian Commercial* in 1922. His contribution to this important series of articles amplifies the theme of persuading public opinion which had formed the introduction to *A Revision of the Treaty*. Introducing the supplements Keynes argues that some of the problems facing Europe are only solved by 'time and labour', but others are man made – 'the offspring of ignorance, remoteness and prejudice' (XVII: 351). Keynes believed that the publication of views and opinions can only serve to bring a 'collective wisdom' to bear on problems out of which 'knowledge and sympathy will grow up, and remedies issue from them' (XVII: 351). He viewed the work of the supplements – and other attempts to bring intelligence to act upon human affairs – as the only means by which the economist (*qua* moral scientist) can bring his 'craft' to exercise an influence over the objects of his study:

How happy are chemists, mathematicians, physicians, and astronomers that the world holds the craft of each to be an unsearchable mystery, and does not seek or pretend to understand it! If it were crypton, harmonics, kidneys, or nebulae we sought to stabilise, we could contemplate the best plan and carry it out in scientific seclusion without ever troubling to make it clear to you, my intelligent but unscientific friends, the readers of this article. But an economist must be humble; his field of thought lies in the public sphere. He cannot accomplish, except by persuasion – and by simplifying. (XVII: 355)

Economics is concerned with the volatile, unpredictable, non-quantifiable forces and elements which are 'stabilized' in the realm of the human mind: it involves dissolving and combining ideas, moods, sentiments and opinions through the alchemy of persuasion and simplification. Economics is a science of morals, and not a science of matter or machines. Later on in the same *Manchester Guardian* article Keynes conjures up the idea of the political world being dragged along by two ill-matched horses. (The metaphor which Plato uses in the *Phaedrus* to describe the soul as a charioteer seeking to control two black (evil) and white (good) horses.) One is a horse composed of 'atmosphere' 'public sentiment', 'cant phrases of the hour' and the 'gradual shifting of what it is correct for the conventional person to think and say'. The other is a horse whose name is: right of action of policy (XVII: 421).

> whereas the creation of atmosphere relies upon sentiment and suggestion and bluff, and must operate on the elements of human nature which are intellectually vaguest, the right policy of action is a realistic business, cool and scientific and technical, not intelligible to the mob, and ill-judging unless it proceeds from what is intellectually clearest. (XVII: 421)

These two horses were doomed to be unhappy mates however they were harnessed together. In the *Manchester Guardian* supplements, as in his later work, Keynes is rather like a circus rider whose great talent it is to stand asride both the horses of opinion and right action and rein in and control their power to serve a common end. This great feat is a trick which only the economist can perform: it is the economist who should be king of the ring because he is 'a better and wiser orator than the general or the lawyer or the oratorical lawyer' (XVII: 432). The economist's task was to open the eyes of policy makers and public opinion. Events could be controlled (II: 3), but only if public and politicians were fully engaged with reality. If the collective will of society could be harnessed, then human beings have it in their power to enter into the march of events and direct them to the greater good (XVII: 438). Blindness and illusion were humanity's greatest enemies.

> The blindness of opinion stands in the way of improvement, rather than material difficulties beyond man's control. ... (the) blind instruments of selection ... must be replaced by deliberate reason. It is many generations since men as individuals began to substitute moral and rational motive as their spring of action in place of blind instinct. They must now do the same thing collectively. (XVII: 453)

Such 'croakings' of a self-confessed Cassandra were collected in 1931 as *Essays in Persuasion*. Although they were written in order to impact on daily affairs Keynes never lost sight of the longer term horizon. It is signficant that, as he notes, amidst the pieces which he wrote to change immediate opinion, there are also essays which take a radical, if not utopian viewpoint of economic problems.

> And here emerges more clearly what is in truth his central thesis throughout – the profound conviction that the economic problem, as one may call it for short, the problem of want and poverty and the economic struggle between classes and nations, is nothing but a frightful muddle, a transitory and an unnecessary muddle. For the western world already has the resources and the technique, if we could create the organisation to use them, capable of reducing the economic problem,

which now absorbs our moral and material energies, to a position of secondary importance. (IX: xviii)

Despite the fact that his croakings (sic) have had such a little effect Keynes proclaims that he still believed that:

> the day is not far off when the economic problem will take a back seat where it belongs, and that the arena of the heart and the head will be occupied, or reoccupied, by our real problems – the problems of life and human relations, of creation and behaviour and religion. (IX: xviii)

The task of persuasion was vital to bringing such a future about, because by changing opinion and engendering a new 'faith', we can also bring a new world into being in which the 'real problems' are addressed:

> For if we consistently act on the optimistic hypothesis, this hypothesis will tend to be realised; whilst by acting on the pessimistic hypothesis we can keep ourselves for ever in the pit of want. (IX: xviii)

The crude, rough, volatile, ignorant stuff which constitutes the primary material of his work in the 1920s and 1930s is public opinion in its various forms. It had to be broken down, destroyed and re-constituted, if civilization were to be re-born. Keynes believed that the world could be redeemed by the effort of changing ideas, aspirations and values. He did not see opinion like a politician, that is as something that had to be followed or manipulated, but as an alchemist: it was a protean force which had to be the object of hard work so as to clarify opinion and transmute values. This process demanded the constant attention of the adept. If change was to be accomplished the modern Cassandra had to be involved in the flow of events, not stuck in an academic ivory tower. His laboratory was the real world, and its problems a world which was as far away from that of Moore, Marshall and the Apostles and Bloomsbury as it was possible to get. In criticizing his old economics teacher, for example, Keynes argued against the academic approach and recommended that economists should leave the 'glory of the quarto to Adam Smith' and instead 'pluck the day, fling pamphlets to the wind, write always *sub specie temporis,* and achieve immortality by accident, if at all' (X: 199). And to the journalist Kingsley Martin he proffered the advice not to take up an academic appointment (at the University College of Wales, Aberystwyth) since international relations was best done outside 'dingy academic circles': better to choose the 'daily task of persuasion' than writing big books (XXVIII: 30). Keynes, of course, did both. He wrote a number of big books in order to influence intellectual opinion which could permeate the wider domains of opinion, as well as numerous letters, articles, radio talks and anything else which gave him an opportunity to get his views across on current affairs.

The Economic Consequences was followed by another important work which shows Keynes forging new instruments of persuasion: *A Tract on Monetary Reform* (1923). In this book Keynes is drawing heavily on his journalism and his desire to change the mind of his readers is most evident. The *Tract* is not simply a book which analyses problems: it also seeks to offer a way by which a transformation in which another crude, rough material, *money*, could be wrought. Money now appears as a substance which can, in wise hands, be so manipulated that it can serve the greater good and release human possibilities. Money (like public opinion) is a base and filthy stuff, but like the alchemist's mercury it had to be 'fixed' and 'stabilized' and used as an agent of transformation. The problems of a monetary economy required, as he commented in 'Does Unemployment need a Drastic Remedy' (1924), *experimentation* to effect a fundamental change in political–economic relationships.

> The next developments of politico-evolution may be found in cooperation between private initiative and the public exchequer. The true socialism of the future will emerge, I think, from an endless variety of experiments directed towards discovering the appropriate spheres of the individual and the social, and the terms of fruitful alliance between these sister instincts. (XIX: 222)

This transformational potential which Keynes saw in a monetary economy becomes clear when we compare Keynes with the work of Georg Simmel whose book on money had been published in 1900 (Simmel, 1990). As Frankel shows, whereas Simmel was concerned with money as a symbol of trust, a means of communication and as a way of life which evolved in civilization to enable men to combat insecurity, uncertainty, and ignorance (Frankel, 1977: 81), Keynes saw money as an illusion, a creation of the state and as a means to attain other goals. It was the 'child (or the changling) of the State and is simply that which is declared by the State from time to time to be a good legal discharge of money contracts' (IV: 6). Whereas Simmel's analysis is pessimistic about the impact of money on human relationships and the longevity of the monetary civilization, Keynes believed that money, though an impure means, could be used to bring about the good society. Again, whereas Simmel sees the story of money as tragedy, Keynes sees it as offering the prospect of completing and perfecting civilization. Simmel gives us a dismal science, but Keynes's philosophy of money shows us the way to developing new techniques for shaping human destiny. Money for Simmel is 'inside' human society and civilization, but for Keynes it is a dreadful power which must be brought under the restraints of human reason to attain an increase in the good. This theme of the possibilities contained within a money economy sounds throughout his writings in the 1920s and 1930s and reaches its fullest expression in *A Treatise on Money* published in 1930. In the 1920s there were also a number of plans for books which did not actually come to fruition that give us a very clear idea as to how his ideas on a monetary economy were developing. In notes for 'An examination of Capitalism', for example (1924–6), he expresses the advantage of capitalism as its potential in respect of the 'mobilization of greedy instincts'. Societies built on the foundations of avaricious instincts – like Babylon – eventually decline and fall (O'Donnell, 1992: 808–902). The problem was, as Keynes saw it, one of releasing the energy of the money economy, whilst at the same time ensuring that capitalism also realized its potential for social justice, the progress of civilization and individual freedom.

Like the *Treatise on Probability*, *A Treatise on Money* marks a point of transition in the development of Keynes's ideas. And just as in the case of probability, the treatise on money was already rather old news by the time of its publication as he was already re-thinking his analysis. The theme of the book(s) is the problem of fluctuating prices and its consequences for the output of a money economy. Keynes aimed to show how the classical view that savings and investment (S and I) were equal to one another was mistaken, and that in conducting economic policy as if they *were*, a capitalist society was undermining the very foundations of its prosperity. The reason for this was that savings and investment were two activities which were distinct and unbalanced: there was *no* automatic mechanism which ensured that all money not spent on consumption would be channelled into investment. The classical theory claimed that there were self-adjusting forces operating in the monetary economy which ensured that increasing savings would trigger increased investment. Keynes shows how, unless banks operate so as to lower the rate of interest, the economy could remain stuck in a slump for a very long time. This linear geometry in which S=I was erroneous since the monetary economy was far more complex a system than the quantity theory of money describes. Savings could very well run ahead of investment thus leading to a situation in which a society becomes wealthier in money terms (savings) but increasingly poorer in real terms. There was no straight line between S and I, but a gap which had to be remedied by the action of central banks acting so as to adjust the rate of interest in order to stimulate investment and deter the desire to hold onto money and engage in speculation. However, in an economy in which the value of money was fixed against gold, and in which public works were ruled out this becomes impossible and the only remedy is 'nature's cure' – the Malthusian solution – so that poverty, low wages, unemployment in the long run bring savings and investment back into balance. But in the long run we are all dead (IV: 65) and the entrepreneurial spirit is moribund. The *Treatise on Money* makes the point that classical theory is blinded by the apparent logic of the money mechanism: in reality, however, the economic system is formed out of (incalculable) human expectations not from a geometry in which the (calculable) sum of S equals the sum on the other side, I. If, therefore, we wish to escape from an economic slump we had to abandon the Laplacean world view in which the economic universe had no need for the hypotheses that a monetary economy requires a hand to keep prices and investment stable and balanced. That the system does need directive intelligence is because it is made from organic material: the opinions, sentiments, and expectations of entrepreneurs. Given this fact, entrepreneurs could be influenced so as to create a national (and international) financial order conducive to promoting a sense of the future which encouraged risk and enterprise, and inhibited hoarding and speculation. If bouts of inflation (investment running ahead of savings) and deflation (savings running ahead of investment) were to be avoided, central banks had to be organized so as to exercise a guiding hand on the way in which savers, investors and entrepreneurs think about the future. Thus the mechanicals had got it completely wrong: it was not puritanical, anal retentive abstinence and thrift which could get the stalled economic machine started again, but the spirit of enterprise.

However, after *A Treatise on Money* Keynes had come to realize that his focus on money and prices was too narrow, and needed to take account of the effect of changes in output in the economy, as well as of the influence of money (GT: xxii). He had also come to the conclusion that the directive intelligence of the banks was not enough to maintain full employment: the state had to accept a wider responsibility for managing the economy. *The General Theory of Employment Interest and Money* (1936) was, as we shall see later in Chapter 4, Keynes's master work which provided a general theory of how the economy as a whole functioned, and how the monetary system could be used as one of the main tools of managing the level of output. Here the alchemy was completed by showing how by regulating the great economic elements the state could realize a short run equilibrium and a long term transformation. In the years following the publication of the *General Theory* he was dogged by ill-health and yet with the outbreak of war Keynes was to find a new lease of life – as a man of action – in contributing to crucial areas of policy making including the budgetary system, national insurance, and full employment on the domestic level and internationally with the US loan and the Bretton Woods agreement. By the outbreak of the war Keynes's ideas had (in part) become broadly accepted by academics, journalists, civil servants and politicians. Typically of Keynes he saw the war as a time of tremendous possibility and a period of transformation in which he was determined to play as full a part as he could in forging a new economic, social and international order.

Keynes's alchemy was a quest to find a way of perfecting the system so that a harmonious condition could be attained by human intervention. Unlike the Newtonian scientists, therefore, he did not see the social universe existing in a state of God-made perfection and order, but a world which was in need of human action to purify it and bring it into new possibilities. He may not have shared the same symbols and metaphors as the alchemist Paracelsus, but he shared the same striving, and the same faith in his own intuitive powers to effect:

> The liberation of gold from dross – i.e., the alchemistic process of the gradual transformation of *materia prima*, the unfinished, nonpurified primal matter, into *materia ultima*, the purest and most accomplished form of matter ... the conquest of natural forces by magic. (Jacobi: 1988: xlvi–vii)

For a generation schooled on Keynesian economics the accomplishment of Keynes was truly magical. Bliss it was to be alive in the Keynesian age. A new heaven and a new earth, all because of one book. When I was young and green I eagerly sought out this book only to find that, as Stewart had warned, it was not an intellectual journey to be undertaken except by the very brave or foolish as it was one which '*even* economists approach with some trepidation' (Stewart, 1967: 264). And yet, this book, more than any other, was credited with banishing one of the greatest evils to beset mankind, mass unemployment. How well I remember reading Michael Stewart's confident assertion that we no longer needed to fear the devil which tormented our parents and grandparents.

> Mass unemployment was brought to an end by the Second World War. It has never returned ... Such a tremedous transformation might be expected to have many casues. But in this case one can point to one cause above all others: the publication in 1936 of a book called *The General Theory of Employment, Interest and Money* by John Maynard Keynes. (Stewart, 1967: 9)

What a book, and what magic! Keynes showed us how he found a way which could heal 'diseased' (sic) capitalism and purify it so as to make it productive and fruitful. For, contrary to its critics, capitalism was not doomed to inevitable decay and decomposition (X: 65), it could be brought back to a new and more vigorous life. Keynes came to free a capitalism 'pregnant' with the 'possibilities of modern enterprise' (X: 327) from the grip of puritanism and renew it with a pre-reformation faith in the potential of the economic arts. In place of the sermons on providence from the financial puritans Keynes proclaimed that the economic forces which brought so much misery to so many could be 'managed' by those adept enough for the task. Thus if Locke (another alchemist) wrote the 'first modern book' (X: xix), then it may be said of Keynes's *General Theory* that it was, perhaps, the last of the ancient books of alchemy. It offered an inspiring prospect which was as commanding and audacious as ever dreamt of by the alchemists of old. For those that read it the *General Theory* offered either a new heaven and a new earth, or a vision of Faust in hell. No wonder that it created a new faith in economics as the master science, and caused others to form their own church during the Keynesian dark age which they had feared might be visited upon a world practising the Keynesian arts. The *General Theory* promised what the ancients had written of long ago: the possibility that human beings might be able to shape, mould and transform what is into what could or ought to be. Like other modern sciences Keynesianism had no use for the chemistry of the alchemists, but it readily adhered to the the great goal of the art: completing and perfecting nature through the union of opposites. As is made clear at the end of the *General Theory* defective capitalism could be healed through the exercise of Paracelsian homeopathy: remedying the disease of capitalist democracy by giving it a very diluted dose of its poisonous opposite: socialism. And, time was short, for if the medicine was not quickly administered society risked the inevitable enantiodromia: democratic capitalism would transmute into totalitarian collectivism.

Keynes, therefore, unlike Marx, did not see war, and the decay of capitalism as the end, but on the contrary, he viewed its decomposition as a source of a vital re-birth. His vision saw human action on the world as transformative. Natural forces are mutable, not immutable inevitable laws of history. Like the alchemists Keynes saw human beings as having a capacity to share in creation and perfect it. This required experimentation: the application of intelligence, feelings as well as reason, judgment, and above all, intuition. Thus Keynes's economics was in essence a radical departure from the world ushered in by the apostles of the Newtonian revolution – but not that of Newton the man. Keynes was really urging us to go back to a time when science and sorcery were as one. Our means of transportation was to be found in Newton's box of hermetic papers.

2. Newton's alchemy and Keynes's moral science

The order of development of Newton's chemical notebook was significant. He did not stumble into alchemy, discover its absurdity, and make his way to sober, 'rational' chemistry. Rather he started with sober chemistry and gave it up rather quickly for what he took to be the greater profundity of alchemy. The philosophical tradition of alchemy had always regarded its knowlege as the secret possession of a select few. The significance of alchemy in his intellectual odyssey lay in the broader vistas it opened up to him, additional categories to supplement and complete the mechanistic ones. (Westfall, 1994: 112, 116, 118)

He told Austin Robinson that his best ideas came to him from 'messing about with figures and seeing what they mean'. He was not the first of the modern statisticians, but the last of the magicians of number. For him numbers were akin to those mystic 'signs' or 'clues' by which the necromancers had tried to uncover the universe. This is the aspect of Newton which most attracted him. (Skidelsky, 1992: 414)

Lord Stewart. What disasters I must suffer too!
Every day we try to save,
but every day our needs increase
and day by day my troubles grow.
Emperor. (after some reflection to Mephistopheles)
Speak Fool. Do you know some further cause for woe?
Mephistopheles. I know of none, and only see the splendor
surrounding you and all your court – Could confidence
be wanting ... where, strengthened by intelligence, good will
and energy of many kinds wait your use ...
Where in the world is something not in short supply?
Someone lacks this, another that, but here the lack is money.
Of course you can't just pick it off the floor,
but Wisdom's skill is getting what's most deeply hidden ...
and if you ask who will extract it, I reply:
a man that nature has endowed with mighty intellect. (Goethe, 1994: 4852–95)

Cambridge in the seventeenth century was, as Keynes notes in his essay on Newton, a centre of alchemical research and had a long established tradition of esoteric philosophy. Alchemy at Cambridge did not, however, come to an end with Sir Isaac Newton. It was revived by the university's three greatest moral scientists: Thomas Malthus, Alfred Marshall and John Maynard Keynes.

The impulse which drives the alchemist is, as Paracelsus argued, a universal (or perhaps the archetypal) desire to transform, and transmute natural forces and substances: 'for alchemy means to carry to its end something that has not yet been completed' (Parcelsus, 1988: 141). For Malthus it meant working with natural laws of God and Newton to remedy the human condition and mitigate evil. Nature and human instincts had to be taken in hand and directed towards a higher individual purpose and a better society. This belief in the ultimate moral claims of economics was to be echoed in the work of Marshall who found in J.S. Mill's *Principles* a new faith to fill the void left by his loss of religious beliefs. For Marshall economics empowered mankind with the capacity to understand natural forces and use them to transform human motivation and social conditions. Finally, Newton's mantle is donned by Keynes for whom economics provided an apparatus which could bring a new capitalism to birth out of the chaos of the old *laissez-faire* system. Like Mill and Marshall Keynes did not read the Reverend Malthus as a harbinger of doom and gloom, but quite the opposite: as a prophet of possibility. As J.S. Mill notes in his *Autobiography*:

> This great doctrine, orginally brought forward as an argument against the indefinite improvability of human affairs, we took up with ardent zeal in the contrary sense, as indicating the sole means of realising that improvability. (Mill, 1924: 74)

Unlike the dreadful Ricardo and his followers the economic alchemists did not accept the notion that the role of the economic adept was to study the laws of nature and let them alone to work themselves out. The economic alchemists held to the philosophy that there was an inner moral purpose in creation: the great task of economics was to complete the work of nature by acting upon conflicting and contradictory exernal forces. From the prime mattter of base instincts and self-interest economists could fabricate a philosophical tincture which could make the world whole and wholesome.

Newton's profound influence on the development of economics may be traced back to the earliest days of political economy. We find clear evidence of Newtonianism, for example, in William Petty's *Political Arithmetick,* and in John Locke. Economic Newtonianism reached its apotheosis in the work of the French Physiocrats whose principal theorist Francois Quesnay advanced the view that there was a rule of nature in the economic affairs of man which ought to be left alone – thus giving rise to the doctrine and rhetoric of *laissez-faire*. Inspired by the problems raised by the Physiocrats, and the idea of a Newtonian universe, Adam Smith was to bring the notion of an economic universe held together by the gravitational pull of self-interest to its most complete formulation. This Newtonian mechanism was subsequently constructed into a formidable theoretical edifice by Ricardo – Keynes's *bête noir*. A break from this mechanical view of economic equilibrium may be discerned in the writings of Malthus, J.S. Mill and Marshall. The work of Mill (claims Marshall) in particular marked a turning point by moving away from a simplistic mechanical view of economy and society by adopting a biological approach and bringing back the 'human element' into a more central position in economics' than it had been allocated in the Ricardian system (Marshall, 1947: 765). The Newtonian inheritance in economics may therefore be divided into two rival camps: on the one hand the rude 'mechanicals' who viewed the natural laws as the mechanism which could be understood and explained by man, but which were ultimately immutable; and on the other, the alchemists, who believed that the forces which drove the economy were mutable, and open to improvement and perfection by the application of human imagination, intelligence and good will. For the mechanicals there was a 'divine or scientific harmony between private interests and public advantage' (IX: 275). Later on in the nineteenth century the old Newtonian mechanism took strength from Darwin and the new found doctrine of natural selection to produce a scientific rationale for letting things alone.

> The principle of the survival of the fittest could be regarded as a vast generalisation of the Ricardian economics. Socialistic interferences became, in the light of this grander synthesis, not merely inexpedient, but impious, as calculated to retard the onward movement of the mighty process by which we ourselves had risen like Aphrodite out of the primeval slime. (IX: 276)

In their different ways Malthus, Marshall and Keynes could not accept the notion that the slime left to itself would produce a higher form of economic life. It had to be shaped, moulded, and formed by a moral vision of its potential and possibilities. Economic alchemists were not propounding a 'dismal science' (as were the crude Newtonians), but on the contrary, were advocates of optimism, hope and faith in the human contribution to the ongoing process of creation and evolution. The nature of their alchemy, however, differed. Malthus and Marshall were heirs of a 'spiritual' alchemy in that they believed in the possibility of transforming human nature. For Malthus this involved 'moral restraint' and the mutability of human passions, whilst Marshall, like Mill, believed in the possibilities of transforming 'character' and human moral evolution. Keynes, on the other hand, did not share this belief in the possibilities of transforming human nature or character, held to what might be described as a more 'chemical' alchemy concerned with managing the elemental forces which shaped the economy as a whole. As he was to express it in the *General Theory*, the task of 'transmuting' human nature should not be confused with 'managing' it (GT: 374). The economic alchemists mirrored Newton's own contradictions: the combination of a belief in the equilibrium of forces, together with the quest for a science which could complete and realize the possibilities contained in elemental forces. Hence, for Marshall, although he shared Adam Smith's low opinion of the motivations of the business classes, he believed that they could be changed, improved, and educated to a higher level. Marshall does not abandon self-interest as a gravitational force, but neither does he throw out the possibilities of benevolence amongst butchers, bakers and candlestick makers. Thus for Marshall there is a Newtonian mechanical equilibrim of supply and demand, but there is also the moral or human dimension which needs to be cultivated and liberated from the baser values. Similarly, Keynes does not reject the power of the 'fundamental' 'natural' and 'undercurrent' 'forces' (XXVII: 444) which tend towards equilibrium, so much as urge the state to accept its responsibilities for managing those forces in the social interest and with a view to achieving the possibilities of the good society. Like Newton 'the man' the economic alchemists struggled with the problem of understanding and explaining the air, fire, water and earth which shaped economic life, whilst at the same time they also concerned themselves with finding ways to balance, shape and *purify* those forces.

Keynes was fascinated by Newton's contribution to the history of ideas and was an acknowledged authority as signified by his invitation to present a paper at the Newton Tercentenary celebrations in 1946. Keynes began collecting Newton's papers in 1936, the same year as the publication of a work which was to revolutionize economic theory and policy, *The General Theory of Employment Interest and Money*. However, his interest in Newton predates the collection of Newton's papers. In his *Treatise on Probability*, for example, Keynes refers to Newton's intuitive powers which he compares with that possessed by 'barbarous and primitive peoples' (TP: 273). Newton's alchemy has been well explored in recent years and in the main they confirm the accuracy of Keynes's interpretation. Newton rejected the Descartean distinction between spirit and matter. He could not accept a mechanical view of the world and was inspired by the Platonic view of the relationship between spirit and the physical world. Newton was attracted to the experimentalism of alchemy as an alternative to Descartes's system of philosophy. Experimentalism offered the prospect of escaping from the Cartesian framework and Newton became convinced of the value of the experimental method as the basis of theorizing, but also of exploring the relationship between mind and spirit, matter and the body. Thus Newton engaged in a considerable amount of alchemy as well as searching for ancient wisdom (*prisca sapientia*) in his extensive theological studies. The seriousness of these activities should not be doubted. Newton worked hard at his alchemy to such an extent that his papers on the subject are, perhaps, one of the largest collections of materials on the ancient art.

The impact of Newton on the development of the arts, social, economic and political thought was immense. It is impossible to conceive of the shape of western thought from the seventeenth century onwards without the towering figure of Newton, father of the Age of Reason. Newtonian mechanics was to prove as attractive to poets as to political economists. The idea of the universe as a clockwork mechanism and of the existence of laws which governed the movement of planets, matter and light greatly influenced the world view of philosophers and economists throughout the eighteenth and nineteenth centuries and imbued social and political philosophy with an assurance which it had lacked until Newton's 'light' dawned. However, this view of Newton as the personification of reason is a gross distortion of Newton the man, as there was much more in the mind of Newton than coldly detached mathematics and experimentalism of the kind that was imitated by the classical economists and portrayed by his biographers and popularizers. There was also a religious and mystical aspect of Newton which displays 'a deep intuition for the limits of the purely mechanical interpretation of nature' (Koyré,1965: 19). This neglect of the other side to Newton was, Koyré argues, to have far-reaching consequences.

> The enthusiastic imitation (or pseudo imitation) of the Newtonian (or pseudo Newtonian) pattern of atomic analysis and reconstruction up to our times has proved to be successful in physics, in chemistry and even in biology, led elsewhere to rather bad results. Thus the unholy alliance of Newton and Locke produced an atomic psychology, which explained (or explained away) mind as a mosaic of 'sensations' and 'ideas' linked together by laws of association (attraction); we have had, too, atomic sociology, which reduced society to a cluster of human atoms, complete and self contained each in itself ... Newton, of course, is by no means responsible for these, and other, *monstra* engendered by the overextension – or aping of his method ... No man can ever be made responsible for the misuse of his work or the misinterpretation of his thought, even if such a misuses or misinterpretation appears to be – or to have been – historically inevitable. (Koyré, 1965: 20)

The gap between the myth and reality of ideas and theories was, of course, to be just as big for Newton's successor, Einstein, who was also destined to be portrayed as the personification of twentieth century intellect, and elevated to the status of a cultural icon. As Friedman and Donley show with respect to Einstein: 'Einstein's person and image have been used to express and support concepts, such as "everything is relative", which in reality he would not have accepted. Image apparently has wider penetration in our culture than idea, so that society at large has accepted only the image of genius, not the genuis itself' (Friedman and Donley, 1985: 194). So, too, recent scholarship reveals that Newton was as much a victim of his image as father of reason and scientific laws as Einstein was later to be victim of his image as father of

$E = MC^2$. And, it may be said in the context of this present essay, so, too, could Keynes be equally said to be more misunderstood as father of 'Keynesianism', than as J.M. Keynes.

By some very astute buying Keynes managed to acquire 130 lots out of the 239 in the sale of the Portsmouth collection in 1936, a few months after the publication of the *General Theory*. At first it appears Keynes was not immediately enthused by the sale, however, once he had become aware of the contents of the lots there was a 'marked change of attitude' (Spargo, 1992: 127). He became so fascinated by these papers that there are stories that during the war Keynes would read them in taxis (although these may be more apocryphal than true). It is evident from the extensive correspondence that in the summer of 1936 he became very interested in the papers and was quite determined to acquire as many as he could. He considered each lot carefully before deciding to bid and was very reluctant to let anyone read them in the following years (Spargo, 1992: 128–9). Of these some 57 manuscripts related to Newton's interest in alchemy (Figala, Harrison and Petzold, 1992). In addition to the papers relating to Newton's alchemical studies Keynes also purchased a good deal of Newton's correspondence and 11 lots of theological papers, together with 8 lots of papers gathered by one of Newton's early biographers, John Conduitt. Keynes also owned Horsley's five volume edition of the collected works, 1779–1785; he had four first editions of the *Principia*; a first edition of the *Optics*; and several editions of *The Chronology of the Ancient Kingdoms*. All in all Keynes assembled one of the finest and most important collection of Newton's papers. Furthermore, he had as much knowledge about their contents as any man alive; indeed, many of the manuscripts had, until Keynes acquired them, never been properly examined and studied since the nineteenth century when much of the theological and alchemical papers were regarded as irrelevant to Newton – the scientist. His essay on Newton must be understood in the context of his earlier essay on the 'End of Laissez-Faire' (published in *Essays in Persuasion*) which reviewed the history and prospects of the political philosophy out of which political economy had sprung. In this essay he argues that it was the economists of the eighteenth century who provided a 'good scientific basis' for liberalism. However, in the process of so doing, economic ideas fell victim to those that Keynes desribes as 'popularisers and vulgarisers'. It was, he argues, the 'language' of the economists which lent itself to a so called *laissez-faire* interpretation. As he notes, the notion itself is not to be found in Smith, Ricardo or Malthus. The 'invisible hand', is also therefore an idea taken out of the context of Smith's economics and moral philosophy. In the light of what he has to say about Newton as victim of his popularizers and vulgarizers, it is clear that Keynes saw the history of liberalism and rationalism as being a victim of its propagators rather than a product of its originators.

Keynes's essay reminds us that Newton rejected the mechanistic philosophy of Descartes, and that the mechanicism of Hobbes, *laissez-faire* economics and Jeremy Bentham owed, perhaps, far more to the Cartesian view of human existence than it did to Isaac Newton, for whom mechanicism was an inadequate approach to understanding God's creation. Newton was greatly influenced by Cambridge neoplatonism (of More and Barrow in particular) which took issue with Descartes's separation of mind and body and wholly opposed a philosophy in which there was no place for spiritual and esoteric ideas. Nature for Newton was both mechanical *and* vegetable and consequently physical phenomena could not be reduced to purely quantitative analysis. His alchemy was based on the notion that *a priori* knowledge was an unsatisfactory basis for natural science: the Royal Art therefore showed the way to inductive and empirical methods as well as opening a doorway into thinking about the universe in ways which encompassed spirit and matter, mind and body and in which geometry and calculation did not exclude the possibilities of alchemy.

In the essay Keynes fundamentally challenged the accepted conventional historical view of Newton as the archetypical rationalist. Quite the contrary: Keynes's Newton was a man who looked on science with the eyes of a magician. Newton's genius is characterized less by reason and experiment than in his great capacity to make intuitive leaps. Newton was, claims Keynes, a man who used science to prove to the rest of the world what he already knew, rather than as a means to actually finding out. Newton, the great high priest of the age of reason, was also absorbed in what we may now regard as the highly unscientific practices of alchemy. This analysis was, as one of the most recent of Newton's biographers R.S. Westfall has commented, a 'decisive break with the established pattern of apotheosing Newton' (Westfall, 1994: 316). Keynes's essay is now acknowleged as being amongst one of the first 'modern' interpretations of Newton, and one which is far less controversial than it was in the 1940s. It was an interpretation which was both a radical departure from biographical conventional wisdom, and also a break from the rather narrow idea of scientific rationality and Newtonian rationalism. In coming to praise Newton the man Keynes was also attempting to bury the kind of mechanical rationalism which had served to underpin *laissez-faire* liberalism. Newton was an alchemist *and* a scientist. He used experiments, but was also deeply intuitive and highly imaginative. He wanted to understand nature, but he also wished to transform and transmute its base metals. This was not the Newton that Adam Smith and the political economists would have recognized. It was this other side of Newton which was so problematical to scholars in the nineteenth century, but Keynes saw his dualism and Janus-like nature as being the key to solving enigmas such as why Newton held to two contradictory optical theories, wave and corpuscular. On the face of it Newton was generally held to be breaking his own rules about allowing an experiment to decide between competing theories. Keynes's Newton, however, is an intuitive magician rather than a rational scientist.

> He was less ordinary, more extraordinary, than the nineteenth century cared to make him out ... In the eighteenth century and since, Newton came to be thought of as the first and the greatest of the modern age of scientists, one who taught us to think on the lines of cold untinctured reason. ... I do not see him in that light. I do not believe that anyone who has pored over the contents of that box which he packed up when he finally left Cambridge in 1689 ... can see him like that. (X: 363)

Keynes's key point is that Newton was not the cold, visionless character that we find in those who claimed to be his disciples, or as portrayed by the likes of Goethe and William Blake. Newton was not the first of the Age of Reason, but far more complex a figure in the history of thought.

> He was the last of the magicians, the last of the Babylonians and Sumarians, the last great mind that looked out on the visible and intellectual world with the same eyes as those who began to build our intellectual inheritance rather less than 10,000 years ago. (X: 363–4)

Newton the alchemist, argues Keynes, was a visionary thinker, and a intuitive scientist as well as an experimentalist. His greatest gift was that of:

> the power of holding continuously in his mind a purely mental problem until he had seen it straight through. I fancy his pre-eminence is due to his muscles of intuition being the strongest and most enduring with which any man has ever been gifted. (X: 364)

Newton would hold on to a problem and wrestle with it until he could devise an experiment to demonstrate what he knew to be the answer. Scientific method was in this sense a means of communicating and changing minds. It was his method of persuading, rather than of discovering. He knew more than he could prove, and, says Keynes: 'The proofs, for what they were worth, were ... dressed up afterwards – they were not the instruments of his discovery.' Keynes relates the story of how he told Halley about planetary motion. Halley asked him if he could prove it, whereupon Newton replied that 'If you'll give me a few days, I'll certainly find you a proof of it' (X: 365). Keynes maintains that the logical dressing up of his ideas bears no resemblance 'to the mental processes by which Newton actually arrived at his conclusions'. He was a magician, says Keynes, because he looked at the universe as a riddle which could be solved by pondering the clues which God had hidden about the creation. In common with another famous student of alchemy, Goethe, Newton (like Keynes) was wholly opposed to the view of scientific inquiry as purely an objective process. As Ronald Gray observes, for example, of Goethe:

> (his) vision was ... essentially the vision of the mystics, the neo-Platonists, the alchemists ... Goethe was more concerned to demonstrate his vision than to give a scrupulously scientific account of the outside world ... (he) was against the strict testing by repeatable experiments ... all of which was for him equivalent to placing Nature on the rack and forcing her to reveal her secrets (an image which Francis Bacon himself one of the founders of modern science, had used). He preferred to see Nature almost as a mistress coming to meet him, confirming what he already perceptively perceived. (Gray, 1967: 122)

Thus in exploring Newton's papers Keynes had found a fellow spirit locked away in the sorcerer's box. He had discovered that the inspiration behind so much of western thought from the seventeenth century onwards was someone whose method of investigation accorded very closely to that of his own. Newton was a mystic who was passionately interested in the study of apocalyptic writings from which he sought to unravel secret truths contained in scripture, church history and the dimensions of Soloman's temple. However, in the end Newton the man of reason was to triumph over the child of magic. Like Prospero, Newton buried his books, and magic was abdured. He was never the same man again, observes Keynes, and he was content to settle down into his life of an eminent and respected public figure. But the public persona veiled a deep conflict: Newton was, says Keynes, a 'Copernicus and Faustus in one'. The box containing the magic was stored away and reason alone remained. However, his deception went further than packing away the magic: the great man also kept another secret about his unorthodox religious beliefs. Newton was a unitarian and he concealed this even to the point of not coming to the aid of those of his persuasion who were to suffer for the confession of those selfsame beliefs. He did not, Keynes points out, murmer a word when Whiston was removed from his professorship for his public admission of unitarian beliefs. His unitarian faith is the reason why he declined holy orders, and why a special dispensation was required for his Chair and fellowship. Newton lived a double life. He was a scientist who practised alchemy and trusted to his intuition, and he was a unitarian in a trinitarian world. Here the underlying irony of Keynes drawing our attention to the contradictions and duality of Newton the man is evident to anyone familiar with Keynes's own life. There was, as his friends would have recognized, much of the Janus personality in Keynes: one part faced Bloomsbury and the other Whitehall.

Keynes took Newton's alchemy seriously as giving an insight into the relationship between intuition, reason and experimentation. He understood the significance of alchemy for Newton, and its importance to our ideas about science in a way which pre-dated recent Newtonian scholarship and is contemporary with Carl Jung's inter-war investigations into alchemy. Keynes records that the scope and character of Newton's alchemical studies were 'hushed-up or at least minimised' by all those who had inspected them in earlier times. Keynes read the greater part of these papers, amounting to over 100,000 words and which compose translations, notes and records of experiments. They show, says Keynes, a man who was living with 'one foot in the middle ages and one foot treading a path of modern science'. But after the publication of the *Principia*, and his transformation into a public servant and one of the 'principal sights of London', his magic was consigned to his box. By this time he has, as Keynes comments:

> become the Sage and Monarch of the Age of Reason. The Sir Isaac Newton of orthodox tradition – the eighteenth century Sir Isaac, so remote from the child magician born in the first half of the seventeenth century – was being built up. Voltaire returning from his trip to London was able to report of Sir Isaac – ''twas his peculiar felicity, not only to be born in a country of liberty, but in an Age when all scholastic impertinences were banished from the World. Reason alone was cultivated and Mankind could be his pupil not his enemy.' Newton, whose secret heresies it had been the study of a lifetime to conceal! (X: 373)

Keynes's account of Newton has, however, a most curious omission: Newton and money. He briefly mentions that Newton became Controller of the Mint, but does not go into any detail about a part of his life which most closely parallels Keynes: the fact that he was heavily involved in maintaining the value of money. Newton was in charge of the mint at a time when the reputation of English money was in deep trouble. The growth of counterfeit money and the practice of clipping had meant that there was a crisis of confidence in the currency. The crisis was so bad that it threatened to bring down the 'Glorious Revolution'. Newton spared no effort to root out those involved in the debasement of money and was responsible for the deaths of 28 men at the gallows. For an economist it is strange that Keynes should not devote a little space to these activities which were of considerable importance. Given his own concerns about money it is doubly perplexing. Here was an example of Newton the alchemist literally turning a base currency into gold, and yet Keynes does not refer to it – although he does briefly footnote in *A Treatise on Money* (VI: 135) and in his notes on ancient currencies (XXVIII: 241). Perhaps he decided to leave this parallel to be reached by those readers knowledgeable enough to make the connection, in which case it may well be that he chose to use the style of the alchemist (leaving arcane clues or hints, such as his oblique reference about Newton's sexual orientation, to be understood by those worthy enough) in writing about an alchemist! No doubt the explanation is more likely to be that he simply had not finished the essay on Newton, and no doubt had he lived to read his paper at the 1946 celebrations he would have taken great delight at making the rather obvious connection between his work as an alchemist and his activities at the Royal Mint.

Amongst Keynes's last written words – apart from official notes – were those concerned with Newton. He contributed to a volume to celebrate George Bernard Shaw's ninetieth birthday. Apart from correcting the odd detail, Keynes was very enthusiastic of the picture of Newton which appears in Shaw's play *In Good King Charles's Golden Days*. He comments that Shaw is right to characterize him as more magician than scientist:

> Newton was seeking the philosopher's stone, the Elixir of Life and the transmutation of base metals into gold. He was indeed a magician who believed that by intense concentration of mind on traditional hermetics and revealed books he could discover the secrets of nature ... whilst his work looked forward, and led back beyond the middle ages to the traditional mysteries of the most ancient East. The words which G.B.S. puts into his mouth are right – 'There are so many more important things to be worked at: transmutations of matter, the elixir of life, the magic of light and colour, above all the secret meaning of the Scriptures'. (X: 377)

Shaw's portrait of Newton emphasizes the importance and absolute centrality of his alchemical quest to his scientific work. GBS's Newton proclaims that:

> My meditations on the ultimate constitution of matter have convinced me that the transmutation of metals, and indeed of all substances must be possible ... The man who begins by doubting the possibility of the philosophers' stone soon finds himself begining to doubt the immortality of the soul. He ends by doubting the existence of the soul. There is no witchcraft about these things. (Shaw, 1985: 30)

Keynes's characterization of Newton as an intuitive alchemical scientist as presented in Shaw's play invites us to reflect on Keynes's own methodology and approach to economic theory and policy. As we shall see, the parallels are close and are heavy with implications both for understanding Keynes as a theorist and for the theory of knowledge which underpinned his liberalism and that of Keynesian political economy.

Keynes argues that Newton's mathematics and experimentation were ways of communicating rather than discovering. So, too, for Keynes himself, his idea that intuitive judgments could form the basis for rational belief was a central philosophical position. He had made his views clear on this point in his *Treatise on Probability*. The Newton essay, which is amongst his last written works, and the *Treatise on Probability* which was amongst his earliest, are then addressing the same issue – the nature of knowledge and the limits of scientific method – in different ways. For Keynes, as apparently for

Newton, logic and proof were just a means of communicating and 'verifying' what he 'knew already'. The essay on Newton, therefore, seeks to confirm the limits of rationality, and the vital role of 'right thinking', and intuitive judgments. And, as Newton's alchemy reflected a certain ambiguity towards pure reason and experimentation, so it is true to say Keynes's ambiguities about the nature of economic knowledge, and the confidence he possessed in his own powers of judgment and capacity to solve problems was akin to the powers that he ascribes to Newton who was 'tempted by the devil to believe that he could reach all the secrets of God and nature by pure power of mind'. It was, of course, a temptation which Keynes himself was no less prone to embrace, and it was an attitude which stands at the very heart of the antagonism between Keynes and his detractors who were to accuse him of creating in the *General Theory* the basis for a scientific theory which had its basis in little more than Keynes's own belief in his mental powers. Hayek, for example, makes the point that:

> Though endowed with supreme mental powers, his thinking was as much influenced by aesthetic and intuitive as by purely rational factors. Knowledge came easily to him and he possessed a remarkable memory. By the intuition which made him sure of the results before he had demonstrated them, and led him to justify the same policies in turn by very different theoretical arguments, made him rather impatient of the slow, painstaking intellectual work by which knowledge is normally advanced. (Hayek, 1978: 287)

Keynes was never a economic scientist in Hayek's sense so much as an economic alchemist. Keynes was writing primarily to change policy rather than for an academic or scientific purpose. The *General Theory* consequently followed a similar pattern to that Keynes ascribed to Newton's *Principia*: the ideas came first, the proofs came later: theory followed policy, and theory dressed up intuition in a form that could change the way people thought about economic problems. Keynes leaves us in no doubt at the end of his essay that Newton's fault was that he was 'tempted by the Devil' to believe in his own power of mind to solve the puzzles of the universe. But, ironically, it was a temptation to which Keynes and his disciples were to prove just as susceptible. Intelligence, the capacity to solve the puzzles and problems of 'the economy', was to constitute a new source of legitimacy and influence for the 'dismal science'. This belief in their capacity to solve problems endowed Keynesianism with a reputation for a highly technocratic notion of 'management'. Perhaps, therefore, what underlay Keynes's reflections on Newton was that he saw in Newton a kind of genetic defect in the rationalism of liberal belief which has been passed on down the line since the seventeenth century. Keynes grasped the truth about Newton's intuitive powers and understood the ambivalence about the relationship between mysticism and science, reason and intuition and the dangers and problems that were to follow – in economics as in other fields of human knowledge – when rational reductionism and Newtonianism were taken too far. Newton illustrated for Keynes the ambiguous and hazy divide which separated Faust from Copernicus; magic and mechanics; intuition and rationality; and alchemy and science.

His paper on Newton was read to an audience at Trinity College Cambridge on Wednesday the 17th July 1946 and later that same week Niels Bohr delivered a lecture, as part of the Newton tercentenary celebrations, on the subject of Newton's and modern atomic mechanics at the Royal Institution. How it would have cheered Keynes to have heard Bohr's analysis of the implications of Newton's methods for the new physics.

> We are here most acutely confronted with the problem of our own position in existence, which occupied Newton so deeply in his later years. Above all, it may in this connection be stressed that speaking of the attitude of a scientist in terms of rationalism and mysticism is essentially ambiguous. In fact, in the ceaseless striving for harmony between content and form we shall always have to do with a fluent border of the regions where some degree of order is established. In this respect, indeed, it is most suggestive that the analysis and synthesis of atomic theory, which in certain respects deals with the simplest of human experience, has so seriously reminded us that in the great drama of life we are at the same time actors and spectators. (Bohr, 1947: 60)

Keynes believed that economics was a moral science: it was not a mechanical Newtonian science, but was in direct line of descent from Newton's alchemy. It was a science which was located in the border territory of reason and mysticism. In this realm human beings were both actors and spectators, object and subject. And given this, economics was consequently both a form of explanation and a means of transformation. This much he had in common with Alfred Marshall. However, Keynes's idea of a moral science was very different to that which was preached by his old teacher. Marshall thought that economics could be used to change human nature and advance the evolution of humanity. As he confessed to Keynes (shortly before his death) in 1924, his economics was a 'sort of religious work for the sake of the human race' (Hill and Keynes, 1989: 195). Having abandoned his Christian faith as a young man Marshall found economics could provide a scientific basis for morality. The *Principles*, for example, opens with the argument that the two major influences on the development of man's character are religion and economics. However, it is the economic forces which have by far the largest impact on shaping and moulding the human character and the 'quality and tone of a man's life' (Marshall, 1947: 13). Economics showed how material progress and moral progress were inextricably interwoven in the story of human evolution. And, far from being the dismal science characterized by Carlyle and Ruskin it offered a new hope for the future of the human race:

> Economists ... have learnt to take a larger and more hopeful view of the possibilities of human progress. They have learnt to trust that the human will, guided by careful thought, can so modify circumstances as to modify character; and thus to bring about new conditions of life still more favourable to character; and therefore to the economic, as well as the moral, well being of the masses of the people ... Now as ever it is their duty to oppose all plausible short cuts to that great end, which would sap the springs of energy and initiative. (Marshall, 1947: 48)

Thus economics was not a 'mathematico–physical' science, but had more in common with biology in giving attention to 'the pliability of human nature, and to the way in which the character effects and is effected by the prevailing methods of the production, distribution and consumption of wealth' (Marshall, 1947: 764). Marshall's idea of the economics *qua* moral science draws on Mill's *Principles of Political Economy* in rejecting the mechanical approach taken by Ricardo and his followers. Economics had to be informed by a sense of 'social duty' (ibid. 765) and a concern with 'inner nature and constitution, as well as the outer form' which are constantly changing (ibid. 772). The economist was therefore part of a gradual evolutionary process:

> It is true that human nature can be modified: new ideals, new opportunities and new methods of action may, as history shows, alter it very much even in a few generations; and this change in human nature has perhaps never covered so wide an area and moved so fast as in the present generation ... But though they wait on it, they may always keep a little in advance of it, promoting the new growth of our higher social nature by giving it some new and higher work to do, some practical ideal of social life, in which the common good overrules individual caprice, even more than it did in the early ages before the sway of individualism had begun. But unselfishness will be the offspring of deliberate will; and, though aided by instinct, individual freedom will then develop itself in collective freedom: a happy contrast to the old order of life, in which individual slavery to custom caused collective slavery and stagnation, broken only by the caprice of despotism or the caprice of revolution. (Marshall, 1947: 752)

The mission of the economist was to promote a world in which the ordinary business of life is more moral, and where deliberateness, self-reliance, shaping decisions by reference to future aims, vigour, cooperation, and self-mastery thrive. As he expresses it in *Industry and Trade* (1919) in a language which would not be out of place in an alchemical treatise:

> The problem of social aims takes on a new form in every age: but underlying all there is the one fundamental principle, viz. that progress mainly depends on the extent to which the strongest, and not merely the highest, forces of human nature can be utilized for the increase of social good ... No utilization of waste gases in the blast furnace can compare with the triumph of making work for the public good pleasurable in itself, and of stimulating men of all classes to great endeavours by other means than that evidence of power which manifests itself by lavish expenditure. (Marshall, 1919: 664–5)

Economics was a moral science which could advance human higher evolution: it was a science of perfectability. The economist ought to be sympatheic to the condition of his fellow man and concerned with the causes of human degradation, and what could be done to improve the material conditions which could develop the higher human faculties. Marshall was, therefore, as Keynes observed, possessed of a dual nature: he was both a preacher and a scientist (X: 173). Economics was a moral science because it sought to understand the conditions which could promote the moral development of mankind. It was an engine for discovering truth and putting it to practical uses. Keynes argues that perhaps this preoccupation to do good led to Marshall undervaluing:

> those intellectual parts of the subject which were not directly connected with human well-being or the conditions of the working classes or the like ... When his intellect chased diagrams and foreign trade and money there was an evangelical moraliser of an imp somewhat inside him that was so ill-advised as to disapprove. Near the end of his life, when the intellect grew dimmer and the preaching imp could rise nearer to the surface to protest against lifelong servitude, he once said: 'If I had to live my life over again I should have devoted it to psychology. Economics has little to do with ideals. If I said much about them I should not be read by business men.' (X: 200)

Marshall was optimistic about the future of capitalist civilization. Although he was sympathetic to socialist ideals, he believed that only a capitalist society could ensure gradual economic progress and improvements in the human character. Economics ought to be driven by the search for practical solutions to 'urgent social problems' (Marshall, 1964: 30) so as to advance the evolution of the species and thereby increase 'the good and diminish the evil influences of economic freedom' (ibid.). His approach was, as he once observed, always 'directed to the problem of poverty' (Marshall, 1926: 205) and the eradication of the evils which economic freedom produced. Inside every man – however poor and disadvantaged – there was a more cultured and refined 'gentleman' waiting to be released from the encumbrances of the lower passions and wants (Marshall, 1923). Over the years he modified his optimism about human perfectability, but he never lost faith in the notion that capitalism had the capacity to create a classless society of gentlemen. His great work was to send out from the mother (sic) university (Cambridge) economists skilled in the science of grappling with the evils of capitalism and whose knowledge deployed with 'cool heads and warm hearts' (Marshall, 1885: 57) could set free the civilized values which could redeem mankind.

Keynes had little taste for Marshall's sermonizing or his morals, but he did agree wholeheartedly with his argument that economics was essentially a moral science. Furthermore, he did not share Marshall's biological/evolutionary framework which believed that human nature could be changed. Marshall was concerned with civilizing the ordinary business of life by the slow transmutation of human nature into a higher form of existence. Keynes states at the close of the *General Theory* how far he departs from the gospel of perfectability preached by his master: 'The task of transmuting human nature must not be confused with the task of managing it' (GT: 374). For Marshall this great task would take a long time. The economist's role was to bring about a change in moral sensibility and social duty through the use of facts and theories. To this end Marshall wrote a bible and preached to men of good will: there could be no leaps in the evolutionary process towards a higher morality. Keynes, on the other hand, wrote no bible, and engaged in persuading opinion formers to change policy since in the long run we are all dead. Keynes was not concerned with human evolution, but in human possibilities contained in the here and now. Marshall wrote gospels (or moralizing asides) to transform individuals (ordinary citizens in their ordinary business of life) whilst Keynes wrote pamphlets to change the minds of opinion leaders (politicians, civil servants, academics, journalists et al.). And yet, although one preached and the other persuaded, both men had a profound belief in economics as an art which could complete nature's handiwork. In this regard the greatest of the Cambridge economists were closer to Newton's alchemy than his supposed science.

There is no evidence that Keynes actually studied the principles of alchemy, but his reading of Newton's papers must have given him an excellent understanding of the subject. When we explore the methods of alchemy, the reasons why Keynes felt so intuitively that he had grasped the essence of Newton the man become very clear. The main features of the art as discussed by modern authorities may be summarized in terms of:

- The belief that through knowledge and experiment human beings could transform nature and purge matter of its impurities (Needham, 1971: 8) And, as Jung notes: 'It is of the essence of the transforming substance to be on the one hand extremely common, even contemptible ... but on the other hand to mean something of great value' (Jung, 1968: 134).
- The belief that truths had been discovered by earlier generations (*prisci theologi*) and that involved de-coding the knowledge of the past and bringing to light that which had been lost or ignored (Thomas, 1973: 511–12).
- Man was part of the process of redemption and was capable of completing and perfecting creation (Jung, 1968: 306).
- The alchemist pursued a quest for reconciling opposites: earth, air, fire and water, and of recombining body, spirit and soul into a higher material and spiritual form of being (Jung, 1968: 147; Gilchrist, 1991: 11–22).

- The practitioner must be free from greed, ambition, and wordly thoughts. He must have faith, and believe that he can succeed (Holmyard, 1957: 37, 143). Alchemy was a 'difficult spiritual quest, since transmutation could not be accomplished until the adept had purged himself of all vices, particularly of covetousness; that is to say, he could not make gold until he had ceased to want to do so' (Thomas, 1973: 768).
- Signs and symbols must only be intelligible to the initiated. It is a secret art in which wisdom speaks in riddles and metaphors. Words are not to be taken literally. The practitioner must exercise imagination and intuition if the puzzles are to be solved (Holmyard, 1990: 30; 125, 142, 153). 'The practice of the art is a hard road and the longest road. The art has no enemies except the ignorant' (Jung, 1968: 315–6).
- Experiments were essentially to confirm and project ideas in material terms. They were the external manifestation of an inner dialogue and imaginative process (Jung, 1968: 245).
- Alchemy was an art in which truth could only be grasped though experience, rather than human reason. 'The alchemists themselves warned: *"Rumpite libros, ne corda vestra rumpantur"* (Rend your books, lest your hearts be rent asunder), and this despite their insistence on study. Experience, not books, is what leads to understanding' (Jung, 1968: 482–3). Intuition, revelation, vision, and insight were part of the art. The alchemist did not just 'experiment', therefore, but *participated* in the transmutation.

The identification of the alchemist with his work is the chief distinction between alchemy and science, for while the scientist attempts to stand outside the experiment in order to obtain 'objective' results, the alchemist only values results that are obtained by personal effort and involvement. (Gilchrist: 1991: 87)

- Alchemists had no problem with the idea of combining theology and chemistry:

for many who practised it the transmutation of metals was symbolical of the transmutation of imperfect man into the state of perfection ... The unity of the world and all things in it was an unshakable belief; there was thus nothing illogical in the combination of mystic theology with practical chemistry. (Holmyard, 1990: 156)

Newton turned to alchemy because he was unhappy with the mechanistic approach: it was not the whole truth. As Westfall comments:

In the mechanical philosophy, Newton had found an approach to nature which radically separated body and spirit, eliminated spirit from the operations of nature, and explained these operations solely by the mechanical necessity of particles of matter in motion. Alchemy, in contrast, offered the quintessential embodiment of all the mechanical philosophy rejected. It looked upon nature as life instead of machine, explained phenomena by the activating agency of spirit, and claimed that all things are generated by the copulation of male and female. ... Newton also met in alchemy another idea that refused to be reconciled with the mechanical philosophy. Where that philosophy insisted on the inertness of matter ... alchemy asserted the existence of active principles in matter as the primary agents of natural phenomena. Especially it asserted the existence of one active agent, the philosophers' stone, the object of the art. Images of every sort were applied to the stone, all expressing a concept of activity utterly at odds with the inertness of mechanical matter. (Westfall, 1994: 117)

In which case, Westfall maintains, Newton's alchemy was signficant in that it was a manifestation of his 'rebellion' against the limits of mechanistic philosophy (Westfall, 1994: 118). This is not to say that he abandoned the mechanical framework, but that he instinctively felt it to be narrow and inadequate. The same might be said with equal force of Keynes's economics. One of the leading authorities on alchemy notes that it is important to understand the twin aspects of the history of the subject:

Alchemy is of a twofold nature, an outward or exoteric and a hidden or esoteric. Exoteric alchemy is concerned with attempts to prepare a substance, the philosophers' stone, or simply the Stone, endowed with the power of transmuting the base metals ... into ... gold or silver ... The belief that it could only be obtained by divine grace and favour led to the development of esoteric or mystical alchemy, and this gradually developed into the devotional system where the mundane transformation of metals became merely symbolic of the transformation of sinful man into a perfect being through prayer and submission to the will of God. (Holmyard, 1990: 16–17)

These two aspects, practical and mystical, were inextricably mixed, however, by the time of Newton, they were beginning to divert into two separate streams. From the exoteric side we find Newton's experimentalism, and from the esoteric, his concern with ancient wisdom and decoding biblical puzzles. As Jung notes, by the eighteenth century the chemical and the hermetic aspects of alchemy had parted company (Jung, 1968: 227–8). In the case of Newton, Keynes shows how one half of his approach – the esoteric – had largely been ignored by his followers eager to portray him as the father of the age of science. The exoteric aspects became fused with Newton's experimentalism, whilst the more secret mystical, theological Newton was forgot and misunderstood. Alchemy was a spiritual or mystical science, it sought to use intuition and experimentation as a method of finding out and using the deep secrets which were buried within matter. This quest required the practitioner to lead an unwordly and good life, and not just to carry out experiments. If the experimenter were unworthy and unclean, and lacked faith there could be no success. In order to turn base metal into gold the alchemist had to undergo a transformation in mind and spirit. In symbolic terms this involved the marriage, unity, death, putrefaction of opposites (King and Queen, Sun and Moon, Light and Dark, Mercury and Sulphur) and their rebirth as an hermaphrodite.

Keynes was in search of a political economy which has a curious similarity to the mysterious science of the alchemists. Like Newton he rejected Cartesian dualism and mechanics and embraced an organic idea of existence and also like Newton he was a practitioner of a *transformative* art: a moral science which aimed to improve capitalist society in the short run, and bring it to a higher perfection and in the long run transform it for our grandchildren. This quest culminates in the publication of *The General Theory of Employment Interest and Money* in 1936. As his ideas developed over the years through his engagement with daily events, Keynes intuitively felt that he had discovered some fundamental truths which, if fully understood, could transform capitalism. This transformation was, however, not to be realized through the destruction of capitalism (as socialists argued), but in releasing the full productive and creative powers of the system. Like the alchemists he believed that human beings were part of a process which would lead to the completion or perfection of nature. Left to itself the natural world of the economy would never be able to realize its full hidden potential. Early on he realized that the key to this mystery lay in the most ancient and complex of human instincts: the desire for money. As for the alchemists, whose science was as old as civilization itself, Keynes came to believe that the answers that he sought were to be found in the power of gold.

3. *Auri sacra fames*: money, sex and religion

The overplus of wealth that lies, lethargic
deep in the soil beneath your territories
still waits to be exploited ...
imagination in its loftiest flight may strain,
but cannot ever do them feeble justice.
Yet minds that can look deep will have
the vast assurance that vast undertakings need.
(Goethe: 1994: 156–7)

This was the clue to Nature which Goethe looked for and believed he had found: the presence of 'polar' forces everywhere in the universe, opposed yet complementary powers which were in conflict and which nevertheless could be brought to a synthesis. This was an idea prominent in neo-Platonist writers, whom Goethe read while young, and in alchemy, where the twin opposites are often designated 'Mercury' and 'Sulphur', and where their union is called the philosophers' stone. (Gray, 1967: 117)

Money, I think, is uncontrollable. Even those of us who have it, we can't control it. Life gets poor-mouthed all the time, yet you seldom hear an unkind word about money. Money, now has to be some *good* shit. (Martin Amis, *Money, a Suicide Note*, 1984)

Sorcerers are supposed to use bodily refuse in persuing their nefarious desires. (Douglas, 1995: 120)

Venturing into the den of the lethargic monster ... I have traced his claims and pedigree so as to show that he has ruled over us rather by hereditary right than by personal merit. (IX: 287)

Keynes's analysis of money was in many respects far from original. The warnings about the dangers of the love of gold are the stuff of which many myths are made. For Keynes's friend, George Bernard Shaw, it was the great moral of Wagner's glorious ring cycle (Shaw, 1923; Donnington, 1974: 50–52). Despite his distaste for religion Keynes's own attitiude is best summed up in the words of St Paul:

For we brought nothing into this world, and it is certain that we carry nothing out ... But they that will be rich fall into temptation and a snare, and into many foolish and hurtful lusts, which drown men in destruction and perdition. For the Love of Money is the root of all evil. (Timothy, 1,6: 7–10)

Karl Marx, of whom Keynes had not a good word to spare, expressed views on the power of money to dominate human beings in terms with which Keynes would have not dissented (Marx, 1970: 179–80). However, although he believed that the love of money was at the root of human evil, Keynes also believed that money was a necessary evil whose powers could be used for good or ill. It was the *love of money* which was problematical. The propensity of mankind to set up money as an end in itself, rather than a means, was the chief cause of much misery and such was its power over the human mind that unless the money instinct could be managed the warnings of saints and philosophers, poets and prophets would come to pass. Money would destroy, warp, and corrupt civilization. For Keynes money was the most important symbol or mediator of human hopes, fears and desires; it was an instrument of value which enabled men to connect the past, present and future in conditions of flux and uncertainty. Money was the essential agent which could effect a transmutation of one thing into another; a characteristic so well captured by Shakespeare's Timon when he cries:

Gold? Yellow, glittering, precious gold? ...
Thus much will make black white; foul fair;
Wrong, right; base, noble; old, young; coward, valiant ...

Because of what Marx described (when using Timon's speech) as the 'omnipotence' of money (Marx, 1970: 180) Keynes believed that men instinctively identify with money and that its fate and that of mankind are inextricably linked and intertwined. When the value of money is insecure and uncertain, civilization rests on the most unstable of foundations. Such was the situation which confronted the world after the Great War and which prompted Keynes in 1919 to embark upon an intellectual journey which was to culminate in the *General Theory*, seventeen years later.

A member of Lloyd George's cabinet (the Earl of Crawford and Balcarres) observed of Keynes during the peace negotiations that: 'I cannot help thinking that he looks at large political problems too much from the aspect of currency and exchange' (in M. Keynes, 1975: 24). From whence came this preoccupation with money? Why should a man who professed a concern with beauty, truth and love become so fascinated with something as sordid as money? We need not stray too far from Marshall's *Principles* for an answer to the question of why the unwordly follower of Moore became so intensely focused on the role of money in human affairs. Marshall had argued that although human motivations were many, various and changeable, it was the money motive which could serve as a measure of motivations which occur in the ordinary business of life. Keynes was quite happy to teach Marshall's (quantity) theory of money until 1914: that is the idea that prices vary with the quantity of money, and the quantity of money determines the price level. And from which it followed that the aim of policy should be to maintain long term price stability which was best achieved through making currencies convertible to gold at a fixed rate of exchange.

To follow his line of development as a monetary expert we may begin with his first book on *Indian Currency and Finance*, published in 1913. The book contains a passing reference to what was to become a major issue later on; the love of gold. He comments on the 'needless accumulation of precious metals' as being 'an uncivilized and wasteful habit' which is having a ruinous effect on the country. If there is hope for India it must lie in leaving off 'their unfurtile habits and to divert their hoards into the channels of productive industry and to the enrichment of their fields' (I: 69–70). Keynes's early ideas on currency also prompt him to set out another important theme which is to run through his later work: the notion that it is possible to institute a rational and more stable system of money. It is not likely, he predicted, that 'we shall leave permanently the most intimate adjustments of our economic organism at the mercy of a lucky prospector, a new chemical process, or a change of ideas in Asia' (I: 71).

Whilst the book was in proof form he was appointed to the Royal Commision on Indian Finance and Currency – at the age of 29. The report which resulted was largely framed by Keynes's ideas, and, although Keynes urged the move towards an Indian gold standard, he displayed a consistently low regard for the essential sterility of gold (XV: 232–3). His early experience in the matter of Indian currency was significant in that it gave him enormous prestige for one so young and brought him public attention. His work on Indian currency shows Keynes as someone who was not simply seeking to apply his theoretical knowledge, but also to *persuade* and bring his ideas and intuitions to influence and shape the events which he was endeavouring to analyse. Any doubts he may have had about the shift from Moore to money must have been banished once and for all by 1913. Within six years of the study of Indian currency he was a senior figure in the Peace negotiations at Paris. During this time his main preoccupation was with the question of population, debt and reparations rather than 'money' as such. In *The Economic Consequences of the Peace* (1919) we get the first indication of how central the twin themes of population and money are to his evolving policy framework. Thus by 1919 Keynes had come to the conclusion that the problem of money lay at the core of the world crisis and the crisis of capitalism in particular. His discussion of money arises as a 'digression' from the issues which figure most strongly in the book, the fear of fecundity, and the problem of uncertainty. The peace settlement, he believed, was the tragic product of the triumph of 'passion and greed' (II: xxv) in human affairs. In a world with growing uncertainty the settlement would only serve to make things worse: as it was so to prove. An age which had felt so secure and permanent had come to an end on the battlefields of France. It was a time which was, in retrospect, an 'economic utopia', an 'Eldorado' (II: 6) which had gone for ever. Keynes's analysis was that the European population problem had begun to improve dramatically from 1870 onwards. Increased supplies of food from America and elsewhere combined with emigration and the efficiency of industrialism meant that Europe had lost sight of the devil of overpopulation which had been an integral consideration of economics throughout the better part of the nineteenth century. This golden age had come to an abrupt end with the outbreak of war in 1914. As the *Treatise on Probability* had shown, stability and certainty are not the lot of humankind. *The Economic Consequences of the Peace* describes what this means in reality.

> The power to become habituated to his surrounding is a marked characteristic of mankind. Very few of us realize with conviction the intensely unusual, complicated, unreliable, temporary nature of the economic organization by which Western Europe has lived for the last half century. We assume some of the most peculiar and temporary of our late advantages as natural, permanent, and to be depended on, and we lay our plans accordingly. On this sandy and false foundation we scheme for social improvement and dress our political platforms, pursue our animosities and particular ambitions, and feel ourselves with enough margin in hand to foster, not assuage, civil conflict in the European family. (II: 1)

The sense of security which made for a contented and stable social order was destroyed by war and in its place was a peace which would be shaped by four main unstable and volatile elements: population; organization; the psychology of society; and the relation of the old world to the new.

First among them was the demon of demographic change. The prospect for the future looked dire indeed as the Malthusian 'devil' of population outgrowing resources had now broken the chains forged in the previous century (II: 6).

> The great events of history are often due to secular changes in the growth of population and other fundamental economic causes, which, escaping their gradual character the notice of contemporary observers are attributed to the follies of statesmen or the fanaticism of atheists. Thus the extraordinary occurrences of the past two years in Russia, that vast upheaval of society, which has overturned what seemed most stable – religion, the basis of property, the ownership of land, as well as forms of government and the hierarchy of classes – may owe more to the deep influences of expanding numbers than to Lenin or to Nicholas; and the disruptive powers of excessive national fecundity may have played a greater part in burtsing the bonds of convention than either the power of ideas or the errors of autocracy. (II: 9)

The threat of human fecundity was made worse by the instability in the organization of trade, distribution and the value of money. To this was added the psychological crisis of capitalism. In the past century, Keynes argues, the system survived because of a 'double bluff or deception' (II: 11). The capitalist class were content to enjoy their wealth in terms of the exercise of 'power which investment gave them to the pleasures of consumption' (ibid.). They worked hard, saved and invested so that the 'cake' got bigger and were restrained by the puritan ethic to find reward in not enjoying their cake, but keeping it. The labouring classes meanwhile accepted inequality because of ignorance or lack of power or were forced and persuaded to go along with the customs, conventions and authorities of a 'well established order of society' (II: 12). Because of this deception the cake kept getting bigger and accumulating capital for the future. In this way the fecundity of compound interest kept pace with the 'fecundity of the species'. Now, however, this age of illusion was at an end. The miracle undreamed of by practitioners of the dismal science in the nineteenth century was looking increasingly fragile. The bluff only worked as long as people were content with a continuous increase in their standard of living and did not increase their numbers, and it was a successful trick for as long as people did not want to consume more of the capital cake. The war had gobbled up a lot of cake: food and resources were no longer cheap, and workers and capitalists wanted bigger slices. Finally, the old world which had torn itself apart in the war had to wake from its frenzy of killing to a world in which the resources of the new world were subject to the law of diminishing returns and rising prices. Europe faced the prospect of not being able to feed itself and of a rapid depression in the standard of living which might mean starvation for some countries. An overpopulated and hungry Europe would not die quietly: some men out of despair will be driven to 'nervous instability', 'hysteria' and madness which could overturn even that economic organization which is left and 'submerge civilization itself' in a desperate attempt to satisfy individual needs. Rather than address these grave problems the peace conference gave way to the baser human instincts of greed and the passion for revenge and thereby served to further destabilize the post-war world by visiting the sins of the parents on their children.

The problems of human fecundity and resources are made infinitely worse by the instability of money, which is considered in the book as 'a digression' from the discussion of production and trade. Money was the most powerful of catalysts in history. It could promote human happiness or 'aggravate evils' (II: 148).

> Lenin is said to have declared that the best way to destroy the Capitalist system
> was to debauch its currency ... As ... inflation proceeds and real value of the

currency fluctuates wildly from month to month, all permanent relations between debtors and creditors, which form the ultimate foundation of capitalism, become so utterly disordered as to be almost meaningless; and the process of wealth-getting degenerates into a gamble and a lottery. Lenin was certainly right. There is no subtler, no surer means of overturning the existing basis of society than to debauch the currency. The process engages all the hidden forces of economic law on the side of destructiveness, and does it in a manner which not one man in a million is able to diagnose. (II: 148–9)

The money instinct was planted so deep in the human mind that we find fluctuations in its value profoundly unsettling (II: 151–2). When people lose their trust in money, they also lose their motivation to be as productive as they could be and choose instead to be more concerned with their own needs: a man will 'keep his produce for himself, dispose of it to his friends and neighbours as a favour or relax his efforts at producing it' (II: 152). An instability in money will also undermine 'genuine' business and feed specu-lation (II: 154). The degradation of money fundamentally disturbs psycho-logical and economic equilibrium. And thus Keynes feared that as a result a sombre vista of inefficiency, unemployment, disorganization, internal con-flict, international hate, war, starvation, pillage and deceit waited in the wings of the peace conference. For an image of what this awful prospect looked like in reality, Keynes suggested that his readers need only to turn to Russia, Hungary and Austria. In these countries the psychological and political consequences of economic change were ample warning to us all of the terrible effects of fecundity, war, disorganization and monetary instabil-ity.

They … are an extant example of how much man can suffer and how far society can decay. Above all, they are the signal to us of how in the final catastrophe the malady of the body passes over into the malady of the mind. Economic privation proceeds by easy stages, and so long as men suffer it patiently the outside world cares little. Physical efficiency and resistance to disease slowly diminish, but life proceeds somehow, until the limit of human endurance is reached at last and counsels of despair and madness stir the sufferers from the lethargy which pro-ceeds the crisis. Then man shakes himself, and the bonds of custom are loosed. The power of ideas is sovereign, and he listens to whatever instructions of hope, illusions or revenge is carried to him on the air. (II: 159)

Happily for England this catastrophy was unlikely, but there were still impor-tant factors as work which required thought and action.

The forces of the nineteenth century have run their course and are exhausted. The economic motives and ideals of that generation no longer satisfy us: we must find a new way and must suffer again the malaise, and finally *the pangs of a new industrial birth*. (II: 161 my emphasis.)

But England also had to live in a world in which the Malthusian devil was loose, with the consequent rise in food prices as Nature fails to keep pace with the birth of babies in other less blessed plots of the earth. If there was to be any hope in this grim state of affairs it requires us to re-learn the Malthusian lessons of directing and regulating the forces of nature and human instincts.

> All that is now open to us is to re-direct, so far as lies in our power, the fundamental economic tendencies which underlie the events of the hour, so that they promote the re-establishment of prosperity and order, instead of leading us deeper into misfortune. (II: 162)

Keynes returned to Malthus and the population problem in his articles in the *Manchester Guardian Commercial* in 1922, especially his pieces entitled 'An economist's view of population', and 'Underlying Principles' (XVII: 440–46; 449–54). They take a gloomy view of the threat posed by a growing population and he identifies it as the 'greatest of all political questions' which had not yet become of political concern. However, he forecast that:

> when the instability of modern society forces the issue, a great transition in human history will have begun, with the endeavour by civilized man to assume conscious control in his own hands away from the blind instincts of mere predominant survival. (XVII: 446)

The reawakened Malthusian devil forced modern man to realize the urgent need to 'substitute moral and religious motive as a spring for action in place of blind instinct' (XVII: 453). The population problem, when mixed with monetary instability, produced a powerful destructive force which, he believed, threatened to blow civilization apart. Rising inflation, and rising populations would lead, he feared, to rising class hatred and growing disillusionment with capitalism. And this theme of managing money and managing population as a remedy for saving capitalism and civilization was to preoccupy his work in the subsequent decades. Although his ideas were to develop over the years, the concern which is expressed in *The Economic Consequences of the Peace* for influencing 'hidden currents' which flow 'continually beneath the surface of political history' through the 'assertion of truth, the unveiling of illusions, the dissipation of hate (and) the enlargement and instruction of men's hearts and minds' (II: 188) remained an ever-constant mission. Greed and passion – which had their springs in the deepest of human instincts, as manifested in the love of money – were to become the main 'hidden currents' which he sought to analyse and control.

Keynes's focus on money as a policy problem, however, may be dated to the July of 1923 when the Bank of England raised the bank rate from 3 to 4 per cent. By this time Keynes had come to the conclusion that stable prices could no longer be achieved through the old classical theory as propounded by Marshall (and himself): gold as a means of stability had to be replaced by intelligent governmental management of the exchange rate. For Keynes it represented the height of foolishness to be following a policy of dear money at a time when unemployment was rising and prices were falling. The decision to raise the bank rate prompted Keynes to launch an attack (in *A Tract on Monetary Reform*) on a policy which he now believed was courting disaster. In a lecture a few days after the publication of the *Tract* he expresses the mood which runs through the book. Modern society, he argued, faced three great evils – profiteering, uncertain expectations, and unemployment. But hope was at hand in economic science which could show how these evils, born of an instability in the standard of value, might be controlled.

> I would like to warn the gentlemen of the City and High Finance that if they do not listen in time to the voice of reason their days may be numbered. I speak to this great city as Jonah spoke to Nineveh ... I prophesy that unless they embrace wisdom in good time, the system upon which they live will work so ill that they will be overwhelmed by irresistible things which they will hate much more than the mild and limited remedies offered them now. (XIX: 158–62)

A Tract on Monetary Reform confirmed Keynes's position as the leading critic of conventional ruling opinion. He was fearful that, if not halted, Britain would lurch towards the gold standard, which it did two years later. In his analysis of the consequences of changes in the value of money contained in the *Tract* Keynes argues that the great fluctuations in the value of money since 1914 has been one of the most significant events in the modern world. The instability in the value of money affects not only personal insecurity, but the relationship between social classes – classified by Keynes in terms of 'investing', 'business' and 'earning' classes. Bouts of inflation and deflation 'inflict' massive redistribution of wealth between these different social groups. In his own time Keynes believed that such was the change in the value of money that it now threatened to subvert the capitalist system as it had evolved since the nineteenth century.

> For a hundred years the system worked, thoughout Europe, with an extraordinary success and facilitated the growth of wealth on an unprecedented scale. To save and to invest became at once the duty and the delight of a large class. The savings were seldom drawn on, and, accumulating at compound interest, made possible the material triumphs which we now all take for granted. The morals, the politics, the literature, and the religion of the age joined in a grand conspiracy for the motion of saving. God and Mammon were reconciled. Peace on earth to men of good means. A rich man could, after all, enter into the Kingdom of Heaven – only if he saved. (IV: 6)

A new harmony sounded from the songs of angels in the celestial spheres: God had so arranged the universe that, as the *Society for Promoting Christian Knowledge* argued, men do 'the greatest service to the public, when they are thinking of nothing but their own gain' (IV: 6). This harmony rested on a highly stable monetary system. However, the unity of God and Mammon, brought about by the gravitational force of self-interest had come to an end in the Great War. The stability in the value of money had deteriorated to the point that:

> it is not safe or fair to combine the social organisation developed during the nineteenth century (and still retained) with a *laisser-faire* policy towards the value of money ... If we are to continue to draw the voluntary savings of the community into 'investments', we must make it a prime object of deliberate State policy that the standard of value, in terms of which they are expressed, should be kept stable. (IV: 16)

Instability in the value of money and rapid fluctuations erode the spirit of enterprise and risk taking. The more insecure businessmen feel, the more likely are they to hold on to their money, rather than invest it. The business-man in order to make money has to resort to becoming a 'profiteer', and a gambler. Whereas in the nineteenth century the entrepreneur was a symbol of respectability and a valuable member of the community, the rapid change in the value of money threatens to topple the capitalist order.

> No man of spirit will consent to remain poor if he believes his betters to have gained their goods by lucky gambling. To convert the business man into the profiteer is to strike a blow at capitalism because it destroys the psychological equilibrium which permits the perpetuance of unequal rewards ... The business man is only tolerable so long as his gains can be held to bear some relation to what, roughly and in some sense, his activities have contributed to society. (IV: 24)

In the wake of the ups and downs of a profiteering-orientated economy had come the unemployment which had brought misery to millions and further depressed the economy. The fluctuation in the value of money had, therefore, generated bouts of two great evils: inflation and deflation. These oscillations were the very 'mortal disease of individualism' which had to be cured by ensuring that: 'there shall never exist any confident expectation either that prices generally are going to fall or that they are going to rise; and also that there shall be no serious risk that a movement, if it does occur, will be a big one'. The answers were not in 'the skies', but were under human control. We can no longer presume a stable measuring-rod of value, it must be a matter of 'deliberate decision':

We can no longer afford to leave it in the category of which the distinguishing characteristics are possessed in different degrees by the weather, the birth-rate and the Constitution – matters which are settled by natural causes, or are the resultant of the separate action of many individuals acting independently, or require a revolution to change them. (IV: 36)

The *Tract* sets out *the* problem which Keynes believed needed to be addressed: the 'instability of the standard of value' as expressed in money (IV: xiv). The 'mortal disease' (IV: 35) which threatens civilization and individualism are the two twin 'evils' of inflation and deflation which undermine the stability of capitalism by destabilizing the measure of value. The consequence of this lack of stability in the value of money are the 'evils' of unemployment, loss of savings, excessive speculative profits and increased feelings of insecurity and higher levels of risk. Keynes argues that we do not have to accept the victory of evil, and urges policy makers (the *Tract* is dedicated to the Court and the Governors of the Bank of England) to realize that there are remedies to hand. In the original *Manchester Guardian* version he selected several cartoons to illustrate his theme and they well reflect his state of mind at the time. One (by Will Dyson), for example, shows a large figure representing 'finance' dressing in morning coat and top hat and holding the symbols of Kingship sitting astride the globe. Looking up at him are a man and a figure of winged peace. The caption reads: 'Let me fix the world's prices: I care not who makes its laws'. Another (again by Dyson) depicts 'prices' as a dark sinister puppet master dressed in top hat and tails with a beast-like shadow who manipulates politicians, the law, prices and speculators. The caption proclaims: 'The power that pulls the strings'.

Keynes's *Tract* is an attempt to show how the economy can be released from the tyranny of these personifications of evil whose antics feed uncertainty and insecurity – especially of the middle classes (IV: 29). In this mood of fear and anxiety about the value of money Keynes was anxious that policy makers would give way to the ancient instinct to turn to gold as a means of restoring stability and relieving this sense of insecurity. However, gold's ancient appeal of being limited by nature herself and thus above human debasement was no longer the case. In the past gold had certain properties which made it attractive as a secure store of wealth and a stable measure of value, but Keynes shows how this no longer held true. Man's mastery over nature has meant that material progress has ceased to be dependent on the discovery of new gold supplies, but was now driven by scientific and technical knowledge and the possibilities of alchemy.

Years may elapse without great improvement in the methods of extracting gold; and then the genius of a chemist may realise past dreams and forgotten hoaxes, transmuting base into precious like Subtle, or extracting gold from sea-water as in the Bubble. Gold is liable to be either too dear or too cheap. In either case, it is too much to expect that a succession of accidents will keep metal steady. (IV: 133)

Thus literally and metaphorically gold was no longer like the sun, outside the sphere of human control and the product of the chance of nature. The value of gold was now determined by the action of powerful central banks – and might yet be controlled by science thus realizing the dreams of ancient adepts of the Royal Art. Yet, despite this gold continued to be seen as a more secure measure of value than that devised by human wisdom. 'Conservatism and scepticism join arms – as they often do. Perhaps superstition comes in too; for gold still enjoys the prestige of its smell and colour' (IV: 132). This reliance on gold to ease the uncertainties of the world was, therefore, little more than a 'barbarous relic' and an illusion which if embraced would have tragic consequences. This desire to return to the gold standard showed modern man to be driven by primordial instincts to place his trust in that which was deemed to be above him and outside the human domain. However, if there was to be any hope for the future we had to realize that this age-old faith in gold had to be replaced by a new faith in the real source of modern progess, knowledge. When Britain returned to the gold standard at a fixed pre-war parity of $4.86 under Winston Churchill he despaired over the prospects for the economy and the impact on unemployment. ('The Economic Consequences of Mr Churchill', IX: 207–30.) In seeking to maintain a high value for the pound (and pushing up the price of exports) the government was prepared to inject a massive dose of unemployment and deflation which he predicted (rightly) would only make matters worse and inflict misery and hardship in the name of a bogus primitive superstition. First in line were the miners who would be offered up as:

victims of the economic juggernaut. They represent in the flesh the 'fundamental adjustments' engineered by the Treasury and the Bank of England to satisfy the impatience of the City fathers to bridge the 'moderate gap' between $4.40 and $4.86. They (and others to follow) are the 'moderate sacrifice' still necessary to ensure the stability of the gold standard … The gold standard, with its dependence on pure chance, its faith in 'automatic adjustments', and its general regardlessness of social detail, is an essential emblem and idol of those who sit on the top tier of the machine. (IX: 2334–5)

Over the next few years Keynes was to argue that the religion of gold had to give way to the new science of monetary management.

Some years later, in April 1930, Keynes's prophecy that the past dreams of the alchemists might come true looked as if the mystery had been solved. Whilst involved in the Macmillan Committee Reginald McKenna told Keynes that a 'new process' had been discovered which offered the prospect of unlimited supplies of gold. This resulted in a most curious episode which was revealed in an envelope discovered amongst his papers in 1979. Reading it one is immediately back in the world of Ben Jonson's *Alchemist*, with Keynes as a gentleman from the City ready to be duped by a charlatan. McKenna told him that a German chemist (by the name of Gladitz) had found a way to produce gold at the cost of one shilling an ounce!! McKenna swore him to secret and told him that:

> In the core of the earth all the elements are present together in minute particles. Thus one would expect lava to have a high metallic content. As a matter of fact lava yields to the ordinary analyst practically nothing but carbon. This must be due, the inventor conceived, to the metals being dispersed into minute quantities, which he called (I think) 'telemons', each particle being encased with a coating of carbon through which ordinary chemical analysis could not pierce. His idea was that by reversing the process the telemons could be released and brought to the surface; that is to say, just as the lava has been slowly cooled down from a great heat, so he would slowly heat it up again to its original temperature. The experiment was performed and on a minute laboratory scale it appeared to be successful. The powdered lava was re-formed into what on being re-cooled became a black vitreous stick very thinly coated with various metals, particularly gold, platinum and iridium. (XX: 160)

This was pure, undiluted alchemy of the kind which Newton would have recognized, and Keynes, whose name (he once noted) rhymed with brains, actually believed it! McKenna even told him that he had already sold some of this gold to the Bank of England, and that the inventor had 'no financial motives for the deception' (XX: 161). Keynes turned his mind to what this could mean from the economic point of view. He concluded that absolute secrecy was essential to secure maximum personal and national advantage. With the ability to produce gold the Bank of England could pay off the country's American debts, and London could seize the leadership of the world economy. The real problem was, he reasoned, how to dispose of such large quantities of gold without arousing suspicion. Secrecy was all if the discovery was to create a new international monetary order. Keynes closes his nineteen page paper musing:

> Is it all true? Is it the greatest hoax in the world? God knows. But I keep my mind open to the possibility of it being at least a part of what it pretends to be. It will be a wonderful last chapter to the long history of gold's dominion over our greedy minds. I look forward with every emotion of satisfaction to the prospect that the world may be forced in my lifetime to the substitution of a scientific control of the lever which works the balancing factor in our economic life. (XX: 165)

This little episode has been somewhat overlooked, but it does reveal much about the way Keynes's mind worked. He trusted and admired McKenna and so when he told him this nonsense Keynes was quite prepared to take the idea

seriously. For Keynes it offered the prospect of ending the power of the
'barbarous relic' (sic), and attaining the philosophers' stone – scientific control over nature and the ability to 'release' the forces which lay buried in the
bowels of the earth. That is what Keynes wanted – a scientific control of the
levers so that men with knowledge and truth could manage the world so as to
bring a new age to birth. There is no evidence to indicate that the whole affair
went beyond this exchange between McKenna and Keynes, but it is equally
evident that he took it very seriously at the time. We can only surmise that, as
he studied Newton's papers, he may have searched for clues as to whether
Newton had actually found out how to square the circle. Perhaps this is why
he was so very protective of the papers in his lifetime, since a few years after
the alchemical encounter with McKenna (in 1932) Keynes was still musing
about the possibility of discovering the secret:

> The day must come and not too far off, when our modern Midases will be filled to
> the teeth and chocking. And that, perhaps, will be the moment which the irony of
> heaven will choose for granting to our chemists the final solution to the problem
> of manufacturing gold, and of reducing its value to that of base metal.

> Witness the famous tale that Ovid told.
> Midas the king, as in his book appears,
> By Phoebus was endowed with asses' ears.
> (XXI: 71–2)

Until such times as the chemists could fulfil the dreams of alchemy, it fell to
the adepts of the economic arts – Faust's intellectual heirs – to show how
money could be controlled and managed.

During the years when he was formulating his ideas on money – which led
in due course to *A Treatise on Money* (1930) – Keynes renewed his interest in
psychology through the study of Freud and Ferenczi and between 1920 and
1926 he was absorbed in the study of ancient currencies. As far as Keynes's
interest in Freud is concerned it has been well established that Keynes was
undoubtedly influenced – like many of his generation – by psychoanalytical
theory (Winslow, 1986, 1989, 1990). In his civil service examinations he did
very much better in psychology than in economics, and by the mid 1920s he
had read a good deal of Freud and his comments in 1929 in defence of Freud
show an unequivocal admiration for his ideas and the insight which his
approach provides.

> Professor Freud seems to me to be endowed, to the degree of genius, with scientific
> imagination which can body forth an abundance of innovating ideas, shattering
> possibilities, working hypotheses, which have sufficient foundation in intuitions
> and common experience to deserve the most patient and unprejudiced examina-
> tion, and which contain, in all probability, both theories which will have to be

discarded or altered out of recognition and also theories of great and permanent significance.

However, his arguments did not rest upon the empirical evidence. Indeed, he thought that very little of Freud's theories would be weakened if:

> it were to be admitted that every case published hitherto had been wholly invented by Professor Freud in order to illustrate his ideas and make them more vivid to the minds of his readers. That is to say, the case for considering them seriously mainly depends on the appeal which they make to our own intuitions as containing something new and true about the way in which human psychology works; and very little indeed upon the so-called inductive verification, so far as the latter have been published up-to-date. I suggest that Freud's partisans might do well to admit this, and on the other hand, that his critics should, without abating their criticism, allow that he deserves exceptionally serious and entirely unpartisan consideration, if only because he does seem to present himself to us, whether we like him or not, as one of the great disturbing, innovating geniuses of our age, that is as a sort of devil. (XXVIII: 392–3)

Freud (1908) had argued that attitudes towards money are the outcome of early psychological experiences. The love of money was an expression of an anal eroticism which develops out of the childish interest in his/her faeces. The experience of toilet training results in a confusion in the mind of the child as the act of excretion is the subject of both parental rewards and punishments. Control over excreting becomes a matter of conflict between parent and child and the refusal of the child to defecate at the command of the parent enables the development of a sense of personal autonomy and control over the sphincter. The child is also attracted to faeces as his personal creation, and yet this object is also regarded as foul and smelly. The relationship of the child to faeces is later projected onto other socially acceptable objects which can be handled and stored. The pleasure in excreta and in retaining faecal matter ultimately develops into a love of money which manifests itself in people whose characters were fixated at this anal stage. Freud argued that the anal personality had three major traits: a desire for order; parsimony or meanness; and a predilection to obstinacy. These traits had associated characteristics such as: cleanliness; conscientiousness; trustworthiness; defiance and revengefulness.

Keynes was attracted to Freud because in so many respects he had arrived at broadly similar conclusions about human psychology in the preceding years – albeit from a different direction, philosophy and economics. Keynes's interest in the psychological aspects of economics and politics may be discerned in his earliest writings. Chapter two of *The Economic Consequences of the Peace* (1919); *A Tract on Monetary Reform* (1923); *A Treatise on Money* (1930) and in two essays: 'A short view of Russia' (1925) and 'The

Economic Possibilities for our Grandchildren' (1930). It is important that we read the *General Theory* (1936) in the context of these earlier works as Keynes makes very clear ideas which are advanced in more obscure economic terminology in the *General Theory*. In *The Economic Consequences of the Peace* Keynes argues that the Victorians had a preference for 'the power which investment gave them to the pleasures of immediate consumption' with the consequence that saving and hoarding money provided a channel for 'all those instincts of puritanism which in other ages has withdrawn itself from the world and has neglected the arts of production as well as those of enjoyment' (II: 11–12). In this puritan fixation with money the Victorians were thus able to 'forget the fertility of the species in a contemplation of the dizzy virtues of compound interest' (II: 13). *The Economic Consequences of the Peace* also provides an early and rare example of Keynes deploying Freud in his analysis of the character of Woodrow Wilson:

> In spite of everything, I believe that his temperament allowed him to leave Paris a really sincere man; and it is probable that to his death he was genuinely convinced that the Treaty contained practically nothing inconsistent with his former professions … For the President to admit that the German reply had force in it was to destroy his self-respect and to disrupt the inner equipoise of his soul, and every instinct of his stubborn nature rose in self-protection. In the language of medical psychology, to suggest to the President that the Treaty was an abandonment of his professions was to touch on the raw a Freudian complex. It was a subject intolerable to discuss, and every subconscious instinct plotted to defeat its further exploration. (II: 34)

Etienne Mantoux, as Harrod notes, accused Keynes of 'dragging … a mention of Freud into the *Economic Consequences of the Peace* in order to titillate the reader', however, as Harrod argues, this charge is inaccurate since: 'The kind of analysis which Keynes gives of President Wilson's character had been common form in his discussions with his friends for more than a dozen years' (Harrod, 1966: 186). As we shall see, his concern with the themes of inner psychological motivation and the consequences of insecurity and uncertainty was to feature thoughout his economic and other writings.

In addition to his study of Freud Keynes was also taken with the study of ancient currencies during the time he was formulating the *Treatise on Money*. The editors of the collected works of Keynes observe of these notes that they 'show Keynes turning his mind in an expected direction' (XXIII: 223). However, reading them they display a real fascination with the topic, which in the light of his comments on the love of money, is perhaps not so very unexpected. They show Keynes to be confirming his instinct or intuitive feeling that money was an absoutely central dynamic of human history and that there was a deep wisdom in the Aristotelean analysis of money which underpinned the success of the ancient world and in the attitude towards usury which existed in medieval and renaissance times.

His notes on ancient currencies begin with a detailed analysis of Aristotle's account (in *The Constitution of Athens*) of Solon's reforms. He concludes that the history of money begins with Solon and that he was:

> the first statesman whom history records as employing the force of law to fit a new standard coin to an existing money of account. The scarcity in Greece of the precious metals must have caused in his age an appreciation of the standard, that is to say a tendency of process to fall, which was intolerably oppressive to that indispensible class in ancient, as in modern, society, which carries on the business of agriculture with borrowed money. As in all ages, the appreciation of the standard called for the remedy of debasement. Solon, perceiving in his wisdom, that in such circumstances the interests of society required that the weight of capitalism and the dead had upon the active workers should be lightened, so became the first of the long line of statesmen ... who throughout the ages of private capitalism, have employed debasement wisely to diminish its weight or rashly to sap its foundations. The sage who first debased the currency for the social good of the citizens was suitably selected by legend to admonish Croesus of the vanity of hoarded riches. Solon represents the genius of Europe, as permanently as Midas depicts the bullionist propensities of Asia. (XXVIII: 226–7)

The same story of wise management of money is to be found elsewhere in ancient history, and in the history of England (from the Plantaganets to the Stuarts) where there was a very stable pattern of price rises and wage increases. Athens, he notes, seems to have been singularly happy in its monetary policy and experience:

> The value of money was steadily falling ... that is to say prices were rising, at a rate which was not injurious to real wages or productive of any awkward economic consequences, and yet as it was just sufficient to relieve debtors ... and afforded the necessary stimulus to enterprise, the Athenians were never faced with the problems of Solon. (XXVIII: 230)

His detailed notes and correspondence which cover the period when he was writing *A Tract on Monetary Reform* and important essays such as 'A Short View of Russia', and 'The End of Laissez-Faire', illustrate how Keynes was trying to make connections between history, psychology and economics in order to prove (to himself) that the love of money was indeed at the root of all evil. He confessed to Lydia in 1924 that although his interest in Babylon and Greece was 'quite absurd' (Hill and Keynes, 1989: 144), he believed it to have inspired him although he was at a loss to explain why. Keynes suggested that it might be that was under some kind of magic spell cast by an ancient Babylonian magician! (Lydia replied that she thought that it was a 'madness' which was a 'treasure of his intellectual spirit' (ibid.).) As

Robert Skidelsky comments, his fascination with ancient money was not an aberration:

> He rummaged in among this ancient debris to verify a couple of intuitions which were to become of key importance to his own thinking: that the use of money as a unit for measuring debts had preceded the use of coin; and that Europe had chosen the path of spending and prosperity, Asia the path of hoarding and stagnation. Thus the problems to which a money-using economy gave rise existed from the dawn of organised life. Keynes was fascinated by the legend of King Midas ... Perhaps he started to see himself in legendary terms – as a Dionysus come to turn Midas's gold back into food and wine; or, more soberly, as a new Solon warning Britain's capitalists of the vanity of hoarded riches. (Skidelsky, 1992: 175)

It is worthwhile mentioning here that his interest in ancient money took place at around the same time he was falling in love with Lydia. Tradition (and scholarship) has it that the first money (gold coin) was minted during the reign of the tyrant Gyges in Lydia. The stories relate how Gyges possessed a ring which made him invisible and thus able to seduce the queen, plot against her husband and obtain the crown for himself (see Plato's *Republic*; and Shell, 1978). Perhaps it is simply little more than a coincidence that the great economist of money should marry a woman called Lydia, a name which is so closely asssociated with the tyrannical power of money – or perhaps it is not! His courtship of and marriage to Lydia Lopokova was of immense significance to his life and work after the First World War. Faust had met his Margarete and Helen and a wide world beyond the confines of Cambridge and Bloomsbury now beckoned. As befitted an alchemist it was a marriage of opposites. Keynes, the homosexual intellectual, man of Whitehall and the City, and Lydia, a Russian ballet dancer, discovered they had a mutal attraction. Lydia was his anima, she was the alchemist's Russian 'dog' (sic) (Hill and Keynes, 1989: 52, 60, 62, 74 et passim) to Faust's French poodle (Edinger, 1990: 23–37). She was the female partner necessary to his alchemical enterprise. As Armand Barbault expresses it:

> Through her extreme sensibility and the mobility of her bodily fluids, the woman is to a certain extent in a favourable position to cross to higher levels and so receive instructions from her partner. His role, on the other hand, is far more earth-bound. He constructs the work on the material plane, at which level the woman stays in the background. She stands, therefore, on the right hand side of the arcana, the 'passive side', the side of the psyche. (cited in Gilchrist, 1991: 59)

We might note in connection with the above observation that Keynes had a close interest in Lydia's 'bodily fluids' and (no doubt in jest) often commented that his own 'cycles' were coincident with her monthly periods!

It is very wrong of you to say that you are an antidote of the elixir. I drew it from you in Paris. It is since then that I am strong. But I'm afraid that it can't last much longer. The moon in its courses will turn my cycle round. My water will become thick, my head fluid, and all small troubles will grow into big ones, courage disappearing. (Hill and Keynes, 1989: 213)

Bloomsbury, of course, despaired of the liason. However, the relationship was from the outset, and remained, deeply passionate, tender, intimate and loving. By 1925 Keynes had achieved at the personal or psychological level a conjunction of opposites which he was subsequently to attain at the theoretical level a decade later. Lydia and Maynard complemented one another and it is difficult to imagine Keynes being able to have gone on to write and do the things he did without the support and love of his 'dog'. She gave him a stability and a sense of security which the critical world of Cambridge and Bloomsbury could never have provided. The marriage fixed and stabilized two people who had been in 'constant oscillation' and 'perpetual motion' (Hill and Keynes, 1989: 16) until they fell in love with one another. Lydia spoke for them both when she wrote:

There was Lydia's lack of stability
only mobility
and sometimes virility.
Then J.M. Keynes ...
with international fameness
swung her into the path of stability. (Hill and Keynes, 1989: 102)

Although Roy Harrod's biography avoided all reference to Keynes's homosexuality, he captured beautifully the pivotal contribution which Lydia made to his life and work as an economist. Lydia, more than anyone or anthing else provided the necessary balance for his creative endeavours.

Creation is a subtle and precarious activity. The creator must be protected for the time from overmuch criticism, else the impluse will die ... While he never lost delight in the erosive and mocking comment on life of his Bloomsbury friends, it may be that he would not have prospered so well had their dialectic been the main background to his work. The curve of the dancer's leap through the air, the tracing and interweaving of lines by motions perfectly designed ... are not achieved without years of hard labour and experience, yet when achieved, they are direct and unimpeded expression of emotion, an outflow of the soul into an appropriate form ... We are far removed from the world of dialectic and debate, of criticism and second thoughts ... Lydia's method was not really compatible with what were now the fixed habits of Bloomsbury ... The oil and water would not mix, and not all Keynes' alchemy could make them. Their temperament and attitude to life were utterly disparate. This did not involve any breach. (Harrod, 1966: 366–9)

It was the miraculous union of contradictions that were embodied in the love of Lydia which provided the vessel in which Keynes was to distil his ideas in the 1920s and 1930s. She was his 'dog', 'jester', 'mare' and 'buzzing bee' (Hill and Keynes, 1989: 257). Like the great economists who combined many gifts (X: 173) Lydia was compounded of numerous qualities. Whilst at King's College in the June of 1924 he contemplated, for example, how she could be so wise:

> You must have spent much time eating apples and talking to the serpent! But I also thought that you combined all ages – a very old woman, a matron, a debu-tante, a girl, a child, an infant; so that you are universal. (Hill and Keynes, 1989: 216)

And that was Lydia for Keynes, the universal woman whose love and sense of Puckish fun was so very necessary to his quest to find a new moral science to replace the moribund ideas of the past. She provided, therefore, as Walter Layton perceptively observed, a stimulus to developing his powers 'by har-monizing the big reserves of (his) emotional nature with (his) intellectual life' (cited in Moggridge, 1992: 395).

His 'Babylonian madness' and preoccupation with money comes to the surface in a vivid form in his essay on Russia, written in 1925 and if read with his ongoing exploration into ancient history and psychology in mind the piece brings clearly to the fore his developing concerns. He had visited Russia with Lydia in September shortly after their marriage as the Cambridge representative at the bicentenary celebrations of the Academy of Sciences. What interested him about Russian communism was its brave attempt to replace the love of money with a new system of values. He saw this as a kind of religious experiment and the attraction of Communism was that it pro-vided a new faith for an age in which religion was dead or dying. Keynes questions if this new religion has the potential to satisfy the yearnings of those who are disillusioned with Christian and egotistical capitalism (IX: 257). Keynes himself admits to finding little to admire in a religion which results in the destruction of human liberty and security, spies on its people, and which 'exalts the boorish proletariat' above the 'intelligensia, who with whatever their faults, are the quality in life and carry the seeds of all human advancement' (IX: 258). And yet, Keynes is attracted by an important doc-trine of the new religion: its attitude towards money.

> in the Russia of the future it is intended that the career of money-making as such, will simply not occur to a respectable young man as a possible opening, any more than a career of a gentleman burglar or acquiring skill in forgery and embezzle-ment. Even the most admirable aspects of the love of money in our existing society, such as thrift and saving, and the attainment of financial security and independendence for one's family, whilst not deemed morally wrong, will be rendered so difficult and impractical as not to be worthwhile ... The effect of

these social changes has been, I think, to make a real change in the predominant attitude towards money, and will probably make a far greater change when a new generation has grown up which has known nothing else ... A society of which this is even partially true is a tremendous innovation. Now all this may prove Utopian, or destructive of true welfare, though, perhaps, not so Utopian, pursued in an intense religious spirit, as it would be if it were pursued in a matter-of-fact way. But is it appropriate to assume, as most of us have assumed hitherto, that it is insincere or wicked. (IX: 260–61)

Although he rejected the totalitarianism of Leninism and its economic theories and policies, Keynes was intrigued by its belief in the need to find a new religion for a new society. It was this religious question which he believed also lay at the heart of the dilemma of modern capitalism. In the past capitalism could lay claim to a moral and religious legitimacy which had disappeared with the triumph of an 'egotistical atomism' (IX: 267). However:

Modern capitalism is absolutely irreligious, without internal union, without much public spirit, often, though not always, a mere congeries of possessors and pursuers. (IX: 267)

If modern capitalism were to survive and defeat Communism it had be be immensely more successful and efficient. In a passage which has a special relevance for Keynes's views about economic growth he argues that there is an alternative to protestant and 'irreligious' capitalism. In the protestant scheme of things business was of the earth and the here and now, whilst religion was for heaven and the hereafter. However, if it is all in the here and now as irreligious capitalism would have it, then there is no 'moral objective in economic progress' and the sole objective of economic policy is to secure progress today – 'we must not sacrifice, even for a day, moral to material advantage' (IX: 268). Keynes is sympathetic to Communism because it was searching for a form of society in which economic progress has a moral objective, and is focused on moral issues. Communism, for all its faults, has grasped the essential moral problem posed by money:

to me it seems clearer every day that the moral problem of our age is concerned with the love of money, with the habitual appeal to the money motive in nine-tenths of the activities of life, with the universal striving after individual economic security as the prime object of endeavour, with the social approbation of money as the measure of constructive success, as with the social appeal to the hoarding instinct as the foundation of the necessary provision for the family and the future. (IX: 268)

And, he believed, if there is to be any hope for the future it lay in a 'revolution in our ways of thinking and feeling about money' (IX: 269). What most interested him about the Russian experiment with the money instinct was the possibility that it might discover a grain of a new ideal. Out of what was foul could come something precious. Thus he concludes his view of Russia on a note of chemical 'elation'.

> Here – one feels at moments – in spite of poverty, simplicity, and oppression, is the laboratory of life. Here the chemicals are being mixed in new combinations, and stink and explode. Something – there is just a chance – might come out. And a chance gives to what is happening in Russia more importance than what is happening (let us say) in the United States of America ... if Russia is going to be a force in the outside world, it will not be the result of Mr Zinovieff's money. Russia will never matter seriously to the rest of us, unless it be as a moral force. (IX: 270)

If he were Russian he could not accept the Soviet regime, but:

> I should feel that my eyes were turned towards, and no longer away from, the possibilities of things; that out of the cruelty and stupidity of Old Russia nothing could ever emerge, but that beneath the cruelty and stupidity of New Russia some speck of the ideal lie hid. (IX: 271)

This is Keynes at his most alchemical. He leaves us with an image of a 'New' Russia purified in a laboratory in which men labour with 'cruelty and stupidity' and the 'compounds of emotional chemistry' (citing Sir Martin Conway, IX: 270) in the hope of extracting from the 'possibility of things' a particle of real philosophers' gold: a 'speck' of a new ideal. Thus although he dismissed the Russian experiment to find new economic techniques, he was more convinced that it had some chance of discovering a new religion (IX: 267).

In 'The End to Laissez-Faire' (1926) Keynes turned his attention to the future of capitalism by tracing the the source of ideas which gave rise to the doctrines of individualism and *laissez-faire* which, he believed, were in a deep crisis. The 1926 essay returns to the theme which had been set out earlier in *A Tract on Monetary Reform*: how the old harmony of opposites (God and Mammon, self-interest and the public interest) no longer held sway in the social and economic universe. A 'miracle' was coming to an end, and the problem facing capitalism was one of devising a new morality and social philosophy which could serve to underpin a new combination of economic efficiency, social justice and individual freedom. He argues that in the nineteenth century a 'miraculous union' (IX: 274) took place between two opposite schools of thought: conservative individualism and socialistic and democratic egalitarianism. It was the economists who were in large part responsible for this 'harmony of opposites' (IX: 274) which resolved the contradiction between private advantage and public good. This was achieved by asserting that the individual and social interests could be made whole by recognizing that the social universe, like the natural universe, was governed by a 'divine harmony'. Keynes portrays Bentham as the source of the 'popular' and 'vulgar' notion that *laissez-faire* was predicated on the 'scientific pretext' that self-interest was the gravitational force in the social universe which ensured the 'miraculous' 'harmony of opposites' of balancing social and private interests. The working of these laws as discovered by the economists and disseminated by the utilitarians meant that there was no conflict between the pursuit of individual interests and the social good. Self interest could also promote the interest of society as a whole. Unfettered private interest operated to the public advantage. The circle had, apparently, been squared. Later Darwin's discoveries could come to the aid of this theory of divine harmony.

> The economists were teaching that wealth, commerce, and machinery were the children of free competition – that free competition had built London. But the Darwinians could go one better than that – free competition had built man. ... The principle of the survival of the fittest could be regarded as a vast generalisation of the Ricardian economics. Socialistic interferences became, in the light of this grander synthesis, not merely expedient, but impious, as calculated to retard the onwards movement of the mighty process by which we ourselves had risen like Aphrodite out of the primeval slime. (IX: 276)

The result of this 'miracle' of the 'harmony of opposites' was that power shifted away from the philosophers to the businessmen. If natural selection worked for human society as for the jungle it followed that progress was led by the hand of commerce. The nineteenth century had found new heroes and new wise men, in the knights of business world. What need we of philosophers when all that was necessary to advance mankind was to set loose that which had been bound and restrained by religion and philosophy: 'the most powerful of human motives, the love of money' (IX: 184). Aphrodite's son did indeed make the world go around.

> Just as Darwin invoked sexual love, acting through sexual selection, as an adjunct to natural selection by competition, to direct evolution along the lines which should be desirable as well as effective, so the individualist invokes the love of money, acting through the pusuit of profit, as an adjunct to natural selection, to bring about the production on the greatest possible scale of what is most strongly desired as measured by exchange value. (IX: 284)

But, says Keynes, although economic Darwinism was a beautifully simple theory, it excluded a more complex reality of a world in which there is no natural or automatic *organic* relationship between individual producers and consumers. Furthermore, and echoing his argument in the *Treatise on Probability*: there is neither 'sufficient foreknowledge of conditions and requirements', or adequate 'opportunities to obtain this foreknowledge' (IX: 284). (These themes of organic relationships and uncertainty are later to be developed in the *General Theory*.) However, the belief that the mechanical, and atomistic divine laws of nature should be left alone was, claims Keynes, the product of the 'popularizers and the vulgarizers' (IX: 277). In the hands of Mrs Marcet, Bishop Whately, Miss Martineau, Bastiat and their ilk economic theories were moulded into a fraudulent science which had little correspondence with the real world in which private and public interests rarely coincide, or in which self interests are always enlightened (IX: 288). The economic 'evils' which were the product of 'risk, uncertainty and ignorance' (IX: 291) are not cured by an unfettered love of money, but on the contrary, only serves to 'aggravate the disease' (IX: 292). If a cure to the 'evils' were to be found it required the recognition that the business man is a 'tarnished idol' who can no longer be entrusted with leading us to 'paradise' (IX: 287). A new age called for a new wisdom, which (his) economics could provide. It required the use of a 'directive intelligence' which drew upon economic data so as to control currency and credit, investment and the quality and quantity of the population (IX: 292). Above all, the problem was one of controlling and channelling the 'intense appeal of money-making and money-loving' as the primary motives forces of the economy and the ordering of our 'affairs in such a way as to appeal to the money-motive as little as possible' IX: 293). This was, however, not a technical matter, but one which involved *psychological* and *moral* issues for society. The task for the economist was to assist in clearing away confusion, and defining what government should do or not do in order to reduce the reliance on the money motive. Capitalism required 'wise management' and a 'new set of convictions' (IX: 294).

Keynes saw money, therefore, as the embodiment of good and evil, and as having the potential for life and death, productivity and sterility. He was manifestly convinced by the Freudian theory of money as excrement, and like the alchemists he saw this excrement as possessing life-giving properties (Silberer, 1971: 124, 140, 142). It was foul stuff which could, in the right conditions, give birth to new life. Left to itself it would rot and decay and be a source of disease, but in the hands of the adept (economist) it could enrich and promote human productivity. What was foul could be fair. The alchemists had sought to fix or stabilize volatile Mercury; Keynes's task was to show how volatile and mercurial money could be stabilized so as to release human productivity and creativity from the rock of conventional wisdom. Writing in 1928 on the devaluation of the French Franc, for example, he comments that now the 'deed is done' the French economy is freed from uncertainty and more able to bring energies that have lain idle back into 'active employment'. Alas for England, however, since unlike France her economy remained held down by an obedience to out-dated 'conventions' (IX: 84–5). The following year (1929) Keynes (with Hubert Henderson) expanded on his criticism of these conventions by supporting Lloyd George's plans to use public spending to stimulate economic recovery.

> A country is enriched not by the mere negative act of an individual not spending all his income on current consumption. It is enriched by the positive act of using these savings to augment the capital equipment of the country. It is not the miser who gets rich; but he who lays his money out in fruitful investment. ... Negation, restriction, inactivity – these are the government's watchwords. Under their leadership we have been forced to button up our waistcoats and compress our lungs. Fears and doubts and hypochondriac precautions are keeping us muffled up indoors. But we are not tottering to our graves. We are healthy children. We need the breath of life. There is nothing to be afraid of. On the contrary. The future holds in store for us far more wealth and economic freedom and possibilities of personal life than the past has ever offered. There is no reason why we should not feel ourselves free to be bold, to be open, to experiment, to take action, to try the possibilities of things. (IX: 123–5)

He developed this theme of possibilities in his essays on 'Clissold' (1928), and in 'The Economic Possibilities for our Grandchildren' published in the same year as *A Treatise on Money* (1930). In his review of H.G. Wells's *The World of William Clissold* Keynes expresses support for Wells's idea that the future ought to be in the hands of scientists, artists and entrepreneurs rather than those of the bankers, workers or left wing intellectuals. If there was to be any hope for the future it meant civilization had to 'harness' human creative energies. Liberalism had to die so that it could be 'born again with firmer features and a clearer will' (IX: 319). The ever present danger is, however, that lacking a religion (creed) creative people will attach their 'abundant libidos' to money – the 'perfect ersatz' (IX: 320). Furthermore, Keynes argues that Wells draws attention to the demographic dimensions of change. He notes that in the future we will all live longer, and there will be a greater proportion of old people in the population than ever before in human history. This trend carries with it the danger that what he later was to talk about in terms of the 'animal spirits' of capitalism would be decline and the 'barren and non-constructive' love of money increase (IX: 316).

> Clissold ... sees more advantage and less disadvantage in this state of affairs than I do. Most love money and security more and creation and construction less, as they get older; and this process begins long before their intelligent judgment is apparently impaired. (IX: 317)

Keynes argues that there needs to be a balance between the 'sex-ridden' creative side of the population and the middle-aged 'money-ridden' old sitting on their unproductive piles of money. Wells shows that the world is moving fast, but not necessarily in a worse or better direction so much as another state of equilibrium. The questions which Keynes poses are '*why* not a better' world?; *how* can change be brought about?; and *who* can provide its 'motive power'? As in the case of the balance between the 'sex-ridden' and 'money-ridden' proportions of the population the answer to these questions lies in the quest for a new harmony of opposites:

> The remoulding of the world needs the touch of the creative Brahma. But at present Brahma is serving science and business, not politics or government. The extreme danger of the world is, in Clissold's words, lest, 'before the creative Brahma can get to work, Siva, in other words the passionate destructiveness of labour awakening to its now needless limitations and privations, may make Brahma's task impossible'. We all feel this, I think. We know that we need urgently to create a milieu in which Brahma can get to work before it is too late. (IX: 319)

Although sharing in Wells's belief in the role of scientists and entrepreneurs in bringing about such a new equilibrium, Keynes is more optimistic about the part universities could play. They could yet become 'temples of Brahma which even Siva will respect' (IX: 320). In 'The Economic Possibilities for our Grandchildren' we find Keynes turning his own mind to science fiction in line with Marshall's recommendation for economists to use their imagination and 'construct edifices of pure crystal' to 'throw side lights on real economic problems' (Marshall, 1947: 782). The essay gives the fullest accounts of the love of money and its social, economic and political implications containing as it does both a hymn to money and a swinging attack on the love of money. Money is represented as both the source of new life and as the bringer of death and disease.

Keynes argues that the standard of living and human progress was somewhat undramatic for the greater part of human history. This was due to two main factors: lack of technological development and the failure of capital accumulation. However, in the sixteenth century the modern age truly begins: it is born out of the treasures of gold and silver brought out the New World. The discovery of vast supplies of precious metal had awakened a protean life force:

> From that time until today the power of accumulation by compound interest, which seems to have been sleeping for many generations, was reborn and renewed its strength. And the power of compound interest over two hundred years is such as to stagger the imagination. (IX: 323)

Out of the alchemy of finance a new age dawned giving rise to rapid scientific and technological development, and the genius of Newton, Darwin and Einstein. The quest for the magic substance which could transform, give new life and immortality was over: the secret compound was 'interest'. Drake had long since turned to dust, but his money lives on and grows, swells and accumulates. 'Such is the power of compound interest' (IX: 324). The new magic had vanquished the old. What need a man have of alchemy when *money* could be made to breed and 'multiply'? Perhaps it is no coincidence that Mercury was both a god of commerce, the hermaphroditic self-impregnating dragon and the water of life, vital to the alchemists' art. Mercury, the messager of the gods, who acts as a link between Olympus and Hades; Mercury, the god of thieves and rogues and of the skilful and dexterous. The secret which Keynes believed he had discovered was how to release life-giving properties enclosed by money. Thus for Keynes money has all of the qualities of mercurial dualism: it was good and bad, it was new life and excreta. The love of money is a 'disease', yet it is an object vital to the health of the economy and for the prospects of human progress. As Mephistopheles proclaims to the ailing Emperor, such are the contradictions of money and the philosophers' stone:

> What is accursed, yet always welcome,
> what ardently desired, and yet chased away,
> what constantly receives our favor,
> yet is denounced and much reviled? (Goethe, 1994: 4743–6)

If, therefore, we could use the reproductive power of capital and the magic of compound interest the future could be bright with possibilities of undreamt advancement. Newton's quest for the philosophers' stone was under his nose all the time at the Royal Mint: it was money. Gold could beget gold as man could beget man, and corn beget corn (Silberer, 1971: 115). The economic problem could be solved – assuming that we tame our own violent impluses (IX: 326).

The economic problem of the struggle for subsistence was, he believed, not the permanent problem of human existence. This struggle for subsistence has come to dominate human nature and shapes all our impulses and deepest instincts – 'for the purposes of solving the economic problem' (IX: 327). However, he looked forward to a time when the economic problem would be solved and 'for the first time since his creation man will be faced with his real and permanent problem – how to use his freedom from pressing economic cares, how to occupy the leisure, which science and compound interest will have won for him, to live wisely and agreeably well' (IX: 328). The evidence of those members of society in the advance guard of this new society suggested to Keynes that the outlook was very depressing. And yet, with more experience, Keynes was optimistic that we shall in time make better use of the freedom from economic problems which are presently the sole preserve of the rich. Once freed from economic struggle:

> We shall be able to rid ourselves of the many pseudo-moral principles which have
> hag-ridden us for two hundred years, by which we have exhalted some of the most

distateful of human qualities into the position of the highest virtues. We shall be able to afford to dare to assess the money-motive at its true value. The love of money as a possession – as distinguished from the love of money as a means to the enjoyments and realities of life – will be recognised for what it is, a somewhat disgusting morbidity, one of those semi-criminal, semi-pathological propensities which one hands over with a shudder to the specialists in mental disease. (IX: 329)

With the love of money recognized as a mental disease:

All kinds of social customs and economic practices, affecting the distribution of wealth and of economic rewards and penalties, which we now maintain at all costs however distasteful and unjust they may be in themselves, because they are tremendously useful in promoting the accumulation of capital, we shall then be free, at last, to discard. (IX: 329)

In this brave new world we can return to the old time religious values: avarice as a vice; usury as misdemeanour; and the love of money acknowledged as little more than a 'detestable' human instinct. We shall not be preoccupied with tomorrow, value ends above means, and take enjoyment in the 'direct enjoyment of things'. Out of evil shall come good, and from base values, the true gold of human freedom. Of course, this will not happen yet:

For at least another hundred years we must pretend to ourselves and to everyone that fair is foul and foul is fair; for foul is useful and fair is not. Avarice and usury and precaution must be our gods for a little longer still. For only they can lead us out of the tunnel of economic necessity into daylight. (IX: 331)

The real question for Keynes is one of the pace of this change in 'psychological' or 'moral' terms. This he believed would depend upon four factors: the control of the population; the avoidance of war and conflict; trusting science to direct 'those matters which are properly the concern of science'; and the 'rate of accumulation as fixed by the margin between our production and consumption'. The latter point was to be examined at length in his *Treatise on Money* in which we once again encounter the power of the puritans he had discussed in *The Economic Consequences of the Peace*. The killjoys were now killing capitalism with their money obsession:

sometimes extreme individualists, who are able, perhaps, to placate ... their suppressed reactions against the distatefulness of capitalism – who draw gloomy satisfaction from the speculative and business losses. The low prices, and the high real wages, accompanied, however, by unemployment, which characterise the typical depression. Nor is it sufficient justification of the latter state of affairs, that necessity being the mother of invention, there are certain economies and technical improvements which the business world will only make under the stimulus of distress; for there are other improvements which will only mature in an atmosphere of optimism and abundance. (V: 246)

The notion that abstinence and saving alone could provide the basis for increasing real wealth is attacked in one of the most vivid passages in *A Treatise on Money*.

> It has been usual to think of the accumulated wealth of the world as having been painfully built up out of the voluntary abstinence of individuals ... But it should be obvious that mere abstinence is not enough to build cities or drain fens ... It is enterprise which builds and improves the world's possessions ... If enterprise is afoot wealth accumulates whatever may be happening to thrift, and if enterprise is asleep, wealth decays whatever thrift may be doing. Thus thrift may be the handmaid and nurse of enterprise. But equally she may not be. And, perhaps, even usually she is not. For enterprise is connected with thrift not directly, but at one remove; and the link which should join them is frequently missing. For the engine which drives enterprise is not thrift, but profit. (VI: 132)

Later on in *A Treatise on Money* this theme of the perverse pleasures to be derived from thrift and holding on to money receives an explicit Freudian and alchemical treatment in a chapter entitled 'Auri Sacra Fames' (the cursed hunger for gold). In this chapter Keynes traces back the origins of money to ancient times and oberves that:

> Dr Freud relates that there are peculiar reasons deep in our subconsciousness why gold in particular should satisfy strong instincts and serve as a symbol. The magical properties, with which Egyptian priestcraft anciently imbued the yellow metal, it has never altogether lost ... Of late years the *auri sacra fames* has sought to envelop itself in a garment of respectability as densely respectable as was ever met with, even in the realms of sex and religion. Whether this was first put on as a necessary armour to win the hard won fight against bimetallism and is still worn, as the gold advocates allege, because gold is the sole prophylactic against the plague of fiat moneys, or whether it is a Freudian cloak, we need not be curious to inquire. But before we proceed, with a scientific and would-be unbiased examination of its claims, we had better remind the reader of what he well knows – namely that gold has become part of the apparatus of conservatism and is one of the matters which we cannot expect to see handled without prejudice. (VI: 259)

He refers the reader to two leading expositions of the theory by Ernest Jones and Sandor Ferenczi. The latter had argued that:

> the adult's symbolic interest in money gets extended not only to objects with similar value or possession (paper money, shares, bankbook, etc.). But whatever form may be assumed by money, the enjoyment at possessing it has its deepest and amplest source in coprophilia. Every sociologist and national economists who examines the facts without prejudice has to reckon with this irrational element. Social problems can be solved only by discovering the real psychology of human beings; speculations about economic conditions alone will never reach the goal. (Ferenczi, 1956: 276–77)

Keynes commends Jones's analysis of the psychological instincts which inform the love and money and his prediction (in 1917) that this would lead to a re-introduction of the gold standard: a prophecy which Keynes notes may be regarded as a 'success for the psycho-analytic method'. Gold, he argues, has become part of the 'apparatus of conservatism' and no longer circulates amongst human beings, or is worshipped as 'little household gods' in purses and tin boxes: it has returned (as in Goethe's *Faust*) to the Earth. Gold now:

> lives underground and is not seen. Gold is out of sight – gone back again into the soil. But when gods are no longer seen in yellow panoply walking the earth, we begin to rationalise them; and it is not long before there is nothing left. (VI: 260)

Gold has taken on a new more subtle body: 'It has become a much more abstract thing'. Gold is now a representative standard of value which only exists as such by being passed around from one central bank to another. And, it is but a small step to the making of a new philosophers' stone, whereby:

> without ever formally renouncing the rule of gold, the quantity of metal actually buried in their vaults may come to stand, by a modern alchemy, for what they please, and its value for what they choose. Thus gold, originally stationed in heaven with his consort silver, as Sun and moon, having first doffed his sacred attributes and come to earth as an autocrat, may next decend to the sober status of a constitutional king with a Cabinet of banks. (VI: 260)

Harrod was somewhat dismissive of the 'Auri Sacra Fames' section of *A Treatise on Money*, describing it as little more than an amusing flight of the imagination. And yet, Harrod concedes the *Treatise* embodies a lifetime of thought and practical experience on monetary matters (Harrod, 1966: 402–3). Furthermore, he also notes that Keynes had a long-standing interest in psychology. In the light of the seriousness of *A Treatise on Money* it is most unlikely that his comments regarding Freud were there for polemical effect. The following year, for example, in a review of the *Treatise* Robertson fixes upon Keynes's idea that monetary restraint and its consequential high unemployment was the outcome of puritanical financiers who conceal their unconscious 'gloomy satisfaction' in the misery their policies create (V: 246). Robertson argues that, contrary to Keynes's viewpoint, such pain was 'in truth an essential phase of the clinical treatment of the trade cycle' rather than a 'mere relic of sadistic barbarism' (Robertson, 1931: 410–11). To which Keynes's unpublished comments were that sadism was indeed at the root of monetary policy and unemployment, but that it stemmed from puritanism rather than barbarism. But, he observes 'at this point pyscho-analysis must take charge and economic analysis withdraw discreetly' (XII: 238). The Freudian references should not, therefore, be discounted, and neither should the chapter's alchemical flavour. As we shall see in Chapter 4, buried wealth and ancient Egypt are images which are also deployed in the *General Theory* (see GT: 129–31). Gold, he argues in *A Treatise on Money,* has undergone a modern transmutation into an 'abstract thing': in the *General Theory* he takes this image further by referring to money as a 'subtle device' (GT: 294). And to complete the metaphor which began with the reference to ancient Egypt he concludes the 'Auri Sacra Fames' section by suggesting that in being transfomed into an abstract, rather than a physical thing, money is a kind of 'modern alchemy'. He drives home the point by invoking the primary al-chemical symbols: Sun, Moon and King. The moon is also to feature as a metaphor in the *General Theory.*

In order to understand what drives the love of money we have to appreciate the impact of uncertainty and the paucity of human knowledge on human behaviour. This had been the subject of his *Treatise on Probability* which had occupied his thoughts a decade earlier. The economy was greatly influenced by those who:

> do not possess even the rudiments of what is required for a valid judgment, and the prey of hopes and fears easily aroused by transient events and as easily dispelled. This is one of the odd characteristics of the Capitalist System under which we live, which, when we are dealing with the real world is not to be overlooked. (VI: 323)

The judgments of buyers and sellers are not focused on 'real trends', but on trying to 'anticipate mob psychology' (VI: 323). And the uncertain, insecure mob will always prefer the short run to the more precarious long run as the time frame for their decisions. These bouts of stimulation and depression in the market place are not unreasonable given the state of uncertainty, but it does mean that it requires skilful management of the 'mob' if 'violent' and large swings in mood (sentiment) are to be avoided. In the years which followed the publication of the *Treatise on Money* Keynes was searching for the right theoretical framework which could guide the management of the economy and control the psychological propensities of capitalism so as to release the 'sleeping' powers of enterprise from the deep subconscious in-stincts which fix upon money as a source of security and pleasure.

Although *A Treatise on Money* shows clearly the influence of German psychology on Keynes's economics, it is apparent that Keynes was not too interested in German sociology. The same year as the publication of the *Treatise* (1930) also witnessed the publication of Talcott Parsons's definitive translation of Max Weber's *The Protestant Ethic and the Spirit of Capitalism.* Keynes is very close to the position advanced by Weber in so many respects and crucially like Weber he argues that, if we are to understand the develop-ment of capitalism, then its ethical basis must be given close consideration. The spirit of modern capitalism was, for both men, a form of organization which was shaped by the protestant religion. And, for both Keynes and Weber a central problem for the twentieth century was the fact that religion was a spent force. For Weber, however, it was the fate of modern man to be imprisoned in an 'iron cage' constructed from protestant ethics and from which there could be no escape until the last ton of coal had been burnt (Weber, 1976: 181). Weber's dismal prospect is that of Goethe's *Faust*: a future which is ruled by: 'Specialists without spirit, sensualists without heart (and which) imagines that it has attained a level of civilization never before achieved' (cited in Weber, 1976: 182). Keynes's views on the impact of protestant ethics almost directly parallel Max Weber's analysis, but crucially he departs from him in adhering to Marshall's faith in the possibility of a new 'alchemy of morality and knowledge' (Kerr, 1969: 130) which could help liberate mankind from the prison of protestantism and help to manage the consequences and possibilities for a civilization in which religion no longer had any power to keep the money instinct in check. Weber therefore shows us an iron cage, whilst Keynes shows us the importance of constantly striving for the philosophers' stone. Weber leaves us with the dismal prospect of an iron cage with nought for our comfort but parliamentary politics and charismatic leadership. In the 1930s, of course, the latter was to have a widespread appeal for both German fascists and Irish socialists, such as Shaw, eager to swear their Faustian pacts with supermen. Keynes's agenda is very different: the search for an optimistic science which could serve to rescue the possibilities of individual freedom from the shackles forged by the dead hand of 'classical' economics. Unlike either Weber or Shaw he had little faith in either politics or charismatic leaders to enhance the prospects for human liberty or increase the sum total of goodness, truth or beauty. The future was in the hands of the economists.

After the publication of *A Treatise on Money* Keynes busied himself with his never-ending task of shaping the policy agenda. In so doing, the theme of releasing the pent-up power of the spirit of enterprise and risk was always at the hub of his arguments. His aim was to show how a money economy provided such immense opportunities for improving the lot of mankind. Money was a major problem, but it was also the primary driving force of human possibilities. In commenting on the slump in December of 1930, for instance, he argues that the 'nightmare' will pass away because 'the resources of nature and men's devices are just as fertile and productive as they were', if not even more so (IX: 126). The slump showed a 'muddle' in running the 'delicate machine' of the economy and provided 'fertile soil' for revolution, agitation and sedition. But when once we have solved the 'magneto' problem there is every hope that the machine will be just as 'fertile and productive' as ever. Policy makers had a responsibility to promote a 'spirit of action', as he expressed it in a BBC broadcast in January

1931. Although the slump was an international problem, people had it in their power to do something, rather than nothing (IX: 137). Housewives could buy goods, and government could spend money on projects that were 'magnificent to the eye, and yet convenient' to put an end to human idleness and waste (IX: 139). This exercise of deliberate control was needed because, as he observed in April 1932, the 'popular mind always rushes to extremes when something occurs to direct attention on the exchange-value of money' (XXI: 63). The enemy of civilization was inaction and inertia and the cure involved government and individuals adopting a sense of 'activity, boldness and enterprise' (IX: 141).

In June 1931 Keynes gave a series of lectures in America dealing with 'An Economic Analysis of Unemployment'. The lectures marked a shift towards the concern with output, employment and equilibrium which were to be explored in the *General Theory*. The lectures summarized for an American audience the arguments which he had put forward in *A Treatise on Money*. From the outset he shows himself to be an optimistic philosopher of possibility. Despite the gloomy prognostications emanating from Moscow that capitalism was in a state of terminal decline, Keynes maintains that it is possible that mankind has it in its power to make its own destiny: we can choose to escape from the economic slump (XIII: 343–4). As he had said in 'The Economic Possibilities for Our Grandchildren' we had to comprehend the enormous potential of capitalism to lead us to an 'economic Eldorado where all our reasonable economic needs would be satisfied' (XIII: 348). With this confidence the spirits of capitalism could be liberated from the dead hand of those 'austere and puritanical souls' for whom boom, expansion, and good times had to be paid for in pain, suffering, poverty and depression. After the self-indulgence of prosperity the economic system had to be purged with the salts of deflation: a 'prolonged liquidation' to put the system right again and into balance (XIII: 349). Nature must run its course. However, as he explained, the central point of *A Treatise on Money* was that there was no 'preordained harmony' in the economic machine which will result in such a self-adjustment in the relationship between savings and investment (XIII: 355). If economic harmony were to be achieved then it ought not to be formed out of the suffering and misery of the unemployed and the poorly paid: human intelligence could devise other more effective and fairer methods (restoration of business confidence, public works, and lower long-term interest rates) than those which involved allowing the economic juggernaut to grind away at the possibilities of capitalist civilization. In concluding his lectures Keynes turned to familiar themes: the opportunities for enlarging human well-being and the prospects of the (Midas) curse of poverty in the midst of wealth.

Thus we need to pay constant conscious attention to the long-term rate of interest for fear that our vast resources may be running to waste through a failure to direct our savings into constructive uses and that this running to waste may interfere with the beneficent operation of compound interest which should, if everything was proceeding smoothly in a well governed society, lead us within a few generations to the complete abolition of oppressive want. (XIII: 367)

In order to make full use of human inventiveness, science, and enterprise the economy had to be planned – as he made clear in a BBC talk in March 1932. In this talk he does not dismiss or belittle the experimental value of communist or fascist planning. Keynes argues that we have to learn from them so as to resolve the extraordinary contradiction of man's capacity to produce material wealth coexisting in a world in which there is 'starvation amidst plenty' – wherein we (like Midas) are unable to 'carry to our mouths the nourishment we have produced by our hands' (XXI: 86–7). He distinguishes between democratic planning and other forms in terms of the former as one which does not seek to 'aggrandise the province of the state for its own sake'. Democratic planning does not aim at:

superseding the individual within the field of operations appropriate to the individual, or of transforming the wage system, or of abolishing the profit motive. Its object is to take hold of the central controls and to govern with deliberate foresight and thus modify and condition the environment within which the individual freely operates with and against other individuals. (XXI: 88)

Where individual action is able to deal with problems the state must act to secure benefits to the wider community. He gives several examples of deliberate planning enlarging the possibilities and potentialities including: transport; rural presevation; location of industry; regulating the level of interest and the rate of investment. In so arguing Keynes's point is that thinking in terms of polarities – planning and democracy – is erroneous: it is 'possible to enjoy the advantage of both worlds' (XXI: 91). The quest was for a new 'miraculous union' between individual and public good.

In 1933 he published a series of articles ('The Means to Prosperity') which presented the fullest account of his thinking prior to the publication of the *General Theory* in 1936 and is best read alongside his essay on Malthus (which he revised at this time). Together they demonstrate how far he had moved from *A Treatise on Money*. Keynes emphasizes in his observations on prosperity that economic problems were oftentimes not due to acts of nature – which were beyond our control, but their origins lay in human inaction and a chronic lack of will.

If our poverty were due to famine or earthquake or war – if we lacked material things and the resources to produce them, we could not expect to find the means to prosperity except in hard work, abstinence, and invention. In fact, our predicament is notoriously of another kind. It comes from some failure in the immaterial devices of the mind, in the workings of the motives which should lead to the decisions and acts of will, necessary to put in movement the resources and technical means we already have. (IX: 336)

The articles argued for action on two fronts: domestic and international. In the case of the latter he urged the institution of a world economic conference to ensure international coordination and cooperation – something which was to command his attention during the war. On the domestic level Keynes had now come to realize the importance of Kahn's theory of the multiplier, and Keynes explains how an injection of money into the economy would stimulate greater economic activity. The alchemy of money meant that modest government spending could breed and make further wealth as people pass on proportions of their income in spending to consume the products and services of others. This was not 'magic' Keynes insisted, but 'a reliable scientific prediction' (IX: 349).

At around the same time when Keynes was putting forward his ideas on the means to prosperity (March/April 1933) he gave a fascinating and badly neglected account of the implications of this new science of wealth: his Dublin lecture entitled *National Self-Sufficency* (published in the *New Statesman* after the World Economic Conference). The lecture has to be read very much in the context of developing the kind of ideas which he had put forward in his essay on 'The Economic Possibilities for our Grandchildren' and in his 1931 American lectures. He makes the point that the economic advantages of the international division of labour are less valid than once they were for a growing number of industrial and agricultural products. The disadvantages of international trade outweigh the benefits, especially in regard of the advantages of 'bringing the producer and the consumer within the ambit of the same national, economic and financial organization' when, given modern technology, most products can be manufactured just as efficiently in one country as another. Moreover:

> as wealth increases, both primary and manufactured products play a smaller relative part in the national economy compared with houses, personal services and local amenities which are not the subject of international exchange. (XXI: 238)

Far from competition in free international trade and foreign ownership of industry being likely to promote peace, Keynes felt that it was setting up strains and bad feelings between nations. Progress – economic growth – as such was not about a spurious and potentially dangerous economic internationalism and 'entanglement', but developing an economic system in which more and more was done locally: 'let goods be homespun whenever it is reasonably and conveniently possible; and above all let finance be primarily national' (XXI: 236). In all of this we should be enthusiastic experimenters in politics and economics so as to ensure that we are not at the 'mercy of world forces' bent on arriving at some kind of 'uniform equilibrium according to the ideal principles of *laissez-faire* capitalism' (XXI: 240–1). In seeking to gain a maximum amount of national self-sufficiency we have to free our-selves from the 'accountants' nightmare' in which society remains poor be-cause it does not 'pay' to be rich, or because we cannot 'afford' to have decent housing and which leads us inexorably to the situation in which:

> We destroy the beauty of the countryside because the unappropriated splendours of nature have no economic value. We are capable of shutting off the sun and the stars because they do not pay a dividend. London is one of the richest cities of the history of civilisation, but it cannot 'afford' the highest standards of achievement of which its own living citizens are capable, because they do not 'pay'. ... We have recently conceived it a moral duty to ruin the tillers of the soil and destroy the age-long traditions attendant on husbandry if we could get a loaf of bread thereby a tenth of a penny cheaper. There was nothing which it was not our duty to sacrifice to this Moloch and Mammon in one; for we faithfully believed that the worship of these monsters would overcome the evil of poverty and lead the next generation safely and comfortably, on the back of compound interest, into eco-nomic peace ... Today we suffer disillusion, not because we are poorer ... but because other values seem to have been sacrificed ... For our economic system is not, in fact, enabling us to exploit to the utmost the possibilities for economic wealth afforded by the progress of our technique ... But once we allow ourselves to be disobedient to the test of an accountant's profit, we have begun to change our civilisation. (XXI: 242–3)

Keynes supported experiments in economic policy as a way of arriving at new arrangments which could offer alternatives to ruling orthodoxy and revolutionary change. The same year (1933) as he backed deValera's dream of an Ireland which valued material wealth only as the basis of right living, Keynes also wrote his famous letter to President Roosevelt in which he proclaimed the President as:

> the trustee for those in every country who seek to mend the evils of our condition by reasoned experiment within the framework of the existing social system. If you fail, rational change will be gravely prejudiced throughout the world, leaving orthodoxy and revolution to fight it out. (XXI: 289)

In the period whilst he was preparing the *General Theory* Keynes naturally became concerned about the growing tensions in Europe and with the threat to civilization posed by fascism and communism. The *General Theory* has to be read within the context of this crisis as he believed that economics as a moral science offered an alternative approach to the religions of the extreme left and right. For example, in a piece dealing with one of the great fruits of compound interest, Einstein, written in 1933, Keynes comments on the Nazi's attack on 'prophets of an ancient race', Marx, Freud and Einstein. They stood condemned by the fascists because they tore at our 'social, personal, and intellectual roots' with an 'objectivity which to the healthy animal seems morbid, depriving everything, as it seems, of the warmth of natural feelings' (XXVIII: 21). Einstein stood for what the Nazi youth see as the very opposite of the 'blond beast'.

> How should they know the glory of the free-ranging intellect and soft objective sympathy and smiling innocence of heart, to which power and money and violence, drink and blood and pomp mean absolutely nothing? (XXVIII: 22)

Then in the following significant passage Keynes offers a highly alchemical image of the human condition. Einstein and the blond beasts are two ends of a spectrum (life and death, creativity and destruction, light and dark, sun and moon, Eros and Thanatos?) which contains a necessary conflict in the extremes of humanity.

> Albert and the blond beasts make up the world between them. *If either cast the other out, life is diminished in its force.* When the barbarians destroy the ancient race as witches, when they refuse to scale heaven on broomsticks, they may be dooming themselves to sink back into the clods which bore them. (XXVIII: 22) (My emphasis)

Opposites and contradictions were the stuff of creation and alchemical creativity. The great task was to work to bring about a harmony of opposing forces. In his BBC talk of 1932 on planning Keynes had argued that even out of the dark forces of fascism and communism there was the possibility of a rebirth of liberalism:

> it is a remarkable and a significant thing that the two most extraordinary political movements of the modern age, approaching their task from opposite moral and emotional poles, should agree in this vital particular – that state planning, that intelligence and deliberation at the centre must supercede the admired disorder of the 19th century. (XXI: 86)

The danger was, however, ever more polarization. A few years later, in 1936, for example, Keynes responds to those who 'blindly' wished to polarize 'everything in terms of Capitalism and Communism' (XXVIII: 56–7). Between November 1934 and January 1935 Keynes engaged in a debate with Shaw and others following an interview between H.G. Wells and Stalin published in the *New Statesman* which offers an insight into his thoughts as he was writing the *General Theory*. The point he makes is that both Marxism and modern liberalism are products of the same system of nineteeth century thought – the 'standard system' of the economists. This system bred two families of dogmatists: those who thought capitalism was 'true and inevitable, and those who thought it true and intolerable' (XXVIII: 32). Until now there had been no third alternative and 'sounder' economic theory. Neither the standard system of the economists or Marxism is satisfactory, and he maintains that the 'pressing task' is for a new system to be developed which will 'justify economists taking their seat beside other scientists' (ibid.). Power had shifted from owners to an impersonal 'salariat': 'In England today no one has personal power' (XXVIII: 34) and therefore the idea of a 'revolution' is anachronistic. Thus, Keynes argues that: 'The problem to-day is first to concert good advice and then to convince the well-intentioned that it is good … There is no massive resistance to a new direction. The risk is of a contrary kind – lest society plunge about in its perplexity and dissatisfaction into something worse' (ibid.). The attractiveness of communism is built upon a 'protest against the emptiness of economic welfare' in capitalist societies and an appeal to ascetic values which idealists find spiritually appealing. Keynes's article prompted a reply from Dora Russell who asked if it was indeed the case that there is no resistance to the alternative he was advocating, why had his ideas not been adopted. Keynes replied:

> Because I have not yet succeeded in convincing either the expert or the ordinary man that I am right. If I am wrong, this will prove to have been fortunate. If, however, I am right, it is, I feel certain, only a matter of time before I convince both; when both are convinced, economic policy will, with the usual time lag, follow suit. (XXVIII: 35)

For Keynes the issue was not one of class warfare or the wickedness of the powerful, so much as knowing what to do:

> I think it is extremely difficult to know what ought to be done, and extremely difficult for those who know (or think they know) to persuade others that they are right – though theories, which are difficult and obscure when they are new and undigested, grow easier by the mere passage of time. I suspect that Bernard Shaw's preference for tyrants is due to his being impressed with the difficulties of persuasion. It is easier to persuade a tyrant to adopt one's policy than to persuade the democracy … But it is not self interest which makes the democracy difficult to persuade. (XXVIII: 36)

Subsequently Shaw urged Keynes to read Marx, and in January 1935 Keynes replied by saying that he failed to see how Marx had 'discovered a clue to the economic riddle' – but that he has!

> To understand my state of mind, however, you have to know that I believe myself to be writing a book on economic theory, which will largely revolutionise – not, I

suppose, at once but in the course of the next ten years – the way the world thinks about economic problems. When my new theory has been duly mixed with politics and feelings and passions, I can't predict what the final upshot will be in its effects on action and affairs. But there will be a great change, and in particular, the Ricardian foundations of Marxism will be knocked away. I can't expect you, or anyone else, to believe this at the present stage. But for myself I don't merely hope what I say – in my own mind I'm quite sure. (XXVIII: 42)

What a claim: a book which would *revolutionize* the way the *world* thinks about economic problems! His theory would show how thinking in terms of opposites could be replaced by a fusion or 'miraculous union' between contradictions: sun and moon; male and female; King and Queen; capitalism and socialism; planning and democracy. Keynes had found a way to square the circle, and attain androgeny: his quest had arrived at a way to rescue and transform capitalism by resolving its contradictions and making it *whole*.

4. Squaring the circle: *The General Theory*

Make a circle out of a man and woman, derive from it a square, and from the square a triangle: make a circle and you will have the philosophers' stone. (*The Rosarium*: cited in Fabricius, 1994: 198)

Science is impersonal, whereas, to succeed, the magician must be entirely involved in the operation. (Nataf, 1994: 54)

Though full of promise, [alchemical] texts invariably contain elaborate devices to deter the unworthy. They are couched in a language often so obscure and so impenetrable that their study requires years and years of devoted attention, of reading and re-reading, before their exegesis even may be attempted. [They] constitute a challenge to the heroic nature of him who seeks to 'innerstand'. Like Theseus, the enquirer confronts the Labyrinth ... Only through reliance on inspired intuition, the golden thread of Ariadne, will the puzzle fall into place and light replace darkness. (Stanislas Klossowski de Rola, 1992: 9)

The purgation of the base metals did not go so far as to deny them the right to exist. It was rather a question of removing all possible obstructions in the path of the developing seed of gold which each was supposed to contain. Translated into human terms, this meant that the passions and desires needed to be sublimated in order to attain harmony. The Freudian expression was in fact used by the alchemists ... the so-called lower impulses were to be refined and brought to a higher level, just as, according to Freud, the anti-social, sexual libido can be sublimated into a socially useful urge. It was not desirable therefore to destroy the baser elements entirely, since only from them could the philosophers' stone be made. (Gray, 1952: 25)

For someone who was trying to influence economic and policy opinion, it is puzzling that the *General Theory* should be so badly constructed as to make grasping the essentials so extremely difficult. As a handbook for a revolution it is without doubt one of the most deeply obscure and (literally) hermetic of volumes. If we compare it with other of his writings aimed at persuading, the *General Theory* comes off very badly. In place of Keynes's lucid prose we have passages so dense that it is quite impossible at times to know quite what he is saying. Perhaps, however, it is this very quality which makes the book so fascinating from the point of view of decoding and deciphering what Keynes is trying to say. It is not an easy book, and Keynes manifestly did not intend that it be so. The book was constructed in such a fashion that we only begin to understand it when we have really engaged with Keynes's thinking as a whole.

In other words, Keynes was writing a book which asked much of the reader. It required the reader to enter into Keynes's mind and exercise sympathy and imagination. Keynes wants us to do some hard work. It is important, therefore, that when we read the *General Theory* we keep in mind what he said to Shaw: 'When my new theory has been duly mixed with politics and feelings and passions, I can't predict what the final upshot will be in its effects on action and affairs'. In literary terms it is an intensely modern work, exhibiting as it does the quality of calling attention to a sense of the interconnectedness of things and for the *reader* to participate in the work of the book. As Sharon Spencer notes of this aspect of the modern novel: 'The open structure is a demand for the reader's acute concentration, and sometimes it is a demand, as well, for his active participation in the recreation of the book' (Spencer, 1971: 57). The *General Theory* is an experiment in thought designed to provoke and persuade the reader into thought, action and 'escape'. It was one of his 'eggs' whose final shape and form could not be known. From the academic and policy point of view this was clearly unsatisfactory as it inevitably gave rise to a discussion – even in his own lifetime – as to what he 'really meant'. The book was therefore seen by Keynes as a catalyst. He hoped that the ideas would stimulate and provoke thought and action. But, what the 'upshot' of this chemistry of theory, politics and feelings would be he did not know. The book is operating at so many levels, and fires off so many ideas which are not pressed home, that we can only conclude that Keynes saw himself as providing a kind of mental laboratory in which we could explore our theories, politics and feelings. He argues at the start of the book that it was the product of a 'long struggle of escape ... from habitual modes of thought and expression' (GT: xxiii). The *General Theory* is not a book designed to create a new prison by imposing a framework to replace the old orthodoxies, but on the contrary, it is designed to foster a new way of thinking which is not as constrained and mechanistic as in the past. This is why he was so antagonistic to the translation of economics into pseudo-scientific mathematical forms of language. The *General Theory* is, in essence, a model for the new moral science – it is a way of thinking about the instrospection and values which shape human thought and behaviour (XIV: 300) in a monetary economy. As moral science the theory was composed of a blend of ideas which we can discern in his earlier work: ethics and politics; economics and psychology; as well as physics. Pigou had hit the nail firmly, fairly and squarely on the head when he noted that:

> Einstein actually did for physics what Mr Keynes believes himself to have done for economics. He developed a far-reaching generalisation under which Newton's results can be subsumed as a special case. But he did not, in announcing his discovery, insinuate, through carefully barbed sentences, that Newton and those who had hitherto followed his lead were a gang of incompetent bunglers. (Pigou, 1936: 18)

When we consider Keynes and his self-proclaimed revolution it is important to keep in mind the revolution in scientific knowledge which was under way in the 1920s and 1930s. As Friedman and Donley observe:

> Twentieth century physics postulated and experimentally validated two new world views, relativity and quantum theory, which differed from the conventional so fundamentally that philosophers and artists were encouraged to assimilate similar revolutionary views into their own disciplines ... Not since the Renaissance had so many creative people paid attention to what was going on in other fields ... New forms had to be created in order to give shape to the new ideas, and the new forms in one discipline often paralleled those in others. The arts became concerned with time as a dimension and with space–time relationships. Physicists found that there was no universal frame of reference, and multiple viewpoints showed up on paintings and in novels ... Relationships between objects became more important than the objects themselves. When physicists discovered they could not simultaneously find a particle's exact position and exact momemtum, they admitted the basic indeterminism inherent in the quantum theory, which gives a probabilistic rather than a causal description of nature. (Friedman and Donley, 1985: 1–2)

The *General Theory* is a child of its time and must be set alongside other explorations in the arts and humanities into the new world discovered by Einstein, Heisenberg, Planck and Bohr. Keynes, like other members of Bloomsbury such as Roger Fry and Virginia Woolf, was fully aware of the implications of the new physics (Friedman and Donley, 1985: 95–9). In 1925, for example, he wrote to Lydia noting that 'lately there is a boom for Einstein, so I am not out of date' (Hill and Keynes, 1989: 280). The following year he wrote an essay on Einstein (X: 282–4) and in his essay on Marshall he recounts a meeting with Max Planck, 'the famous originator of the Quantum Theory' (X: 186). The development of Keynes's ideas which culminates in the *General Theory* took place in the context of a post-Newtonian world. The old 'classical' view of the clockwork universe had been shown to be no longer valid as a 'general' theory and Keynes was evidently alive to the ideas which were, after all, the stuff of newspaper headlines. At a popular level the new physics was seen as signaling the end of a deterministic view of the universe. Russell's *ABC of Relativity* (1925) – which was originally composed for a series of articles in *The Nation* – interpreted relativity as an argument which pointed unequivocally in an indeterministic direction and towards greater *possibilities* for mankind free from the deterministic science of the past. As Russell concludes in his *Outline of Philosophy* (1927):

> The world presented for our belief by a philosophy based upon modern science is in many ways less alien to ourselves than the world of matter conceived in former centuries. The events that happen in our minds are part of the course of nature. ... The physical world, as far as science can show at present, is perhaps less rigidly

determined by causal laws than it was it was thought to be ... There is no need to think of ourselves as powerless and small in the grip of vast cosmic forces ... From the point of view of human life, it is not important to be able to create energy; what is important is to be able to direct energy into this or that channel, and this we can do more as our knowledge of science increases. Since men first began to think, the forces of nature have oppressed them; earthquakes, floods, pestilences, and famines have filled them with terror. Now at last, thanks to science, mankind are discovering how to avoid much of the suffering that such events have hitherto entailed. ... It would be well if human beings had a sense ... of the possibilities of greater things to come. (Russell, 1970: 311–12)

As far as popular science was concerned classical mechanics had been buried by Einstein, Planck, Heisenberg and Bohr. Although published after the *General Theory,* Sir James Jeans's book on *Physics and Philosophy* (1943) expresses the feeling which was widespread in the 1920s and 1930s that the new physics had revolutionary implications for humanity. The misbehaving electron had shown the deficiencies of the old paradigm (Jeans, 1981: 202). The new physics empowered mankind with the realization that, as the universe existed in the mind, not as a machine, we can exercise 'guidance through a fiat which is our own' (Jeans, 1981: 205).

The new physics shows us a universe which looks as though it might conceivably form a substitute dwelling-place for free men, and not a mere shelter for brutes – a home in which it may at least be possible for us to mould events to our desires and live lives of endeavour and achievement ... What remains is ... very different from the full-blooded matter and the forbidding materialism of the Victorian scientist. His objective and material universe is proved to consist of little more than constructs of our own minds. In this and in other ways modern physics has moved in the direction of mentalism. (Jeans, 1981: 216)

Keynes wished to move economics in the very same direction: from determinism to a 'mentalism' which confronted a world of *probabilities,* and not certainties. By the time of his letter to Shaw he had finally grasped the scale of his revolution: he would revolutionize economics by showing how limited was the old classical model to a world in which the economic electrons misbehaved and did not tick and tock in accordance with their theory. Furthermore, he could show how economists did not have to stand on the sidelines in a state of pseudo objectivity, but could participate in shaping and moulding events and 'chanelling' human energy. Now at last he was ready to abandon the Newtonian mechanics of classical economics and embrace Newtonian alchemy. The *General Theory*, therefore, marks the passing of the mechanical age in economics as Einstein's general theory had marked its demise in physics.

As someone who was, first and foremost, *policy* orientated, Keynes saw the working out of these ideas as something which was discovered through the application of his framework to day-to-day events and problems: there was no one 'Keynesian' solution or economic policy. Given the uncertainty and flux which existed in the real world a 'general theory' as a general panacea was not what he had in mind.

> we must recognise that only experience can show how far the common will, embodied in the policy of the State, ought to be directed to increasing and supplementing the inducement to invest; and how far it is safe to stimulate the average propensity to consume. (GT: 377)

The object of the *General Theory* is, as he makes clear, not to provide 'a machine or method of blind manipulation which will furnish an infallible answer' (GT: 297), but on the contrary, a method of thinking in an 'organized and intelligent' way about the complex interactions which take place in the economy *as a whole*. This complexity cannot be captured by mathematical economics which can lead to blind manipulation of symbols and result in losing sight of the 'complex interdependencies of the real world' (GT: 297–8). Keynes's economics was no science which involved a precise universal formula for the transmutation of capitalism. Like alchemy there was no:

> formula which if followed to the letter, would bring about the desired end. There are only principles of operation that the alchemist must apply with a high level of awareness and judgment. Indeed, the process, with all its potential set-backs and problems, is itself the education of the alchemist, and until he has developed his own skills and insights through this he cannot perfect the Work. (Gilchrist, 1991: 7)

Keynes made the point after the *General Theory*'s publication that he hoped that: 'If the simple basic ideas can become familiar and acceptable, time and experience and the collaboration of a number of minds will discover the best way of expressing them' (XIV: 111). For Keynes 'time and experience' was absolutely central to the 'revolution'. The *General Theory* was not intended to be a definitive 'academic' statement but a set of laboratory tools for economic experimentation. In the *General Theory* we see Keynes the alchemist mixing and distilling ideas and intuitions from various sources. As Moggridge comments:

> Keynes' wide reading, plus his formal neglect of his predecessors while writing, meant, when coupled with the industry of the academic world, that it was, and is, possible to find a precursor for almost every idea in his work, as numerous issues of economic journals and scholarly monographs have proved beyond doubt. (Moggridge in M. Keynes (ed.), 1975: 75)

These ideas drawn from economics, as well as psychology, mathematics, philosophy and ethics, composed the elements which he was to combine in the

General Theory. This intellectual chemistry is the source of the book's obscurity and its genius. By the time of its publication Keynes had come to believe that he had formulated a model of the economic system which could be used to bring about a capitalism free from mass unemployment and the extremes of boom and bust, inflation and deflation, and the extremes in the distribution of wealth and income. In the right hands, and with the right feelings, his book offered the possibility of a new mastery over economic forces. He had shown how to square the circle and resolve the contradictions which socialists (such as Shaw) were convinced would ultimately destroy capitalism.

Whereas the classical school (descended from Ricardo) saw the economy as a Newtonian atomistic machine which, if left to itself, would attain a balance and equilibrium, Keynes viewed the world in a more organic way: like an alchemist he saw man as active in the redemption of inter-related natural forces. The *General Theory* is rejecting the atomistic, dualistic, objectivist, and deterministic version of Newtonianism which underpinned the 'classical' physics of the economists, and is pointing the way to a *policy science* more suited to an age in which mankind had to come to terms with uncertainty. In this regard, although the *General Theory* was a very different book to Marshall's *Principles*, it is informed by the same kind of attitude towards the role of economics as having a part to play in improving man's 'limited but effective control over natural development by forecasting the future and preparing the way for the next step' and which called for 'courage and caution, for resource and steadfastness, for penetrating insight and for breadth of view' (Marshall, 1947: 248). The *General Theory* is a book which is concerned with what Marshall expressed as 'balancing the forces in the life and decay of people' (Marshall, 1947: 323). Keynes's aim was one with Marshall in seeking to 'unveil the mysteries of the growth and decay of custom and other phenomena which we are not any longer contented to take as ultimate and insoluble facts given by nature' (Marshall, 1947: 775). The numerous references to Marshall in the *General Theory* show how far he has moved from Marshall's economic theory, but they belie the fact that he remained very much a pupil of Marshall's moral science. However, in seeking to lead a revolution he has naturally to emphasize how his theory differs from previous theories. Hence, in the German and Japanese preface, he begins by denying his old master and confessing that he too had been in error: he was a 'priest' of economic orthodoxy who has converted to Protestantism (GT: xxiv). And yet, the *General Theory* is essentially not moving in leaps, but is far more of a development of and transition from the economics of Marshall, even though he rejects his theory of money and interest and much else besides. So, if he were to influence and change inside and outside opinion and 'do any good' then he had to 'appear unorthodox, troublesome, dangerous, disobedient to them that begat us' (IX: 306).

The *General Theory* aimed to show how the power for good could be set free from the shackles of the Ricardian prison in which market forces were as fixed as the law of gravity. In the years preceding the *General Theory* Keynes was 'struggling' to find a way to work this transformation through changing opinion and policy. Although human nature could not be 'transmuted' (GT: 374) opinions, ideas, beliefs *could* be shaped and re-formed. Human nature was unalterable, but the human mind *was* amenable to argument and persuasion. As he had stated in *A Treatise on Money* (1930), there was nothing inevitable about depression or economic slumps. Their cause was *policy*, and therefore 'avoidable':

> Yet it is evident that the policy could not have been radically different, unless the mentality and ideas of our rulers had also been greatly changed. That is to say, what has occurred is not exactly an accident; it has been deeply rooted in our general way of doing things. But, granted that the past belongs to the past, need we be fatalistic about the future also? If we leave matters to cure themselves, the results may be disastrous ... our present regime of capitalistic individualism will assuredly be replaced by a far-reaching socialism. (VI: 345–6)

Keynes's mission was to show that, despite the dismal theories of the classical school or of Karl Marx, economic forces were not beyond our control. The problem was setting out a theory which could demonstrate how we could wrest control away from blind economic forces and human psychological propensities. The *General Theory* is his handbook for a revolutionary rebirth of capitalism as the engine of human progress and the enlarger of human possibilities.

He concludes his preface (to the English edition) by saying that it was the product of a long struggle to 'escape' from 'habitual modes of thought and expression' – and adds that 'so must the reading of it be for most readers if the author's assult upon them is to be successful'. Although the ideas are 'extremely simple' and 'obvious' he confesses that they are 'laboriously expressed' (GT: xxiii). This is so, he argues, because he requires his readers to go through a kind of mental experiment. It is *designed* to be difficult so that at the end of the process his 'simple ideas' can penetrate into 'every corner' of the mind. For someone who is trying to influence policy this is indeed an odd kind of approach. He is saying to the reader that if you want to know my mind, you have to work with me: the reader is part of the experiment. This book, he says, is a 'long struggle', and it has been written in such a way that simple ideas are hidden under 'laborious' modes of expression. This quite deliberate obscuratism of the *General Theory* finds a parallel in Newton's *Principia* (1686). Newton rewrote part three of the book so that it could only be understood by those who had fully mastered the ideas contained in the proceeding two books. Since its publication the *General Theory* has more than fulfilled the author's hermetic intention, in developing a reputation for being an important book which is not actually read, and which has largely been propagated by the interpretations of others. But the obscuratism of the book was no accident. Keynes meant it to be a trial. It is often compared to books such as Darwin's *Origin of Species*, or Marx's *Das Capital* (Hansen, 1953: ix), and yet unlike either of these and other important books of the last hundred years or so Keynes's *General Theory* steadfastly retains it reputation as requiring a great deal of sweat, time, pain and devotion on the part of the reader (Hansen, 1953: xi). Like the alchemists he believed that his readers had to undergo a process of mental purification if they were to make the leap into a new way of thinking and feeling. The 'simple ideas' of the book have to be hunted down with all the diligence employed by Newton in pursuit of his Greene Lyon (Dobbs, 1975). By 1939 Keynes had came to realize that the plan to make the book a 'struggle' was problematic. He notes in the preface to the French edition that if he were writing afresh he would 'endeavour to free [himself] from this fault and state [his] position in a more clear-cut manner' (GT: xxxi). This he never did and so we are left with a book which makes no attempt to be 'clear-cut' but wilfully takes us on a winding journey of discovery. Here and there Keynes leaves clues and markers as to his 'simple ideas' and intimations of the magic spells which he believes can transform capitalism. The promise is escape – a word he uses three times in nine lines – from the evils of mass unemployment and the defects of a capitalism which, if not reformed, threatens to put an end to individual freedom and civilization as we know it.

Before we set off Keynes gives us a thread which we must trace through the book as we struggle to break out of the Newtonian *laissez-faire* labyrinth. We have to hold on to this very tightly if we are to enter into Keynes's mind: 'A monetary economy is essentially one in which changing views about the future are capable of influencing the quantity of employment and not merely its direction' (GT: xxii). As the future cannot be known Keynes leads us through a model designed to illuminate a world in which human decision making takes place in the context of uncertainty, ignorance and flux. Money is the key which opens the door to those psychological propensities of human beings which ultimately shape and determine economic conditions. Knowing and understanding these inclinations we no longer have to be driven along by these dark forces but can direct and use them to realize the good society. In his 'clear cut' mood (in the French preface) he gives the reader another thread to hold:

> as soon as we know the propensity to consume and to save (as I call it), that is the result for the community as a whole of the individual psychological inclinations as to how to dispose of given incomes, we can calculate what level of incomes,

and therefore what level of output and employment, is in profit-equilibrium with a given level of investment ... (the multiplier) ... Or again, it becomes evident that an increased propensity to save will *ceteris paribus* contract incomes and output; whilst an increased inducement to invest will expand them. We are thus able to analyse the factors which determine the income and output of the system as a whole; – we have, in the most exact sense, a theory of employment. (GT: xxxiii)

Another important clue to find comes in the preface in a remark which is almost an aside, but contains a central idea which he develops more fully after the publication of the book.

The writer of a book such as this, treading on unfamiliar paths, is extremely dependent on criticism and conversation if he is to avoid an undue proportion of mistakes. It is astonishing what foolish things one can temporarily believe if one thinks too long alone, particularly in economics (along with other moral sciences), where it is often impossible to bring one's ideas to a conclusive test either formal or experimental. (GT: xxiii)

This is, therefore, a work of moral science. And, if we are to understand this notion we have to follow a trail to other writings in other books, especially Malthus. As is clear from the references to Malthus in the *General Theory* – and from his comment in the Japanese edition which notes that his book 'traces its descent from Malthus' (GT: xxix) – we have to go off and read his essay on Malthus if we are to understand the direction from which Keynes is coming and the direction he wants us to follow. On this journey we have to have an eye on the ideas of the past, as well as on the conditions of the present and the prospects for the future: we have to keep our wits about us. As Winch observes, for Malthus: 'Preaching morality was secondary to the role of the moral scientist capable of elucidating principles, assessing their application to the real world, and attempting to gain support for them' (Winch, 1987: 99). Malthus did not keep his moral principles and his work as a scientist in separate compartments. This was something which clearly distinguished him from other political economists and in particular what made him an entirely different kind of economist to Ricardo. More than anyone else – apart from Moore – Keynes identified most strongly with the ideas of the good Reverend. If we are to understand Keynes's quest for a new moral science we have to understand the relationship between his economics and the work of Thomas Malthus.

Keynes regarded Malthus as the founding father of an economics based on moral and political philosophy, rather than mathematics and crude Newtonianism. The *General Theory* is therefore a book written in the light cast by Malthus's insights and intuitions. As he argued after the *General Theory* his aim was 'to do justice to schools of thought which the classicals have treated as imbecile for the last hundred years'. This showed that, 'I am not really so great an innovator ... but have important predecessors and am returning to an age-long tradition of common sense' (XIII: 552). Keynes's concern with the 'Malthusian devil' (II: 6) of overpopulation is evident throughout his writings. As we noted earlier, in chapter two of *The Economic Consequences of the Peace* he argues that the fundamental problem for the future was how to feed, clothe and house Europe's growing population. What had happened in Russia could well happen elsewhere: civilizations could be destabilized by the 'disruptive power of national fecundity' (II: 8–9). It is fear of human fecundity which prompts Keynes to believe that it is only by making the most productive use of resources can we hope to bind up the devil – hence the absolutely crucial role of the economist. In the essay on 'The Economic Possibilities for our Grandchildren' the 'power to control population' is seen as an essential precondition of the possibility of 'economic bliss' (IX: 331). In his essay on 'The End of Laissez-faire' he argues that three forms of management were necessary for curing the diseases of individualism: the exercise of 'directive intelligence' over money; the management of savings and investment; and the management of the population (IX: 292). And in his essay 'Am I a Liberal?' he refers to the centrality of the 'sex question' and issues such as the 'use of contraceptives, marriage laws, sexual offences and abnormalities, the economic position of women, [and] the economic position of the family' (IX: 302). These questions, he felt, 'interlock with economic issues' and cannot be evaded even though they were not discussed openly in political debate (IX: 303). Keynes's Mathusianism was a vitally important aspect of his thought and if we are to enter fully into what he has to say we need to set his ideas in the context of Malthus's political economy. The *General Theory* opens with Keynes arguing that economics took a wrong turn when it followed in the lines of development marked out by Ricardo, rather than Malthus. Economists were subsequently to occupy another world far removed from the realities discovered by Malthus (GT: 33). Read in this light the aim of the *General Theory* is to take us back to the point at which it all began to go wrong and show us how, by adopting a Malthusian framework, we can once again return to the real world. So, let us put down our copy of the *General Theory* and reach for Keynes's essay on Malthus.

The *General Theory* contains an oblique reference to this 'moral science' (GT: xxiii) but, apart from his theory of effective demand, Keynes does not go into any detail on Malthus's conception of the moral sciences. In his essay on Malthus he includes a large quote from the conclusion to the *Essay on Population* (X: 105–6) and it is in this work we find the other part of Malthus which also provides a point of entry into Keynes's own idea of economics *qua* moral science. The *Essay on Population* (vol. 1) paints a notoriously dismal picture of the human condition in which population inexorably outgrows resources. The growth of population, Malthus believed, was subject to

two checks: the positive checks of vice, misery, famine, epidemics and violence, and the preventive checks of moral restraint, late marriage and chastity.
In primitive societies the positive checks of raw nature are the main forces
which operate to cull the human population. However, in more 'civilized'
societies human beings were capable of exerting reason, moral choice, and
economic calculation to manage their reproduction. It was the peculiar fac-
ulty of man that he has power of reasoning which 'enables him to calculate
distant consequences' and control the 'dictates of nature' (Malthus, vol. 1,
1958: 12–13). Civilized man has a capacity for 'preventative foresight'
(Malthus, vol. 1, 1958: 236) which can restrain his powerful sexual urges.
The Malthusian vision is one in which sexuality contains the potential or
possibility of good and evil, life and death.

> An implicit obedience to the impluses of our natural passions would lead us to the
> wildest and most fatal extravagances; and yet we have the strongest reasons for
> believing that all these passions are so necessary to our being, that they could not
> be generally weakened or diminished, without injuring our happiness. After the
> desire of food, the most powerful and general of our desires is the passion
> between the sexes ... Of the happiness spread over human life by this passion very
> few are unconscious. Virtuous love, exalted by friendship seems to be that sort of
> mixture of sensual and intellectual enjoyment, particularly suited to the nature of
> man, and most powerfully caculated to awaken the sympathies of the soul ...
> Perhaps there is scarcely a man, who has once experienced the genuine delight of
> virtuous love, however great his intellectual pleasures may have been, who does
> not look back to that period as the sunny spot in his whole life, where his
> imagination loves most to bask, which he recollects and contemplates with the
> fondest of regrets, and which he would wish to live over again. We have ... great
> reason to believe that the passion between the sexes has the most powerful ten-
> dency to soften and meliorate the human character, and keep it alive to all the
> kindlier emotions of benevolence and pity. (Malthus, vol. 2, 1958: 153–5)

What is required to ensure that civilization is not destroyed by natural laws
which cannot be 'diminished' or 'altered' (Malthus, vol. 2, 1958: 159) is that
individuals have to 'regulate' and 'direct' their instincts. There was hope, as
he concludes (in the passage cited at length by Keynes), for a 'gradual and
progressive improvement in human society' in the dissemination of a moral
and political philosophy which shows how to 'counteract' the laws of nature
(Malthus, vol. 2, 1958: 261–2; cited in Keynes, X: 105–6). The educated
classes have it in their power to regulate and direct their natural impulses so
as to ensure that their desire for immediate sexual gratification is contained
and restrained. Human passions have to be tamed by rational and moral
calculation about future economic prospects. As for the lower classes, there
appeared to be little prospect of sexual instincts being subject to rational
restraint. The 'positive' checks were the primary means of keeping their
numbers down. If not, the growing ignorant and discontented 'mob' threat-

ened the very foundations of constitutional governance. Over the years, however, Malthus became less pessimistic about the possibility of using moral restraints to contain the basic instincts of the lower orders. Knowledge of natural laws could set them free from their sexual slavery. Thus although he was critical of allowing government to do anything to improve the lot of the poor on a physical level, he was very committed to raising their mental condition through a national education system.

Keynes shared in all essentials Malthus's dualistic idea of human instincts, and an economics which was rooted in understanding the human instincts which were under the surface of visible economic life. He thought Malthus was the greatest of the economists because, unlike Ricardo, he based his ideas on a real world which was close to human experience (GT: 192). Malthus saw sexuality as the essential force which shaped human destiny for good or ill. *The Principles of Population* predated the later concerns of Freud and others in considering the relationship of sexuality and civilization. In Malthus we find the essential Freudian argument that the continued existence of society required that we control our sexual impluses, and that if we fail to do so civilization will crumble. Malthus gives us an image of sexuality as containing the primary conflict of opposites which found expression in social, economic and political life. It was the cause of life, but also the bringer of death, misery, and war. Sex was both good and evil, necessary and dangerous, creative and destructive. Human passions could not be changed, diminished or altered but only 'directed' and 'regulated'. Keynes shared Malthus's fear of the population devil because it could be so destabilizing and induce such insecurity that it unleashed other evil spirits from the dark pits which contained primitive human instincts. Chief of these malign spirits was the love of money. It was the other side of Malthus's devil. For Malthus the source of so much human misery as well as joy were the penis and vagina. To these Keynes added the Freudian perspective on the role of the anus and excreta in human history. Both front and back were sources of good. Money and population were necessary to sustain life, but they could also bring death. For Malthus 'moral restraint' held the key to human happiness: 'Industry cannot exist without foresight and security' (Malthus, vol. 2, 1958: 143). However, whereas for Malthus this foresight and security were the fruits of individual 'moral restraint', direction and control, for Keynes the age when the passions could be restrained by *individual* moral restaint was long gone. Now, it fell to the *state* to provide the foresight (GT: 164) which could create a more secure environment in which enterprise could thrive. In the modern age, Keynes believed, it was only the use of economic knowledge and not Victorian morality, which could save us from the fate predicted by the Rev. Malthus. As the peace settlement of 1919 had shown, if human destiny were to be entrusted to politicians, the prospect was indeed dismal for us all. As Malthus had concluded in the later editions of his essay on population, God-given human reason meant that men could beat the devil. Keynes's Malthus is therefore not the figure of popular imagination or of the 'economic sophists' (X: 104). His Malthus is someone whose thought developed like a chrysalis (another form of egg) to produce a beautiful master economist who was concerned with solving human problems – albeit through transforming human character. He, too, was interested in unemployment and finding a cure to the economic malaise through 'free expenditure, public works and a policy of expansionism' (X: 107). For Keynes, Malthus raised:

> The voice of objective reason ... against a deep instinct which the human evolutionary struggle had been implanting from the commencement of life; and man's mind, in the conscious pursuit of happiness, was daring to demand the reins of government from out of the hands of the unconscious urge for mere predominant survival. (X: 85)

This too was Keynes's dare voiced in the *General Theory*. The book demands that the 'reins of government' be wrenched from the grasp of unconscious urges so as to release human possibility from the psychological propensities which ruled economic life.

In keeping with his belief that economics was fundamentally a moral science it is significant that Keynes concludes the *General Theory* with the words 'good or evil'. At one level the book can be read as a journey through contradictory and opposing forces, and in the course of this journey Keynes is going to show us how what we thought of as good (thrift) is the source of much evil, and how what we may think of as being evil (consumption) is the source of much good. Keynes shows us how economics can open the door to understanding the ancient conflicts and contradictions inherent in the sterile love of money, and how the curse visited upon Midas is the inescapable destiny of all those societies and individuals who choose to store up wealth rather than use it for life and for the attainment of the good. As we weave our way through the *General Theory* we encounter the embodiments of the battle of good and evil: the investor who thinks in the long term, takes risks, creates real wealth; the hoarder who prefers to hold on to his money and feed on the interest it makes; and the speculator blinded by the vice of Onanism. On our journey we will come to know the embodiment of animal spirits in the entrepreneur. We will learn that our life enhancing friend is no calculating machine and that the role of the state is to change the institutional environment of capitalism so as to set his animal spirits free to do their work. We will encounter the hot Sol and the watery Luna of the social universe: risk taking, intelligent, animal spirited masculine enterprise and capricious, shy, hysterical, emotional and cautious feminine liquidity.

Chapter 1 is but one paragraph long, plus a footnote. Keynes describes the book as a 'general' theory so as to differentiate it from the dominant 'classical' school and its postulates. What is striking is that it immediately invites comparison with Einstein. Keynes's revolution involves showing that Newtonian clockwork economics is a special case in the same sense as was argued in respect of physics in *The General Theory of Relativity*. Like Einstein, Keynes is not arguing that the Newtonian model is wrong, but that it is *inadequate* as a *general* explanation. It is positing, therefore, *complementarity* rather than incommensurability (as Bohr was to argue in respect of Newtonian, Einsteinian and Quantum physics). Keynes wants us to think differently about the economic universe: we have to realize that the old geometry will not suffice to guide and plot a course for policy making in an economy in which mass unemployment exists and persists. This theme is developed more explicitly a few pages on, in chapter 2, when he argues:

> if the classical theory is only applicable to the case of full employment, it is fallacious to apply it to the problems of involuntary unemployment – if there be such a thing (and who will deny it?). The classical theorists resemble Euclidean geometers in a non-Euclidean world who, discovering that in experience straight lines apparently parallel often meet, rebuke the lines for not keeping straight – as the only remedy for the unfortunate collisions which are occurring. Yet in truth, there is no remedy except to throw over the axiom of parallels and to to work out a non-Euclidean geometry. Something similar is required to-day in economics. We need to ... work out the behaviour of a system in which involuntary unemployment in the strict sense is possible. (GT: 16–17)

This passage is a direct reference to Bernhard Riemann's 'elliptic geometry' which showed the limitations of Euclid's axioms on curved surfaces: parallel lines do not always behave according to the postulations of Euclidean geometry. It was, of course, Riemann's geometry that was a starting point for Einstein's critique of Newtonian physics as being a *partial,* rather than a *general* theory. Keynes is arguing that we need to work out a new non-Euclidean economics which is more appropriate to a world which does not move in a straight deterministic line. Sometimes the sum of the interior angles of a triangle does not equal the two right angles. Sometimes economic reality does not fit with an economic theory which assumes that the great clockwork economic machine moves in the direction of an equilibrium in which there is full employment. Einstein shows us a universe which was not as linear and deterministic as Newton's laws maintained. Keynes aims to show that the classical theory of economics is just as inadequate to understanding the real world.

In chapters 2 and 3 Keynes's objective is to briefly set up the classical approach as being a form of Euclidean geometry in a non-Euclidean, post-Newtonian world. The parts of the machine do not relate to one another in the way the classical school believes. The rude mechanicals are victims of an 'optical illusion' in thinking that the laws of supply and demand generally or always work in the way they claim. In the *General Theory* as in the *Theory of Relativity* appearances can be very deceptive. The laws of classical economics are the equivalent of Euclid's 'axiom of parallels' (sic) and may be subjected to just the same kind of criticism as advanced by Bernhard Riemann in the nineteenth century and Einstein in the twentieth: there *are* conditions in which the axioms do not hold. These axioms were dangerous because they lead to a whole theory of public policy in which:

> the social advantages of private and national thrift, the traditional attitude towards the rate of interest, the classical theory of unemployment, the quantity of money, the unqualified advantages of *laissez-faire* in respect of foreign trade and much else which we shall have to question. (GT: 21)

Keynes argues that the lines do not behave in a *real* world in accordance to axioms which have partial validity: real wages do *not* equal the marginal disutility of existing employment; there *is* involuntary unemployment; savings do *not* equal investment; supply does *not* create its own demand. Above all, as chapter three details, there *may* be times when demand is not effective in bringing about an active and productive economy. The nexus of decision which links the present and future are *not* linked in a simple way (GT: 21). That this is so is because the economy is not a mindless machine, or a collection of atoms, but an organic set of relationships and the product of human psychology (GT: 27).

In these early chapters Keynes names the propagators of the belief that human beings were helpless in the face of evil: Ricardo and his heirs. In so doing he is quite ruthless in heaping on the heads of the 'classical' theorists the blame for errors and their practical consequences. Chief amongst the modern sons of Ricardo is Pigou who is targeted as the exponent of a theory of unemployment which suggests that it will all come right in the end if we leave things alone and let falling wages do the trick. This 'austere' doctrine is condemned by Keynes as serving to: 'explain much social injustice and apparent cruelty as an inevitable incident in the scheme of progress, and the attempt to change such things as likely on the whole to do more harm than good' (GT: 33).

Book one (chapter 3) is all about heroes and villains. Our hero is Malthus, and our villain is Ricardo. Keynes explains that the (Malthusian) notion that sometimes there is insufficiency of effective demand in the economy is a factor which is intimately related to the level of investment. In turn investment is influenced by a 'complex' set of other factors which are not mechanical, as in the classical model, but psychological. These propensities have characteristics which, like Riemann's geometry, gives rise to paradoxes and anomalies in the real world, as opposed to the behaviour of lines on a flat surface. It is not simply wages which provide the mechanism by which the system can determine employment levels: we have to take account of human desires to consume and invest. When once we rid ourselves of the Euclidean axioms of classical economics we can then see the reality of the distortions and paradoxes which actually occur in the real world.

> This analysis supplies us with an explanation of the paradox of poverty in the midst of plenty. For the mere existence of an insufficiency of demand may, and often will, bring the increase of employment to a standstill before a level of full employment has been reached. This insufficiency of effective demand will inhibit the process of production in spite of the fact that the marginal product of labour still exceeds in value the marginal disutility of employment. (GT: 30–31)

Futhermore, our non-Euclidean economics will show that, paradoxically, the richer a community becomes, the wider becomes the gap between what is produced and its actual potential to produce, with the consequence that the gap between the rich and poor, and the employed and the unemployed, capitalist and worker, grows ever wider. Rich societies have to confront the problem of having an inherent tendency towards an insufficiency of demand and a weak propensity to consume in relation to the actual capacities of the economic system. Falling wage rates will do nothing to remedy this situation, but will only make matters worse. The solution lies in the opposite direction to that advocated by the classical model: towards increasing the levels of consumption and investment, rather than increasing savings and reducing wages to price workers back into employment. But we live in a Ricardian world in which the problem of aggregate demand does not exist. The doctrine justifies the actions of individual capitalists and public authorities and is supported by academic economists (notably Pigou) who are 'unmoved by the lack of correspondence between the results of their theory and the facts of observation' (GT: 33). The classical model, therefore, is assuming that straight lines behave in a way that they are supposed to behave, and assuming the actual difficulties of a real world away (GT: 34). The *General Theory* wants to challenge the logical superstructure of assumptions which supports so much 'social injustice' and 'cruelty' (GT: 33): it wants to do for economics what Riemann had done for geometry.

Book two follows directly after the discussion of the way in which Malthus's principle of effective demand disappeared in the Ricardian conquest of English economics. The aim is to show that, in order to escape from the economic gardens of the classical economists where all is for the best if we leave well alone, we have to abandon the language which helps to create the 'optical illusions' of ruling economic theory. If economics is to be renewed we have to rid ourselves of the old discourse so that we can see the world as it really is. It is the alchemical method of *solve et coagula* (dissolve and combine): before we can go any further we have to dissolve away the classical conceptual framework before we can proceed to combine the ideas which follow into a new model. In particular Keynes tells us (chapter 4) that we must discard the notions of 'national dividend', the 'stock of real capital' and 'the general price level': 'we can get on better without them' (GT: 39). Next (chapter 5), we have to understand that expectations are crucial to explaining how output and employment are determined. Finally (chapters 6 and 7), we must abandon the classical framework of savings and investment, and think in terms of decisions to consume, or not to consume, invest, or not to invest; that is, in terms of psychological habits and propensities, rather than self-adjusting mechanisms which regulate savings and investment. The economic model which we are about to enter is one in which individual decisions about consuming or not consuming have far-reaching social consequences: this model requires that we divest ourselves of atomistic assumptions and ways of seeing and view human interactions in terms of wholes and not parts.

> It is true that, when an individual saves he increases his own wealth. But the conclusion that he also increases the aggregate wealth fails to allow for the possibility that an act of individual saving may react on someone else's savings and hence on someone else's wealth. (GT: 83–4)

There are no forces in this economic universe which 'harmonises the liberty' of individual interests and the social good: what is good for the part, may be bad for the whole. Keynes's framework, based on human propensities and psychological motivations, will enable us to move from the Ricardian/ Newtonian world where the economic behaviour of human beings in the aggregate is assumed to be like the behaviour of the individual, and where what is good for the individual is good for the whole, to a world in which there is tension and conflict between individual and social good. This is an alchemical world in which harmony has to be brought about by human agency, and in which there are paradoxes and uncertainties which must be addressed, not ignored, and in which possibilities and potentialities have to be released. Having established this proposition Keynes is now ready to examine economic propensities and demonstrate what actually determines the volume of employment in the economy as a whole.

Book three introduces a core concept in Keynes's theory: the propensity to consume. Here we encounter the 'fundamental psychological law':

> upon which we are entitled to depend with great confidence both *a priori* from our knowledge of human nature and from the detailed facts of experience, is that men are disposed, as a rule and on the average, to increase their consumption as their income increases, but not as much as the increase in their income. (GT: 96)

The psychological law having been established as the primary objective factor determining the propensity to consume Keynes then introduces us to the 'subjective factors' which provide the forces for change over time and place. The location of chapter 9 prior to the chapter on the multiplier (10) is significant. Having introduced his revolutionary concept of the propensity to consume (chapter 8) and prior to explaining the multiplier (10) Keynes returns us to the kind of economics that we find in Marshall's *Principles*: geography, race, education, religion, and moral values all have a part to play in shaping motives. In his analysis of the 'subjective' factors involved in the propensity to consume he sets out a list of characters who would not be out of place in a Victorian melodrama or the closing scenes from Goethe's *Faust*. Enter stage left, the good, the bad and the foolish! On the one side we have brothers Precaution, Foresight, Calculation, Improvement, Independence, Enterprise, Pride, and Avarice; on the other, sisters Enjoyment, Shortsightedness, Generosity, Miscalulation, Ostentation and Extravagance. These primal forces of human motivation are not constant:

> the strength of all these motives will vary enormously according to the institutions and organisation of the economic society which we presume, according to habits formed by race, education, convention, religion and current morals, according to present hopes and past experience, according to the scale and technique of capital equipment, and according to the prevailing distribution of wealth and the established standards of life. (GT: 109)

This is Marshall's economics: a world in which nature does not move in leaps, but gradually and slowly. Thus he argues that the *General Theory* will assume that, given the 'slow effects' of secular progress and 'far-reaching change' and the 'more or less permanent social structure of the community' and the consequent distribution of wealth, we can disregard the 'subjective factors' on the pattern of saving and spending. Subjective factors do not move in leaps and therefore 'Virtue and vice play no part'. In the volatile short run saving and spending is held to depend on 'how far the rate of interest is favourable to investment, after taking account of the marginal efficiency of capital' (GT: 111–12). This fact leads on to the relationship of consumption to investment. We have arrived at the magic of the multiplier. We enter a circle in which Marshall's big book has little power to restore full employment and equilibrium. Keynes is going to show us the trick.

See how it's done!
Make ten of one,
and let two be,
make even three,
then you'll be rich.
Cast out the four!

... from five and six
make seven and eight,
and now you're done:
The nine is one,
and ten is none
(Goethe, 1994: 2540–50)

Here we are with Faust in the Witches' kitchen and before the ailing Emperor as the secret of multiplication is disclosed. With this key – the 'philosophers' multiplying stone' (Fabricius, 1994: 176–7) – we can safely enter into the rose garden of book four wherein we will have to confront expectations, uncertainties and animal spirits and where we will encounter the conflict between the great opposites of the economic system: liquidity and hoarding versus enterprise and investment.

In chapter 10, therefore, we find one of the most potent of modern spells: how to multiply money. The chapter has some of the few pages of the *General Theory* that actually contains mathematical symbols which show how to 'escape from the sufferings of unemployment' (GT: 131). It is best read alongside his earlier comments on the sterility of money and the Midas effect. Here we find Keynes demonstrating how wealth can be grown through stimulating consumption. The theory is sufficiently well known not to be set out in too much detail: drawing on Kahn's work on the multiplier Keynes posits that the key to increasing employment is the fact that an increase in income is passed on to others, and that these increases multiply to generate a higher level of employment and investment. The multiplier turned the morality of the puritan economy upside-down. Out of what was deemed 'wasteful' and bad could come forth that which was productive and in the general good (GT: 128–9). Playfully Keynes concludes the chapter with the argument that, with the multiplier, we now possess the great secret which can transform a private vice into a public virtue. He had found a new source of the 'fabled wealth' of ancient times. Keynes had shown how money could grow and breed new life. He had indeed mastered the alchemist's art and found how to make true *philosophical* gold that enriched and fulfilled human life rather than serving only to destroy and corrupt it. Like the gold of the alchemists it had to be buried so as to ferment and grow, as in the dictum: 'Sow your gold in the white foliated earth' (Fabricius, 1994: 142). The answer to our economic problems lies (as Faust discovered) in the realm of Plutus and Pluto.

> If the Treasury were to fill old bottles with bank notes, bury them at suitable depths in disused coal-mines, which are then filled up to the surface with town rubbish, and leave it to private enterprise on well-tried principles of *laissez-faire* to dig the notes up again ... there need be no more unemployment and, with the help of the repercussions, the real income of the community, and its capital wealth also, would probably become a good deal greater than it actually is. It would,

indeed, be more sensible to build houses and the like; but there are more political and practical difficulties in the way of this, the above would be better than nothing. The analogy between this expedient and the gold-mines of the real world is complete. At periods when gold is available at suitable depths experience shows that the real wealth of the world increases rapidly; and when but little of it is so available our wealth suffers stagnation or decline. Thus gold-mines are of the greatest value to civilization. (GT: 129–30)

Or, as Goethe put it:

Take hoe and spade, and dig yourself,
this peasant labor will augment your greatness,
and from the soil you'll liberate a heard of golden calfs. ...
the philosophers' stone could be in their possession,
but there'd be no philosopher to use it. (Goethe, 1994: 5039–42)

Book four opens in chapter 11 with the definition of the marginal efficiency of capital and is a pointer towards the crux of his argument: the impact of expectations of future yields. The classical theory by contrast is shown by Keynes to be based on an unreal world in which expectations about the future have no place. This is followed by an analysis of long term expectation (chapter 12) and then a discussion of the theory of the rate of interest (chapter 13) which focuses on the myth of automaticity contained in the classical framework. Keynes needs to explain how this notion that the economic machine supposedly works so that lower spending and lower interest rates will serve to increase investment is without foundation in fact. His outlook on the 'mechanism of the economic system' suggests that the reality is very different: falling spending brings about disequilibrium and rising unemployment. At the centre of part four we find an analysis of the two great polarities: liquidity and capital. Chapter 15 is an essay on the allure of liquid wealth and the difficulties in conducting policy so as to manage the desire for liquidity. The theme that runs through this part of the book is the sheer difficulty in formulating policy for an economic system which is so inherently subject to waves of optimism and pessimism, confidence and insecurity. Book four describes an age of anxiety and mass movements of opinion which make the tasks of economic policy making infinitely more complex than in the past. The chief reason is that capricious substance, 'mass psychology' (GT: 170) and its relationship to the monetary economy. Formulating monetary policy involves securing the confidence of public opinion (GT: 203): the old magic and rituals will no longer work the trick. Book four seeks to show us why the old nostrums have lost their potency and lay the basis for a new policy rite: economic management.

Chapter 12 of the *General Theory* addresses a main concern of Marshall's closing chapter of the *Principles*: failing confidence and what can be done to remedy its 'evils' (sic). The purpose of this crucial chapter of the *General Theory* becomes much clearer when we view it through Marshall's arguments. Marshall notes that the collapse in confidence is the main cause of falling investment and demand.

> For when confidence has been shaken by failures, capital cannot be got to start new companies and extend old ones. Projects for new railways meet with no favour, ships lie idle, and there are no orders for new ships. There is scarcely any demand for the work of navvies, and not much for the work of the building and the engine-making trades ... the diminution of the demand for their wares makes them demand less of other trades. Thus commercial disorganization spreads ... The chief cause of the evil is a want of confidence. The greater part of it could be removed almost at an instant if confidence could return, touch all industries with her magic wand, and make them continue their production and their demand for the wares of others. (Marshall, 1947: 710)

For Marshall – unlike Keynes – there is no 'magic wand'. He is dismissive (like J.S. Mill and Keynes) of collectivist arguments that government ownership would do anything more than make matters far worse. The chapter which contains Marshall's thoughts on confidence is entiled 'Progress in relation to standards of life'. Economic progress was to be obtained through a rise in the 'standard of life', by which he meant 'the standard of activities adjusted to wants'. A rise in the standard of life involved increasing 'intelligence, energy and self-respect' and a consequent enlargement of 'care and judgment with regard to expenditure and consumption' (Marshall, 1947: 689). And it is a rise in the standard of life which will be the chief cause of increasing the national wealth (dividend) in (the long) time. Marshall therefore, does put forward a number of policies to remedy the falling confidence, including: help for those who, due to physical, mental or moral incapacity are unable to work; improving the skills of the working classes; controlling 'malignant' forms of speculation; stimulating the growth of economic 'chivalry' or service to the public wellbeing; developing the 'higher faculties' of the young; and arranging work so that parents can spend more time with their children. The deficiency in confidence has no quick fix. Not the least of the reasons for this condition is that 'the elements of human nature which have been developed during centuries of war and violence, and sordid and gross pleasures, cannot be greatly changed in the course of a single generation' (Marshall, 1947: 721). Human nature cannot be easily 'transformed' – except in the long run by 'slow' and 'solid' progress (Marshall, 1947: 722).

Chapter 12 of the *General Theory*, however, shows us a 'magic wand' which does not serve to transform human nature, but manage (in the short run) confidence, and speculation and promote enterprise and creativity in the face of uncertainty. Although the chapter takes off from a point at which Marshall's *Principles* concludes (the issue of confidence) Keynes transports us to a very different universe to that inhabited by Marshall and the classical school. The chapter is located at the very centre of the book and contains in many respects the essence of his revolution in economic thinking. From here we may go back to understand where he is coming from and how he differs and agrees with from Marshall *et al.*, or we may travel forward to explore the policy and theoretical implications of his analysis of expectations. In this chapter we leave the world of Newtonian economics and a stable economic universe far behind and bravely go where no economist had ever gone before: into a post-Newtonian cosmos where human beings have to deal with the fact that stability is a 'special case' and that the whole system is fundamentally unstable, full of uncertainty and chance. It marks an important transition from the non-Euclidean geometry contained in the preceding pages to the evolving Newtonian alchemy which is manifested in full in chapter 24. This *quantum* economics provides the rationale for the economic alchemy in that its shows us a picture of an economy in which the human mind interacts with economic forces – something which is absent from both the Newtonian machine and Einstein's universe. Keynes offers us the prospect of being able to 'defeat' the 'dark forces of time and ignorance' (GT: 155) and thereby transform capitalism. In this chapter Keynes presents us with an image of an economy which is more like that we find in the physics of Max Planck, Werner Heisenberg and Niels Bohr than in Albert Einstein or Isaac Newton. In the language of the *Treaty on Probability* it is a world governed by the mathematics of Poincaré, rather than the probability of Laplace.

- The economic system is full of uncertainty. The only certainty is that there are no certainties. We inhabit a realm of probability where knowledge is slight and often negligible.
- It is a system in which the economic gods *do* play dice, as well as Roulette, Snap and Old Maid. It is a system driven by chance, rather than determinstic laws.
- The system is fundamentally unstable and psychologically 'hysterical'. Small changes which seemingly have nothing whatever to do with the economy can have catastrophic effects. A change in the weather, or butterflies in the stomachs of investors, speculators and entrepreneurs can cause waves of optimism and pessimism to batter the economy. Animal spirits can melt and thaw.
- In the chapter Keynes describes a system in which the relationship between subject and object – the observer and the observed – is unlike that assumed by Newton or Einstein. In Keynes's world the expectations of people affect the present. At another level, Keynes is not simply seeking to analyse economic forces, he wishes his theory to interact with the economy and change it. Ideas *matter* and alter reality.

- We are in a world which is uncertain, indeterminate and discontinuous where the simple causalities of the classical theory of the economy – like that of the account of classical physics – no longer exists. Economic reality is not 'out there', in an objective sense, but is something which is *mental* and not mechanical.
- Because of the psychological nature of the system, it cannot be broken up into parts – like a machine – but must be understood in terms of its interconnectedness, polarities and antimonies. It must be viewed as a *whole.*

This is a chapter, therefore, which is unlike any other we have thus encountered as it is concerned with 'actual observation of markets and business psychology' and is consequently operating at an entirely different level to most of the book. This is also the chapter which is the most personal: it resonates with the themes of the *Treatise on Probability*; in its pages we hear the voices of trusted financial adepts, Oswald Falk and the French alchemist (sic) Marcel Labordère (Skidelsky, 1992: 275–6 et passim) whose intuitions and insights he respected and valued; here too we find Keynes's own transformation from a speculating, gambling batchelor, to the married investor. We also hear intimations of the Cambridge oral tradition in an analysis on speculation which is redolent of Marshall's views (Dardi and Gallegati, 1992).

The chapter begins by making a rare reference back to the *Treatise on Probability*, chapter six, which is conerned with the issue of the 'weight of argument'. Keynes had argued here that increasing relevant information will always serve to give more weight to a proposition. The greater the weight of argument the more certain and the more confident do we become about the basis upon which we are taking our decision. In the *General Theory* Keynes develops this thesis by observing that we tend to be more confident as we become more certain. And, as we can know more about the present than the future, human decision making will inevitably be somewhat biased in favour of exaggerating the existing knowledge and situations. In practice we tend to project the existing state of affairs into the future. Our long-term expectations are not simply the outcome of our forecasts of what is probable, but they also involve the question of how confident we feel about the forecast we have made. The decisions about whether to save or invest, hold money, or real assests, therefore, ultimately depends on the 'state of psychological long-term expectation' (GT: 147–8). However, as Keynes points out, the analysis of the state of confidence had (until this chapter) not been closely studied by economists. Keynes believes that it is only through 'actual observation of markets and business psychology' that we can explain long-term expectations and the consequences which fluctuations in confidence can have on the economy as a whole. The problem we have to place at the forefront of our mind is that of the 'extreme precariousness' of our knowledge of the future: it is usually 'very slight and often negligible'. And yet, once upon a time when capitalism was in the hands of risk-taking individuals, business men were prepared to play the game with skill and invest without troubling themselves for 'precise', 'cold' calculations: people were prepared to take a chance and construct railways, mines, and farms. The key point that Keynes makes is that whereas in the past decisions were made by those with direct involvement in enterprises, modern capitalism has torn asunder the connection between individuals, communities and business.

> Decisions to invest in private business of the old-fashioned type were ... decisions largely irrevocable, not only for the community as a whole, but also for the individual. With the separation between ownership and management which prevails to-day and with the development of organised investment markets, a new factor of great importance has entered in, which sometimes facilitates but sometimes adds greatly to the instability of the system. (GT: 150–1)

Modern financial institutions have severed the relationship between investment and the 'community as a whole'. The stock exchange is geared to quick profits and immediate gain with disastrous results for the communities who pay the ultimate price for this institutionalized hysteria.

> It is as though a farmer, having tapped his barometer after breakfast, could decide to remove his capital from the farming business between 10 and 11 in the morning and reconsider whether he should return to it later in the week. (GT: 151)

Modern day Pharaohs are more likely to keep their money liquid than build Pyramids. Business had been ripped out of the local community and an organic relationship between business, industry and the community had been destroyed. The modern stock market and the rise of the joint-stock company had, therefore, radically changed capitalism by making the economy subject to the preference for the short term and liquidity amongst investors who are driven by 'convention', that is the assumption that 'the existing state of affairs will continue indefinitely, except in so far as we have specific reasons to expect a change' (GT: 152). The modern investor relying on such convention will have a preference for investments which are 'safe' in the short run. The investor will tend to operate so as to arrange investments in a liquid way for the *individual* – so he can make money – whilst for the *community* investment remains 'fixed' (GT: 153). Modern capitalism is therefore built on a high degree of precariousness. The factors which influence this uncertainty include: investment is dominated by those who have no special knowledge or commitment; the value of investments fluctuates excessively; the valuation of investments is determined by the outcome of 'the mass psychology of a large number of ignorant individuals' (GT: 154); investment decisions by professional investors are informed by average opinion which has a preference for the short term and the liquid; and the fluctuating confidence of the lending institutions.

Keynes argues that consideration of the psychology of expectation has such an important role to play in understanding the modern economy that it 'should not lie beyond the purview of the economist' (GT: 158). The trend within modern capitalism has been that at certain periods speculation – 'the activity of forecasting the psychology of the market' (ibid.) – predominates over the activity of forecasting the yield of an asset over the long term (enterprise).

> Thus the professional investor is forced to concern himself with the anticipation of impending changes, in the news or in the atmosphere, of the kind by which experience shows that the mass psychology of the market is most influenced. This is the inevitable result of investment markets organized with a view to so-called 'liquidity'. Of the maxims of orthodox finance, none, surely, is more anti-social than the fetish of liquidity ... It forgets that there is no such thing as liquidity of investment for the community as a whole. The social object of skilled investment should be to defeat the dark forces of time and ignorance which envelop our future. (GT: 155)

Speculation – in distinction to investment and entrepreneurship – is a powerful aspect of the 'dark forces' which threaten us. In *A Treatise on Money* Keynes set out in quite explicit Freudian terms the deep instincts which lay at the heart of the 'fetish of liquidity' – anal eroticism. In the *General Theory* this picture of the erotic economy is completed, but in less sensationalist and in a more discrete form. The forces of anal eroticism are joined with the the the consequences of a substitute form of masturbation: gambling. It is important to note that unlike his ideas on the anal character there is no direct evidence that Keynes was aware of Freud's theory of masturbation. However, it is quite beyond belief that, given his preoccupation with his sexuality (he kept detailed records of his own masturbation), the frankness of Bloomsbury in such matters, his propensities for gambling and his familiarity with Freudian analysis, we should think that he would not have known about it. If he signals (very clearly) that we should think of money in Freudian terms, why should we not continue in this line of thought to reach the seemingly inevitable conclusion that 'speculation' was also to be viewed from the perspective of psychoanalysis? In his essay on 'Am I a Liberal?', for example, Keynes refers to gambling as a 'drug' (IX: 303) and in the *General Theory* he analyses the 'addictive' nature of speculative gambling. Freud's theory – that masturbation was the 'primal addiction' – was made known to Fliess as early as 1897 (Gay, 1988: 100). His paper which developed the idea ('Dostoevsky and Parricide') was published in German in 1928 and in English the following year. In it he traces the condition back to the point when the child substitutes gambling for the (vice) of masturbation:

> and the emphasis laid upon the passionate activity of the hands betrays this derivation. Indeed, the passion for play is an equivalent of the old complusion to masturbate; 'playing' is the actual word used in the nursery to describe the activity of the hands upon the genitals. (Freud, 1985: 459)

When we consider that Keynes was actually circumcised at eight years old to stop him masturbating (Skidelsky, 1983: 66) and had a preoccupation with hands (Moggridge, 1992: 23) – so much so that he would keep them stuffed up his sleeves like a monk – we can only surmize that Freud's theory of masturbation as involving castration fears, hands (Freud, 1977: 316–7) and links with gambling, must have had a special meaning for him. Another indication of how close in his mind were the sterility of the money motive and sexuality comes across in a quite remarkable observation which he makes in the Macmillan committee when he refers to excessive savings as wasted resources and he alludes to the story of Onan in the Bible who, rather than dutifully beget children by his brother's dead wife, chose to spill his 'seed on the ground' (XX: 75, 95, 137). The selfish behaviour met with Yahweh's greatest displeasure and occasioned Onan's demise. Keynes was fond of using the story to convey a very graphic image of how wasteful saving is as a purely self-regarding act. It ultimately brings death, rather than new life. Onan chooses masturbation because the child would not be regarded as his, and therefore he will not do his duty by his brother. Like selfish undutiful saving Keynes regarded speculation (something in which he himself actively engaged) as essentially an activity focused in on itself. The speculator's game is to 'beat the gun' (sic) (GT: 155) by reading the psychology of the market. It is a form of gambling on how other gamblers will react. The speculator is driven by a sense of 'life is not long enough' (GT: 157) to take risks for the hope of immediate gain: 'Human nature desires quick results, there is a peculiar zest in making money quickly, and remoter gains are discounted by the average man at a very high rate' (GT: 157).

Alas, like all 'desires' there is a price to be paid for indulging in speculation:

> The game of professional investment is intolerably boring and over-exacting to anyone who is entirely exempt from the gambling instinct; whilst he who has it must pay to this propensity the appropriate toll. (GT: 157)

Speculation, like Onanism, can make you go blind! Speculation is self-fixated, self-regarding and self-referential: it is preoccupied with keeping its eyes on the psychology of the crowd. It consequently thrives and grows fat on uncertainty, volatility, and instability. Enterprise, on the other hand, does not suffer from the short-sightedness of those possessed by the 'gambling instinct' as it is concerned with the yield of assets 'over their whole life' (GT: 158), and if it is to do well it requires stability, a sense of confidence, convention and certainty.

If not taken to excess the activity of speculation does little harm. However, the organization of stock markets have provided just the right conditions for this sterile self-regarding speculation to thrive. In a brilliant and often quoted passage Keynes warns of the dire social consequences.

> Speculators may do no harm as bubbles on a steady stream of enterprise. But the position is serious when enterprise becomes the bubble on a whirlpool of speculation. When the capital development of a country becomes a by-product of the activities of a casino, the job is likely to be ill-done. (GT: 159)

Enterprise is associated with the 'life': it is a 'steady stream' of productive activity. The fruits of economic Onanism (speculation) are ultimately barren and if gamblers predominate over entrepreneurs, the results will ill-serve 'social purpose' and *laissez-faire* capitalism (GT: 159). The speculator is the embodiment of economic Onanism: playing around and gambling with no thought of anything but his immididate gratification. Keynes argues that, like casinos, stock markets should be 'inaccessible and expensive' if the occasions for 'sin' (sic) are to be reduced. In contrast to the image of sinful masturbators Keynes offers a solution of which Marshall and Malthus would have wholeheartedly endorsed: marriage.

> The spectacle of modern investment markets has sometimes moved me towards the conclusion that to make the purchase of an investment permanent and indissoluble, like marriage, except by reason of death or other grave cause, might be a useful remedy for our contemporary evils. For this would force the investor to direct his mind to the long-term prospects and to those only. (GT: 160)

The erotic passions which lead inexorably to decay and destruction must be bound and 'moral restraint' be exercised so that the lust for self-gratification is controlled by rational consideration of the social good. Whenever the economy is in the hands of the anal retentives (hoarders) or the masturbators (speculators) there will be a dismal outcome. Greed and gambling are dangerous instincts to loose upon the world. Of course (as Malthus argued), passions will not be removed from human nature. Those who play with the stuff of economic life as if it were a game of chance will always be with us. As Keynes argues at the end of the book, the 'addiction' (GT: 374) to speculative activity has therefore to be played for 'lower stakes' and be subject to more restraint ('rules and limitations', GT: 374) and with the 'odds loaded against' the gambler (GT: 381).

Modern capitalism has therefore an inbuilt and growing tendency to be subject to high levels of uncertainty, precariousness and instability, with the result that the speculators are left to play with our resources whilst the creative, optimistic, risk-taking 'animal spirits' are depressed. As Mephistopheles observes:

Take my word for it, anyone who thinks too much
is like an animal that in a barren heath
some evil spirit drives around in circles
while all about lie fine green pastures
(Goethe, 1994: 1830–33)

Business men and policy makers confront an unstable and unpredictable environment in which economic decisions are not predicated on entirely rational grounds derived from mathematical calculation.

Most, probably, of our decisions to do with something positive, the full consequences of which will be drawn over many days to come, can only be taken as a result of animal spirits – of a spontaneous urge to action rather than inaction, and not as the outcome of a weighted average of quantitative benefits multiplied by quantitative probabilities. (GT: 162)

If the optimism of the animal spirit falters so too does the entrepreneurial spirit. The ups and downs of the 'animal spirit' gives rise to the exaggerated slumps and depressions in the economic cycle. Keynes believed that it was dangerous to allow the economy to be subject to mass psychology. The economy all too often could fall victim of a disturbance in the average businessman. The analysis of the conditions for investment therefore needed to take account of 'the nerves and hysteria and even the digestions and reactions to the weather of those upon whose spontaneous activity it largely depends' (GT: 162). This is not to say that human economic behaviour is entirely driven by 'irrational psychology', but that when expectations are disturbed and the future uncertain, fluctuations in sentiment occur which have enormous consequences for the economy as a whole. There has been a good deal of confusion surrounding the notion of 'animal spirits' contained in the *General Theory*. The source of the idea has been variously located in ancient Greece (Plato's *Republic*) and Babylon (Fitzgibbons, 1988: 85; Dow and Dow, 1985; Mini, 1994: 229–30). However, if we keep in mind that Keynes saw himself in the line of English high intelligentsia going back to Locke and Hume, then the context of animal spirits is rather obvious, and springs from a stream of thought much nearer home. Yolton tells us that the term animal spirits was widespread in the seventeenth and eighteenth centuries and refers to the theory that the nerves were hollow tubes which contain a fluid which is responsible for bodily motion and awareness (Yolton, 1993:

11). We find the notion of 'animal spirits' in Locke and Hume as well as in Descartes and Malebranche and it is evidently this idea to which Keynes is directing our attention – rather than some kind of reference to duty we find in Plato. One passage in Locke provides an important insight into Keynes's use of the term in the *General Theory*. The passage occurs in a section where Locke concedes that it may well be that some aspects of human thinking are caused by innate involuntary animal spirits rather than deliberate thought.

> Custom settles habits of thinking in the understanding as well as of determining in the will, and of motions in the body: all which seem to be but trains of motion in the animal spirits, which, once set a-going, continue in the same steps they have been used to; which by often treading are worn into a smooth path, and the motion in it becomes easy and, as it were, natural. As far as we can comprehend thinking, thus *ideas* seem to be produced in our minds; or, if they are not, this may serve to explain their following one another in an habitual train, when once they are put into that track, as well as it does to explain such motions of the body. A musician used to any tune will find that, let it but once begin in his head, the *ideas* of the several notes of it will follow one another orderly in his understanding, without any care or attention as regularly as his fingers move orderly over the keys of the organ to play out the tune he has begun, though his unattentive thoughts be elsewhere a-wandering. Whether the natural cause of these *ideas*, as well as of that regular dancing of his fingers be the motion of his animal spirits, I will not determine how probable soever by this instance, it appears to be so; but this may help us a little to conceive of intellectual habits and of the tying together of *ideas*. (Locke, 1995: 219–20)

Hume argues in a similar way that:

> We learn from anatomy, that the immediate object of power in voluntary motion, is not the member itself which is moved, but certain muscles, and nerves, and animal spirits, and perhaps, something still more minute and more unknown, through which the motion is successively propagated, ere it reach the member itself whose motion is the immediate object of volition. Can there be a more certain proof, that the power, by which this whole operation is performed, so far from being directly and fully known by an inward sentiment or consciousness, is to the last degree, mysterious and unintelligible? (Hume, 1975: 66)

Read in the context of what Keynes has to say about custom and habits it is clear that in this *Lockean* and *Humean* sense the failure of animal spirits has to do with a mysterious and unpredictable loss of nerve. Like the musician who suddenly cannot remember where his fingers should go, the investor finds that he no longer has the nerve to play the market and take risks. The economy is, in this sense, subject to a nervous failure or breakdown in the confidence of entrepreneurs who have to fall back on reason, and deliberate thought and *calculation,* rather than trust to their instincts. This idea of animal spirits is also evident in the *Treatise on Probability* where he refers to impulses and instincts which are 'refined by reason and enlarged by experience' (TP: 275). Enterprise has its source in the intuitive, primitive, risk-taking and animalistic aspects of human psychology. When the 'animal spirits' dim and fail there is a diminution of the vital fluids which flow through the (organic) economic system. This dimension of the human mind is not about calculation, or cognitive mechanics: it is located in that place in the subconscious where mind and matter, spirit and body meet. The psychological forces which inform long-term expectations means that the economic system has a natural tendency towards developing a self-focused, self-referencing pattern of decision making. Economic Onanism thus engenders a highly unstable system in which human beings are not motivated by 'reasonable calculation' supported by 'animal spirits' (GT: 162), but by attempts to make money in the short run predicated on calculable expectations of profit and loss. However, as Keynes had examined at great length in the *Treatise on Probability* (in response to Moore's arguments for following convention, certainty, and calculation):

> human decisions affecting the future, whether personal or political or economic, cannot depend on strict mathematical expectation, since the basis for making such calculations does not exist; and that it is our innate urge to activity which makes the wheels go round, our rational selves, calculating where we can, but often falling back for our motive on whim, or sentiment or chance. (GT: 162–3)

When once we understand the psychological factors at work in the economy then we can explain the defects of the market mechanism, and what is more, be able to do something about them. In the chapters following chapter 12 (13 to 17) Keynes proceeds to explore the general theory in terms of the rate of interest; the psychology of business liquidity preference; and the nature of interest and money. His aim here is to destroy the assumptive world of classical economics by showing how the rate of interest is but one factor operating in a complex set of inter-relationships; and that the classical model has a very deficient theory of money and business behaviour. The forces which determine employment behave in such a way that it does not follow, for example, that because the quantity of money has been increased, interest rates will fall, since at the same time liquidity preference may be increasing at a faster rate than the quantity of money. If we think of money as a 'drink which stimulates the system to activity' we must be aware that there 'may be several slips between cup and lip' (GT: 173), and that money may serve to make some relationships rather 'sticky', than facilitate better fluidity (GT: 238–9). The various factors (savings, investment, the rate of interest, the propensity to consume and the marginal efficiency of capital) exist in a state of organic interaction: the relationships are not deterministic in the classical sense since a fall in spending does not lead to a lower rate of interest, and then higher investment. The economic system is not that kind of machine (GT: 185). The classical world of Ricardo is consequently revealed to be little more than an hypothesis, 'remote from experience' (GT: 192). And thus Keynes explains once again (in chapters 15, 16, 17) that what needs to be considered is the actual psychology of business decision making; why saving does not stimulate investment; and why the desire to hold money wealth has no automatic connection with the growth of productive investment. The transfer of wealth (saving) is something quite distinct from the creation of new wealth. Thus wealthy societies can be getting poorer all the time (GT: 219). What the rate of interest does, therefore, is not regulate savings and investment, so much as set a 'limit to the level of employment' (GT: 222). Faced with the uncertainty of human existence those with wealth will choose to hold that wealth in liquid form if they believe that they can get a better rate of interest on money than from the prospective yields from investment in real assets. This behaviour enriches the owner of wealth, but impoverishes the community as a whole.

The issue of central policy importance was how, given the nature of modern capitalism, could the effects of ignorance about the future – which opens the doors on the desire to hold money – be managed so as to create the right kind of environment in which reasonable calculation and animal spirits could engender risk and enterprise. Keynes argues that he expects to see the state – which is in a position to make long-term calculations and take risks – assume more responsibility for organizing investment to the 'general social advantage' (GT: 164).

The theme of uncertainty and its consequences is taken up later in his notes on the trade cycle in which Keynes examines the recurrence of boom and bust, optimism and pessimism, which characterizes the capitalist system over time. Expectations about the future play a crucial part in determining the scale of new investment. They are subject to 'shifting and unreliable evidence' and are subject to 'violent changes' (GT: 315). The cycles of economic activity are determined by 'the uncontrollable and disobedient psychology of the business world' (GT: 317) and something as precarious as 'confidence' is not susceptible to control in individualistic capitalism. If we are to avoid the wild swings of confidence and investment, captalism had to alter the way in which investment is organized:

> It is not reasonable that a sensible community should be content to remain independent on fortuitous and often wasteful mitigations when once we understand the influences upon which effective demand depends. (GT: 220)

> In conditions of *laissez-faire* the avoidance of wide fluctuations in employment may ... prove impossible without a far-reaching change in the psychology of investment markets such as there is no reason to expect. I conclude that the duty

ordering the current volume of investment cannot safely be left in private hands. (GT: 320)

Policy making had to be concerned with guiding the psychological propensities to save, consume and invest so as to ensure that society could avoid the wild and dangerous oscillations which result in unemployment and the miseries which attend it. Keynes did not want to abolish capitalism, or individualism, but remedy their deficiencies. Economic alchemy is an artful science of refining and purifying a decaying system. As he states at the end of the book:

> individualism, if it can be purged of its defects and its abuses, is the best safeguard of personal liberty in the sense that, compared with any other system, it greatly widens the field for the exercise of personal choice, and the loss of which is the greatest of all the losses of the homogenous totalitarian state. (GT: 380)

If we read this notion of 'purging' (a Freudian and alchemical slip!) individualism in the context of his analysis of the love of money, it is clear that for Keynes the chief defect which needed to be remedied was the attitude towards money and the power which money loving calculators exercised. Apart from over population, and the pressure for markets it is the anal sadistic personalities for whom war produced a 'pleasurable excitement' (GT: 381) and businessmen who hoarded and played with their money rather than invest it who posed the greatest threats to civilization. It was, above all, *uncertainty* which provided an essential condition in which these personalities thrived. The 'social object' of policy was to invest skilfully so as to 'defeat the dark forces of time and ignorance which envelop our future' (GT: 155) since:

> There is no clear evidence from experience that the investment policy which is socially advantageous coincides with that which is most profitable. It needs *more* intelligence to defeat the forces of time and our ignorance of the future. (GT: 157)

Uncertainty can, if unchecked, prompt the passion for liquidity which drives further bouts of instability. Money is central because it is 'a link between the present and the future' (GT: 293). Expectations about the future affect the decision making in the present, and thus:

> Money in its significant attributes is, above all, a subtle device for linking the present to the future; and we cannot even begin to discuss the effect of changing expectations on current activities except in monetary terms. We cannot get rid of money even by abolishing gold and silver and legal tender instruments. So long as there exists any durable asset, it is capable of possessing monetary attributes, and therefore, of giving rise to the characteristic problems of a monetary economy. (GT: 293–4)

If we did not come to understand the nature on a money economy, and make the right policy adjustments then an ancient curse would be visted upon us. Looking to Britain and America in his own day Keynes saw examples of stagnation, poverty and low productivity in a money rich economy.

> The post-war experiences of Great Britain and the United States are ... examples of how an accumulation of wealth, so large that its marginal efficiency has fallen more rapidly than the rate of interest can fall in the face of prevailing institutional and pyschological factors, can interfere, in conditions mainly of *laissez-faire*, with a reasonable level of employment and with the standard of life which the technical conditions of production are capable of furnishing. It follows that of two equal communities, having the same technique but different stocks of capital, the community with the smaller stocks of capital may be able for the time being to enjoy a higher standard of life than the community with the larger stock; though when the poorer community has caught up the rich ... then both alike will suffer the fate of Midas. This disturbing conclusion depends, of course, on the assumption that the propensity to consume and the rate of invetsment are not deliberately controlled in the social interest but are mainly left to the influence of *laissez-faire*. (GT: 219)

This image of death (Midas would have starved had he not repented) is driven home by Keynes noting that in the past the wealthy in order to repent of their sins or prepare a place for their afterlife at least built pyramids and cathedrals which increased the 'real national dividend of useful goods and services' (GT: 220).

Keynes believed that now we 'know' the secret of effective demand it is not reasonable or sensible for a society to have to wait upon the whims of fortune. Having penetrated the secrets of economic forces he, like the hermetic philosophers of old, believed that he could 'achieve great things in the world transforming nature and using natural forces' (Haeffner, 1994: 114). Although the Midas myth revealed an essential truth about the 'natural tendencies' which shape economic conditions it illustrated a 'world as it has been, and not a necessary principle which cannot be changed' (GT: 254). The role of the state was ultimately to so manage money – that mercurial 'link between the present and the future' and between inner mental states and society – so that we can aim to have a less uncertain, and a more stationary environment:

> Let us assume that the steps are taken to ensure that the rate of interest is consistent with the rate of investment which corresponds to full employment. Let us assume, further, that State action enters in as a balancing factor to provide that the growth of capital equipment shall be such as to approach saturation point at a rate which does not put a disproportionate burden on the standard of life of the present generation. On such assumptions I should guess that a properly run community equipped with modern technical resources, of which the population is not increasing rapidly, ought to be able to bring down the marginal efficiency of

capital in equilibrium approximately to zero within a generation; so that we should attain the conditions of a quasi-stationary community where change and progress would result only from changes in technique, taste, population and institutions. ... A man would still be free to accumulate his earned income with a view to spending it at a later date. But his accumulation would not grow. He would simply be in the position of Pope's father, who, when he retired from business, carried a chest of guineas with him to his villa at Twickenham and met his household expenses from it as required. (GT: 220–1)

The aim is, therefore, what Mill termed a 'stationary state'. Progress takes place more in moral, or aesthetic, terms, rather than in the pursuit of economic growth for its own sake. This becomes clear when we read these remarks on Pope's father in the context of what he had argued earlier in his essay on 'The Economic possibilities for our Grandchildren' (1930) and his Dublin lecture of 1933

Let us, for the sake of argument, suppose that a hundred years hence we are all of us, on average, eight times better off in the economic sense than we are today. Assuredly there need be nothing to surprise us here. Now it is true that the needs of human beings may seem to be insatiable. But they fall into two classes – those needs which are absolute in the sense that we feel them whatever the situation of our fellow human beings may be, and those which are relative in the sense that we feel them only if their satisfaction lifts us above, makes us feel superior to, our fellows. Needs of the second class, those which satisfy the desire for superiority, may indeed be insatiable; for the higher the general level, the higher still are they. But this is not so true of the absolute needs – a point may soon be reached, much sooner perhaps than we all of us are aware of, when these needs are satisfied in the sense that we prefer to devote our further energies to non-economic purposes. (IX: 326)

In this regard Keynes shows himself to be in a tradition of asceticism which may be traced back to Adam Smith, James and J.S. Mill and Marshall which had a low opinion of the accumulation of wealth and consumption for its own sake (see Reisman, 1986: 25–6; Winch, 1970: 42). Keynes believed that, properly managed, economic forces can be directed and planned to promote a world in which absolute need has been met, and mankind will be free of the economic problem and able to explore what are the central problems of existence: truth, beauty, knowledge, human relationships and the arts of life. At such a point in history the love of money – and the liquidity fetish – will no longer hold us captive. Keynes never propounded the kind of growth mania which 'Keynesians' were to deploy in the post-war era. This is evident in 'How to Avoid a Slump', published the year after the *General Theory* when he argues that the maintenance of prosperity and economic stability depends upon investment, but also upon patterns of consumption.

Up to a point individual saving can allow an advantageous way of postponing consumption. But beyond that point it is for the community as a whole both an absurdity and a disaster. *The natural evolution should be towards a decent level of consumption for everyone; and when that is high enough, towards the occupation of our energies in the non-economic interest of our lives. Thus we need to be slowly reconstructing our social system with these ends in view.* This is a large matter, not to be embarked upon here. But, in particular and in detail, the relief of taxation, when the time comes for that, will do most for the general welfare if it is so directed as to increase the purchasing power of those who have most need to consume more. (XXI: 393–4) (My emphasis)

At the close of chapter 17 in the *General Theory* Keynes states his views on what drives progress in quite unambiguous terms.

That the world after several millennia of steady individual saving is so poor as it is in accumulated capital assets, is to be explained, in my opinion, neither by the improvident propensities of mankind, nor even by the destruction of war, but by the high liquidity-premiums formerly attaching to the ownership of land and now attaching to money. I differ from the older view expressed by Marshall with unusual dogmatic force in his *Principles of Economics*: 'Everyone is aware that the accumulation of wealth is held in check by the preference which the great mass of humanity have for present over deferred gratifications, or in other words, by their unwillingnes to "wait".' (GT: 242)

Thus the crux of the matter for Keynes is the relationship of human uncertainty to money wealth, rather than human improvidence. Wealth and poverty are not the outcome of moral inadequacy, but of human instincts and psychological propensities. We are not quite out of the Ricardian world (GT: 244) at the end of chapter 17. But before we move on to kill the two dragons – the classical approaches to wages and prices – which we encountered at the start of the book, Keynes gathers all his 'threads' together and provides us with a summation of the Great Work: the instruments to be used to bring about a purified capitalism and an economic system made whole. In true alchemical tradition it involves three forces to be brought into a new relationship with one another if the great work of achieving economic equilibrium and full employment is to be accomplished. For the alchemist it was body, soul and spirit and for Keynes it involves three 'ultimate independent variables', consisting of:

(1) the three fundamental psychological factors, namely the psychological propensity to consume, the psychological attitude to liquidity and the psychological expectation of future yield from capital-assets, (2) the wage-unit as determined by bargains reached between employers and employed, and (3) the quantity of money as determined by the action of the central bank. (GT: 247)

These factors together determined the national income and the quantity of employment. The task is to select the variables which can be 'deliberately controlled or managed by central authority in the kind of system in which we actually live' (GT: 247). The goal of policy is to bring the three independent variables into a relationship that could attain the equilibrium which *laissez-faire* economic forces could not reach unaided by intervention. Art *could* perfect nature and experimentation *could* combine extremes to produce a new kind of economic system. Keynes says that at this stage in the book we have to 'pull together the threads' of the argument and clarify the central 'elements' of his system before proceeding further. As the factors which shape the economy are essentially psychological they can change without much warning. The economists' mercury like the philosophers' mercury is labile and 'unstable' stuff and requires vigilance, experience and intuition if the 'material' is to be worked upon successfully. The task is to select those variables which can be deliberately controlled: the propensity to consume and hold liquid wealth; the expectation of future capital yields; wage bargains; and the quantity of money. But, of course, reality is more complex than is represented in these few factors. We should not think that in so controlling these elements we can do anything more than make the problem of achieving full employment 'more manageable'. By thinking in terms of his model Keynes argues that we are thereby free to apply our 'practical intuition (which can take account of a more detailed complex of facts than can be treated on general principles)'. This means that in simplifying the material upon which we have to work becomes 'less intractable' (GT: 249). Practical intuition and experience has to take account of an economic system in which there is a ghost in the machine: the existence of human psychology that results in a situation where things happen which are not 'logically necessary'. The economic machine does not work in practice as the classical theorists suppose: B does not follow in a linear, logical sequence from A. For although modern capitalism is prone to considerable fluctuation, it does not tend towards a 'violent instability': the economic system can remain in a state of chronic 'sub-normal activity' for long periods of time. Fluctuations in the machine 'may start briskly but seem to wear themselves out before they have proceeded to extremes' (GT: 250). The 'psychological propensities of the modern world' (GT: 250) – which Newtonian economics had excluded – inhibit the economic machine functioning in the way they assume. Our 'actual experience' shows that the machine can oscillate around a position in which there are no extremes (in employment or prices), but a good deal of sub-optimality, inefficiency, inequality and unfairness. And thus we confront the Midas paradox outlined in chapter three: 'poverty in the midst of plenty'. The economic system can, despite the apparent illogicality of it all, lead to a situation in which 'the richer the country, the wider will be the gap between the actual and the potential production; and therefore the more obvious and outrageous the defects of the economic system' (GT: 31). The capitalist system can therefore be a machine in which negative feedback does *not* occur: there is no self-adjustment of economic relationships. Indeed, the system can exist for long periods in which defects and failings are positively reinforced, but the system still oscillates around a level at which there are no 'violent' bouts of instability. As the final pages of the book make clear capitalism might well survive in this condition, but it was unlikely if liberal democratic civilization could last very much longer if it did not address the social and political consequences of the growing gap between the actual and potential performance of the economy. But, this is the shadow of what is or must be, given the free functioning of a world machine impelled by the laws of logical necessity. These laws, however, govern a world 'as it is or has been', not a world that *can* be (GT: 254). Holding firmly on to these 'threads' we now enter into book five and investigate the mechanical illusion that money, wages, and prices are as self-adjusting as they look.

Keynes argues that it is only now, at the very end of our journey, that we can finally confront the misguided theories which we first glimpsed at the start of the book. Before we can understand his critique of the ruling orthodoxy he has had to lead us through the labyrinth of his method: the twists and turns were a necessary preamble to the two-headed monster dwelling at the centre of the maze. His argument seeks to show how reductions in money wages as a solution to unemployment is erroneous and actually serves to make things worse. There are, he maintains, no grounds for believing that a flexible wages policy in an uncontrolled monetary system is capable of producing a state of full employment on a continuous basis. Cutting wages, he shows, is unjust, unfair and advantageous to the rentier class. Furthermore, cutting wages may well serve to increase price instability such that it is only in authoritarian societies where flexible wages policies could function. Wages policies which introduce uncertainty and volatility into money wages were consequently a threat to capitalist democracy, not its means of salvation. The aim must be to fix and 'stabilize' money wages, not to increase their volatility by greater 'flexibility'. Having dispatched the wages argument, and marked it out by placing Pigou's head on the battlements of chapter nineteen (appendix, pp. 272–9), Keynes sets out to deal with the other head of the dragon, prices. However, before making the attack Keynes steps back to equip us with one last weapon, the employment function. Employment, he shows, is not a function of wages: it is far more complex than this and is related to the way in which the economic system works as a whole. This is expressed in several pages of algebra – one of the few parts of the book which resorts to mathematics. Although he notes that if we 'rightly dislike algebra' we can cut them out (GT: 280). (Algebra, we might note here, was closely associated with alchemy because of the sound which was similar to the name of a famous Arabian adept, Al-Djaber. It also involved arcane procedures which only the initiated could comprehend!) Employment has to do with demand in the economy, which in turn, of course, is related to the propensity to consume, investment and interest rates. The classical school has failed to grasp the conflicts and antimonies which drive the system. Ruling orthodoxy has not understood the tension between rising prices and falling demand and the essential organic unity of the economy and thus has propagated the fallacy that the free movement of prices in response to supply and demand will serve to bring the great machine back into balance. The mechanism of the classical approach which views the forces of supply and demand as ultimately maintaining equilibrium through the price 'mechanism' has taken us to a world in which we are 'lost in a haze where nothing is clear and everything is possible' (GT: 292). The concluding chapter (21) aims to bring us back to earth.

> We have all of us become used to finding ourselves sometimes on the one side of the moon and sometimes on the other, without knowing what route or journey connects them, related apparently, after the fashion of our waking and dreaming lives. (GT: 292–3)

That old devil moon (the 'nocturnal, subterranean and subconscious part of man's world' (Fabricius, 1994: 25)) has led us astray and its hazy light has misled us into dividing what should be united: the theory of value and distribution on the one hand and money on the other. But, says Keynes, what has been divided must now be made whole:

> So long as we limit ourselves to the study of the individual industry or firm on the assumption that the aggregate quantity of employed resources is constant, and provisionally that the conditions of other industries or firms are unchanged, it is true that we we are not concerned with the significant characteristics of money. But as soon as we pass to the problem of what determines output and employment as a whole, we require the complete theory of a monetary economy. (GT: 293)

Economics has led a 'double life' (sic) and Keynes is now ready to show how the subject and its object of study can be made whole. Keynes is our guide out of the lost atomistic world in which 'nothing is clear' and the strangest things are possible – despite the *theory* which says that they should not be so. We have to pass from the moonlit theories of a certain world which tends towards equilibrium, into a real world which is full of uncertainty and which tends towards patterns of shifting or punctuated equilibrium. We have to pass from a world in which natural laws rule the affairs of men as they do the movement of sister moon in her orbit, to a world in which the human mind acts upon and influences the real world. It is a quantum leap: we have to accept that human beings stand in a relationship to their world which is totally unlike that which is implicit in the idea of the Newtonian world machine. In asking us to pass from the atomistic economics of the classical school into an organic economics we also, in a sense, have to pass from a Newtonian physics into the world of Newton's alchemy, and from Newtonian mechanics into the uncertainties of quantum theory.

> we might make our line of division between the theory of stationary equilibrium and the theory of shifting equilibrium – meaning by the latter the theory of a system in which changing views about the future are capable of influencing the present situation. *For the importance of money essentially flows from its being a link between the present and the future* ... Or we can pass from this simplified propaedeutic to the problems of the real world in which our previous expectations are liable to disappointment and expectations concerning the future affect what we do to-day. It is when we have made this transition that the peculiar properties of money as a link between the present and the future must enter into our calculations. But, although the theory of shifting equilibrium must necessarily be pursued in terms of a monetary economy, it remains a theory of value and distribution and not a separate 'theory of value'. Money in its significant attributes is, above all, a subtle device for linking the present to the future; and we cannot even begin to discuss the effect of changing expectations on current activities except in monetary terms. We cannot get rid of money even by abolishing gold and silver and legal tender instruments. So long as there exists any durable asset, it is capable of possessing monetary attributes, and therefore of giving rise to the characteristic problems of a monetary economy. (GT: 293–4)

This passage is of vital importance to coming to grips with Keynes's revolutionary way of thinking. It links his early concerns with uncertainty as first set out in the *Treatise on Probability* with his later investigations as an economist into money, with the conclusions he had reached about the economy as a whole by the time of the *General Theory*. The future and the present interact: time is not a one way street, or a straight line. Ideas about the future influence the present: and it is money which makes this possible. Significantly, from the standpoint of our investigation of Keynes's economics as a form of alchemy he refers to money in explicitly alchemical terms: it is a 'subtle device'. By coincidence, in alchemy the production of the *corpus subtile* was, as Jung argues, the ultimate aim of the hermetic arts: 'the attainment of immortality through the transformation of the body' (Jung, 1968: 428). Fabricius tells us that subtle body was formed from the distillation of all the four elements: it is the quintessence or the fifth element in which 'the elements are contained in their original unity and synthetic form' (Fabricius, 1994: 200). Keynes has finally disclosed the key to economic understanding: it is in the quintessence as revealed in (apppropriately enough) book five. Money is a link between the present and the future, a subtle device. And like the subtle device of the alchemists it is immortal. We cannot destroy it, even if we abolish gold and silver. It is, as the ancients once thought, the fifth element! Keynes's economics had succeeded where Newton's alchemy had failed: he had discovered the *corpus subtile* of the social universe. Having realized that the unifying idea is uncertainty in a monetary economy the old economics which portrays a world of market mechanisms turning the wheels of economic life towards equilibrium is of little use to modern man. The *General Theory* does not give us a 'machine or method of blind manipulation' so as to provide an 'infallible answer' (GT: 297). Keynes's economics is radically different: it is a method of thinking for an uncertain, unstable, neurotic world in which all the factors of economic life and the human mind interact and change one another in an organic (or in a Newtonian sense 'vegetable') way. Hence, economic theory and practice which are over-reliant on mechanical and mathematical modes of thinking are very dangerous because they make us 'lose sight of the complexities and interdependencies of the real world in a maze of pretentious and unhelpful symbols' (GT: 298). The unemployed and low paid are the ultimate victims and scapegoats of this way of thinking about economic problems. Demand and supply, wages, investment, interest and money and other economic forces fly about, conflict, and are shaped by human expectations, fears and anxieties in ways that cannot possibly be encapsulated in economics *qua* a branch of mechanics. Keynes urges us to recognize that the classical model is hopelessly inadequate as a way of thinking given the conditions which pertain in a world of mass unemployment coexisting in a supposed equilibrium. The 'balance of forces' (GT: 308) that existed in nineteenth century capitalism which provided for levels of investment sufficient to generate high levels of employment have disappeared, leaving behind the malign spirit *laissez-faire*. But, this concluding chapter emphasizes, the price mechanism or the mechanism of the market has demonstrably failed to facilitate human progress, creativity and possibilities. Productive investment has become less attractive than making money and in order to keep up their profits the rentier class plays games with bouts of boom and bust, inflation and deflation. Keynes describes a world composed of unstable 'elements' whose complex interactions give rise to an economic system which cannot be *fully* comprehended by the way of thinking devised by Smith, Ricardo or Marshall. Taken as a whole the economy comprises a volatile mix of forces which cannot be regulated by the price mechanism so as to arrive at a point of equilibrium in which there exists *real* wealth in the lives of *real* people and their communities. The classical school's eyes are focused on the money economy, rather than the real economy in which mass unemployment and the curse of poverty amidst plenty is all too evident. However, Keynes is optimistic. We can stabilize human desires for money and liquid wealth so as to make *investment* a more attractive source of real wealth. Only then can we achieve a steady growth in wages, stability in prices and a more productive economy. Thus ends the fifth book:

the most stable, and the least easily shifted element in our contemporary economy has been hitherto, and may prove to be in the future, the minimum rate of interest acceptable to the generality of wealth owners ... the long-run relationship between the national income and the quantity of money will depend on liquidity-preferences. And the long-run stability or instability of prices will depend on the strength of the upward trend of the wage unit ... compared with the rate of increase in the efficiency of the productive system. (GT: 309)

We turn the page and in book six we are out of the economists' garden which we had entered in book one (GT: 33). Keynes shows how to deal with the trade cycle in the light of of the theory he has just developed (chapter 22). He seeks to confirm his new theory by reference to ancient wisdom and the intuition of 'cranks' (chapter 23). And finally, we are shown the promised land, the garden of the philosophers and the possibilities which these 'visionary hopes' contain.

Book six comprises three chapters (22, 23, 24) on the theme of 'Short notes suggested by the general theory'. One way to look at these three chapters is in terms of time – a central theme of the book. Chapter 22, on the trade cycle, looks at the big picture of how booms and slumps fluctuate over time. Keynes points to the role of the propensity to consume, the preference for holding money, and the marginal efficiency of capital in the ups and downs of the economic cycle. He considers various explanations (over investment, rates of interest, under consumption and employment) as being inadequate and concludes with a discussion of Jevons's theory. Keynes's argument is that economic cycles are not beyond the wit of man to control by taking account of the waves of optimism and pessimism which pertain in investment. The secret lies in adjusting the propensity to consume, the incentives to invest and the preference for holding liquid assets. Adopting this framework the great fluctuations which cause so much human misery and unemployment are not inevitable. Boom does not have to give way to a depression and economic life does not have to be at the mercy of erratic business psychology. Signficantly, the chapter concludes with a review of Jevons's theory which explained the trade cycle as shaped by good and bad harvests, and solar variations (sunspots). Although Keynes is sympathetic to the notion that harvests could affect the optimism and pessimism of investors (see also his essay on Jevons, CW: X: 122–6) he rejects this idea as having any relevance for a modern industrial society which is no longer subject to the whims of mother nature and celestial forces. In place of the notion of economic life being determined by the vacillations of earth, air, fire and water, Keynes argues that we do not have to be victims, we can take charge of our destiny. Human optimism and pessimism can be so shaped as to lead to a world in which bouts of optimism are not followed, as day is night by economic darkness. The answer, he believes, is in so ordering the economic variables that slumps may be abolished and replaced by a permanent 'quasi-boom'. From the standpoint of Jevons's theory of the economic cycle as determined by sunspots Keynes gives us a new vision of a humanity liberated from the forces of nature and uncontrollable human psychology. An ancient curse can be lifted and with knowledge we can escape the fate of past generations and avoid the extreme fluctuations which have long characterized the trade cycle.

The following chapter (23) deals with mercantilism, usuary, stamped money and theories of under-consumption. In his notes on mercantilism Keynes seeks to bring out how the intuitive ideas of the past, and works of more recent 'cranks' contain a grain of truth which has been ignored by scholars and policy makers and has lived on 'furtively, below the surface and in the underworlds of Karl Marx, Silvio Gesell and Major Douglas' (GT: 32). There was, he argues, a wisdom in their belief in low interest rates, and their antipathy to usuary: 'The early pioneers of economic thinking may have hit upon their maxims of practical wisdom without having had much cognisance of the underlying theoretical grounds' (GT: 340). History shows that there has been:

> a chronic tendency throughout human history for the propensity to save to be stronger than the inducement to invest. The weakness of the inducement to invest has been at all times the key to the economic problem. Today the explanation of the weakness of this inducement may chiefly lie in the extent of existing accumulations; whereas formerly, risks and hazards of all kinds may have played a larger part. But the result is the same. The desire by the individual to augment his personal wealth by abstaining from consumption has usually been stronger than the inducement to the entrepreneur to augment of the national wealth by employing labour on the construction of durable assets. (GT: 347–8)

Giving India as an example, Keynes points towards the consequences for a country when an excessive preference ('a strong passion') for liquidity results in impoverishment for the greater proportion of the people (GT: 337). In the face of the dominant view of money and interest, the mercantalists believed in a more ancient and deep seated doctrine which the age of *laissez-faire* chose to ignore:

> I mean the doctrine that the rate of interest is not self-adjusting at the level best suited to the social advantage but constantly tends to rise too high, so that a wise government is concerned to curb it by statute and custom and even by invoking the moral law. Provisions against usuary are amongst the most ancient economic practices of which we have record. The destruction of the inducement to invest by an excessive liquidity-preference was the outstanding evil, the prime impediment to the growth of wealth, in the ancient and medieval worlds. (GT: 351)

Given the uncertainty in human affairs, and a world which no-one reckons to be safe, it has proved to be the case thoughout human history that there will be an inherent preference for liquidity and a tendency for interest rates to rise to levels that will inhibit risk and entrepreneurial investment. Keynes calls his readers to appreciate the wisdom of the ancients on this point:

> I was brought up to believe that the attitude of the Medieval Church to the rate of interest was inherently absurd, and that the subtle discussions aimed at distinguishing the return on money-loans from the return to active investment were merely jesuitical attempts to find a practical escape from a foolish theory. But I now read these discussions as an honest intellectual effort to keep separate what the classical theory has inextricably confused together, namely, the rate of interest and the marginal efficiency of capital. For it now seems clear that the disquisitions of the schoolmen should allow the schedule of the marginal efficiency of capital to be high, whilst using rule and custom and the moral law to keep down the rate of interest. (GT: 351–2)

However, as he continues, moral arguments were deployed in respect of the virtues of saving as opposed to the profligacy of consumption. Again, a search through the less well-respected texts of the past (and the present) reveal that there is a body of thought which has 'ascribed the evils of unemployment ... to the insufficiency of the propensity to consume' (GT: 35). Keynes cites Bernard Mandeville's *Fable of the Bees* as an illustration of how an endorsement of the virtues of spending and the wickedness of saving called down 'the opproprium of two centuries of moralists and economists' who urged thrift in the individual and the state:

> Petty's 'entertainments, magnificent shews, triumphal arches, etc.' gave place to the penny-wisdom of Gladstonian finance and to a state system which 'could not afford' hospitals, open spaces, noble buildings, even the preservation of its ancient monuments, far less the spendours of music and drama, all of which were consigned to the private charity or magnanimity of improvident individuals. The doctrine did not appear in respectable circles for another century, until in the later phase of Malthus the notion of the insufficiency of effective demand takes a definite place as a scientific explanation of unemployment. (GT: 362)

In more recent times the view that unemployment may be caused by underconsumption has largely been advanced by theorists who were not taken seriously – 'heretics' such as Hobson and Mummery, Gesell and Major Douglas – who followed their intuition rather than adhere to the logic of an erroneous ruling opinion. Gesell, for example, receives – as Keynes admits – an amount of space (five pages) in the *General Theory* that is completely disproportionate to his importance in order to show the value of 'imperfectly analysed intuitions' (GT: 353) and his 'moral quality' (GT: 355). He commends the preface to Gesell's *Natural Economic Order* with the words: 'I believe that the future will learn more from the spirit of Gesell than from that of Marx ... The answer to Marxism is, I think, to be found along the lines of this preface' (GT: 355).

For many Keynes's use of these 'cranks' was, as Harrod commented, merely a 'tendentious attempt to glorify imbeciles' (XII: 555). Harrod could not believe that 'Malthus, splendid as he was as a population theorist, contributed much of value to economics, in which he was always muddled' (Harrod, 1966: 460). And yet, Keynes had an alchemist's fixation with examining all manner of weird and wonderful stuff in order to find out if a secret was buried amongst the musings of others, no matter how imbecilic. Keynes certainly did not think that Malthus was of no consequence as evidenced by the Malthusianism which runs throughout his economics (*qua* moral science) and not simply in the matter of 'effective demand'. Thus although many might dismiss the writings of 'cranks' Keynes took them terribly seriously. He was quite happy with the notion that an intuitive seeker might have stumbled upon a nugget of truth. However dubious the source, Keynes would pan for grains of untutored wisdom which he used to confirm his own sense of being on the right lines. This is the author of the *Treatise on Probability* speaking: as his observations on *The Golden Bough* make clear, truth may be found amongst what is regarded by many as irrational, unscientific nonsense (TP: 273–4).

Having placed one foot firmly in the past in chapter 23 Keynes concludes with his other foot in the future. Looking into his crystal ball Keynes considers what kind of practical social philosophy towards which the *General Theory* might lead. In the previous chapter Keynes has used ancient wisdom to confirm his transmutation of fundamental values: saving is bad, consumption is good. In the closing chapter he shows how, because of the fact that the rich will no longer hoard their wealth, but spend it and enrich society, 'one of the chief social justifications of great inequality is therefore removed' (GT: 373). Given this, what is required is not a political revolution, but a revolution in ideas: capitalism was controllable and transformable. Through the direction of the inducement to invest and the propensity to consume capitalism could be transformed. This required that, rather than seeking to abolish many human instincts (which were seen as base and evil by socialists), they had to be managed so as to provide the motivating force for continuing progress. In the words of Faust's shadow: in allowing evil we might thereby produce good.

> I believe that there is social and psychological justification for significant inequalities of incomes and wealth, but not for such large disparities as exist today. There are valuable human activities which require the motive of money-making and the environment of private wealth-ownership for their full fruition. Moreover, dangerous human proclivities can be canalised into comparatively harmless channels by the existence of opportunities for money-making and private wealth, which, if they cannot be satisfied in this way, may find their outlet in cruelty, the reckless pusuit of personal power and authority, and other forms of self-aggran-

disement. It is better that a man should tyrannise over his bank balance than over his fellow citizens; and whilst the former is sometimes denounced as being but a means to the latter, sometimes at least it is an alternative. But it is not necessary for the stimulation of these proclivities that the game should be played for such high stakes as at present. Much lower stakes will serve the purpose equally well, as soon as the players are accustomed to them. *The task of transmuting human nature must not be confused with the task of managing it.* Though in the ideal commonwealth men may have been taught or inspired or bred to take no interest in the stakes, it may still be wise and prudent statesmanship to allow the game to be played, subject to rules and limitations, so long as the average man, or even a significant section of the community, is in fact strongly addicted to the money-making passion. (GT: 374) (My emphasis)

The great task, therefore, was not to transmute *human nature* (as it was for Malthus, Mill and Marshall) but to 'manage' and 'harness' (IX: 284) it. Where socialists had got it wrong was in their belief that human nature could be transmuted. However, fundamental characteristics – such as the love of money – could not so easily be abolished. Nature had to be 'managed', and passions had to be canalized so that their force could be turned into a useful energy to drive the engine of progess. By adjusting taxation, the rate of interest and in 'other ways' capitalism could be 'gradually' transformed so as to 'realize the full potentialities of production' (GT: 379). Individualism could be 'purged' (another alchemical term) of its defects and abuses and self-interest could be made purer thus serving to enhance personal freedom and efficiency. Thus the end result of Keynesian alchemy is that which was strived for by the practitioners of the ancient arts: androgeny. Keynes argues for a middle way which was neither *laissez-faire* capitalism or totalitarian socialism, but an hermaphroditic system which combined and united opposites in a more wholesome economic 'rebis' which his enemies found monstrous and perverted. He thus achieved, perhaps, a kind of social androgeneity that closely paralleled and reflected his own sexual orientation and which Hession suggests was an important aspect of his tremendous creativity (Hession, 1984, 15 et passim). Just as Newton and the economists he most admired had a capacity to combine a variety of gifts to form a creative approach to knowledge, so Keynes clearly came to believe that only in a system which sought to experiment with contradictory elements could individualistic capitalism be reborn. The goal of economics was to show how the full productive capacity of capitalism could be released from its base defects and abuses. Unlike the socialists, therefore, Keynes does not see this transformation coming about through the abolition of evils – such as inequality and money making – but on the contrary, in so structuring the game and harnessing human instincts that evils can serve the greater good. Like the alchemists, Keynes did not wish to go against nature, but perfect it by harmonizing its contradictory energies. Forces had to be used, not destroyed: it was *dualism* (mind/matter, black/white, certainty/uncertainty, capitalism/socialism) which had to be abandoned.

For Malthus massive overpopulation could threaten democracy, and for Keynes the great danger which now confronted civilization was the possibility that mass unemployment and the inequitable distribution of wealth would bring an end to the age of democracy and bring about a new age of dictators and tyrants. His analysis showed how unemployment could be cured, and the shadow of totalitarianism banished by adeptly managing the very forces which could destroy individualistic capitalism. The disease required homeopathy, not radical surgery. In the penultimate section of chapter 24 Keynes uses an explicitly Malthusian theme: population. He argues that dictators may fan the flames of 'natural bellicosity', but it is the pressure of population (and markets) which have played the 'predominant part' in the history of the nineteenth century and might do so again. Then, in a passage which echoes Malthus's belief that if we could only tame overpopulation we could put an end to war (Malthus, vol. 2, 1958: 164), Keynes gives us his vision of a world in which, when mass unemployment is solved (and population controlled), the economic causes of war would be reduced. Nation shall speak peace unto nation and swords be hammered into tradable goods and services, if they can:

> learn to provide themselves with full employment by their domestic policy (and, we must add, if they can also attain equilibrium in the trend of their population), there need be no important economic forces calculated to set the interest of one country against that of its neighbours. ... International trade would cease to be what it is, namely, a desperate expedient to maintain employment at home by forcing sales on foreign markets and restricting purchases, which, if successful, will merely shift the problem of unemployment to the neighbour which is worsted in the struggle, but a willing and unimpeded exchange of goods and services in conditions of mutal advantage. (GT: 383)

Finally, he ends with three questions:

> Is the fulfilment of these ideas a visionary hope? Have they insufficient roots in the motives which govern the evolution of political society? Are the interests which they will thwart stronger and more obvious than those which they will serve? (GT: 383)

To these he declines to give an answer as it would 'need a volume of a different character from this one to indicate even in outline the practical measures in which they might be gradually clothed' (GT: 383). The *General Theory* in this sense is a 'potent' (sic) body of ideas which would be 'gradually clothed' by practical and mental experimentation.

Next to his comment that 'in the long run we are all dead' (IV: 65) the closing paragraph of the *General Theory* are amongst his most well-known words:

> the ideas of economists and political philosophers, both when they are right and when they are wrong, are more powerful than is commonly understood. Indeed the world is ruled by little else. Practical men, who believe themselves to be quite exempt from any intellectual influences, are usually the slaves of some defunct economist. Madmen in authority, who hear voices in the air, are distilling their frenzy from some academic scribbler of a few years back. I am sure that the power of vested interests is vastly exaggerated compared with the gradual encroachment of ideas. (GT: 383)

It is an indeterministic (quantum) world in which the mind alters reality. The world is ruled by ideas, from which it follows that if we can bring about change in the world of ideas, then we can change the real world. Even those who think that they are practical men, far removed from the world of ideas, are pulled by the strings held by men of ideas. The future is shaped by ideas about the present: and the present is shaped by our ideas about the future. Compared with this power of ideas, interests are – in the long run – somewhat ineffectual as sources of change. Ultimately it is 'ideas, not vested interests, which are dangerous for good or evil' (GT: 384).

After such great labours Keynes rested and for the remainder of his life he was to focus on clarifying and applying his theoretical framework in correspondence and in articles and broadcasts. In an article on 'Art and the State' written in 1936, for example, Keynes had earlier made the point that a defining characteristic of the nineteenth and twentieth centuries has been its attitude to the so-called 'non-economic':

> The ancient world knew that the public needed circuses as well as bread. And, policy apart, its rulers for their own glory and satisfaction expended an important proportion of the national wealth on ceremony, works of art and magnificent buildings. These policies, habits and traditions were not confined to the Greek and Roman world ... But there commenced in the eighteenth century and reached a climax in the nineteenth a new view of the functions of the state and of society, which still govern us today. This view of the utilitarian and economic – one might almost say financial – ideal, as the sole, respectable purpose of the community as a whole; the most dreadful heresy, perhaps, which has ever gained the ear of a civilized people ... We have persuaded ourselves that it is positively wicked for the state to spend a halfpenny on non-economic purposes. (XXVIII: 341–2)

Keynes (the disciple of Moore) attacked the puritanical attitude towards the role of the arts in society and urged that the state take an active part in stimulating the arts so as to enrich the life of the individuals and the community as a whole. Keynes's vision encompassed an idea of a society which was not driven by the purely economic and the utilitarian but by the pursuit of beauty which would actually serve to promote economic as well as social well-being.

> Taking London as our example, we should demolish the majority of existing buildings on the south bank ... and lay out these districts as the most magnificent, the most commodius and healthy working-class district in the world ... (with) parks, squares, boulevards, and every delight which skill and fancy can devise. Why should not all London be the equal of St James's Park and its surroundings? The river front might become one of the sights of the world with a range of terraces and buildings rising from the river. The schools of South London should have the dignity of universities with courts, colonnades, and fountains, libraries, galleries, dining-halls, cinemas, and theatres for their own use. Into this scheme there should be introduced the utmost variety. All our architects and engineers and artists should have the opportunity to embody the various imaginations, not of peevish, stunted, and disillusioned beings, but of peaceful and satisfied spirits who belong to the renaissance. (XXVIII: 348)

In late 1936 Keynes wrote an article for the *Quarterly Journal of Economics* which was published in February, 1937. The article brings out a number of points about the central and fundamental ideas contained in the *General Theory*. Above all the article sought to describe in clear terms how he differed from his 'classical' critics. Ricardo, Marshall, Pigou and others, he argues were:

> dealing with a system in which the amount of factors employed was given and the other relevant facts were known or more or less certain ... at any given time facts and expectations were assumed to be given in a definite and calculable form; and risks, of which, though admitted, not much notice was taken, were supposed to be capable of an exact actuarial computation. The calculus of probability, though mention of it was kept in the background, was supposed to be capable of reducing uncertainty to the same calculable status as that of certainty itself; just as in the Benthamite calculus of pains and pleasures or of advantage and disadvantage, by which the Benthamite philosophy assumed men to be influenced in their general ethical behaviour. (XIV: 112–13)

The classical economists assumed a certain world which, like Newton's universal machine, could be reduced to a set of relationships which were calculable. But, this is not so. The economic world is not composed of forces which could be calculated in the kind of way advanced by Laplace, Bentham or Ricardo. The whole point is that *we do not know*. Time and chance mean that we can only have the 'vaguest idea' of the consequences of our decisions and actions. Thus because our knowledge about the future is 'fluctuating, vague and uncertain' (XIV: 113) the classical model is not adequate as a theory of the real economy which is full of uncertainty and instability. It is uncertain because, in so many respects, we have 'no scientific basis on which to calculate probability whatever. We simply do not know' (XIV: 113–14). Given this, how do 'practical men' make decisions? Keynes argues that in the real world decision makers rely on three main techniques:

- Assume that the present is a serviceable guide to the future and ignore the prospects of future changes about which we can no nothing.
- Assume that existing opinion has correctly summed-up future prospects, until something new or relevant comes into the picture.
- Individuals fall back on the judgment of the majority, or the average, and rely on conventional opinion.

Now, because this is how *real* people respond in a *real* world which is uncertain, the economic system is nothing like the model which underpins the classical way of thinking. The mechanicals had gravely underestimated the impact of the 'concealed factors of utter doubt, precariousness, hope and fear' (IX: 122) and overestminated the knowledge which we can possess. Real decision are based on a 'flimsy foundation' which is not very stable, consequently:

> it is subject to sudden and violent changes. The practice of calmness and immobility of certainty and security, suddenly breaks down. New fears and hopes will, without warning, take charge of human conduct. The forces of disillusion may suddenly impose a new conventional basis of valuation. All these pretty, polite techniques, made for a well-panelled boardroom and a nicely regulated market, are liable to collapse. At all times the vague panic fears and equally vague and unreasoned hopes are not really lulled, and lie but a little way below the surface. (XIV: 114–5)

Into this realm of uncertainty comes money which can serve as unit of account and a store of wealth.

> So we are told without a smile on the face. ... it is a recognised characteristic of money as a store of wealth that it is barren; whereas practically every other form of storing wealth yields some interest or profit. Why should anyone outside a lunatic asylum wish to use money as a store of wealth? Because, partly on reasonable and partly on instinctive grounds, our desire to hold money as a store of wealth is a barometer of the degree of our distrust of our own future. Even though this feeling about money is itself conventional or instinctive, it operates, so to speak at a deeper level of our motivation. It takes charge at the moments when the higher, more precarious conventions have weakened. The possession of actual money lulls our disquietude; and the premium which we require to make us part with money is the measure of the degree of our disquietude. (XIV: 115–16)

But, as he had realized after *A Treatise on Money,* the role of money has to be placed in the context of the way in which the system as a *whole* works (XIV:

119). This is the second major difference between Keynes and the mechanicals. The *General Theory* insists that if we wish to understand a money economy we cannot do so by taking an atomistic view and analyse the parts: the economy has to be seen as comprising microcosmic and macrocosmic forces which interact and interpenetrate. (In alchemy this was pictured as two triangles in the shape of the star of David.) Keynes's *General Theory* is therefore a theory of why output and unemployment fluctuate, but it is also a policy science. Like the alchemists Keynes was not simply seeking to 'diagnose', but was in search of a 'cure' (XIV: 122). And also like the alchemists, Keynes's elixir was not and could never be *the* cure: there was no single formula for the philosophers' stone. The *General Theory*, therefore, was not a universal panacea, but a way of thinking about the ailments of and cures for a money economy.

The themes of uncertainty and Benthamite calculation in the *Quarterly Journal of Economics* article were developed later in his lecture to the Eugenics Society in February 1937.

> The future never resembles the past – as we well know. But, generally speaking, our imagination and our knowledge are too weak to tell us what particular changes to expect. We do not know what the future holds. Nevertheless, as living and moving beings, we are forced to act. Peace and comfort of mind require that we should hide from ourselves how little we foresee. Yet we must be guided by some hypothesis. We tend, therefore, to substitute for the knowledge which is unattainable certain conventions ... This is how we act in practice. Though it was, I think, an ingredient in the complacency of the nineteenth century that, in their philosophical reflections on human behaviour, they accepted an extraordinary contraption of the Benthamite school. (XIV: 124)

And in a letter to Townsend in 1938 he expanded on this:

> Generally speaking, in making a decision we have before us a large number of alternatives, none of which is demonstrably more 'rational' than the others ... To avoid being in the position of Buridan's ass, we fall back, therefore ... on motives of another kind, which are not 'rational' in the sense of being concerned with the evaluation of consequences, but are decided by habit, instinct, preference, desire, will, etc. (XXIX: 294)

In the *General Theory* Keynes does not address the 'Mathusian devil' in any detail, so much as focus on his notion of deficiency of demand. However, in his Eugenics Society lecture he stresses that population is crucial to analysing the economy – whether it is on the increase or on the decline. In the case of Britain he believed that the trend would be downwards. But, this does not mean that he departs from the Malthusian model – quite the opposite, since a falling population will only mean a rising standard of living if resources or consumption continue to rise.

For we have now learned that we have another devil at our elbow at least as fierce as the Malthusian – namely the devil of unemployment escaping through the breakdown in effective demand. Perhaps we could call this devil too a Malthusian devil, since it was Malthus himself who first told us about him ... Malthus was no less disturbed by the facts of unemployment as he saw them round him and sought ... to rationalise that problem too. Now when Malthusian devil P is chained up, Malthusian devil U is liable to break loose. When devil P of Population is chained up, we are free of one menace; but we are more exposed to the other devil U of Unemployed Resources than we were before. (XIV: 131–2)

A decline in population would not improve the standard of life unless a policy of more equal distribution of incomes and of 'forcing down' the rate of interest is also implemented. Thus although we may chain up one Malthusian devil – overpopulation – policy makers have to be very careful in the future that they did not unleash another – unemployment – which would be 'still fiercer and intractable' (XIV: 133). In other words, although we may well be able to restain our fecundity, controlling the love of money would prove to be infinitely more problematic than sexual desire.

After the *General Theory* Keynes put forward the clearest account of his notion of economics as a moral science and perhaps the most cogent exposition of the philosophy contained in the *Treatise on Probability* and worked out in the *General Theory*. In the debate about Tinbergen he was to show his hostility to the notion that economics ought to imitate the natural sciences. If only Keynes's observations on the nature of economics had been taken more seriously and more to heart the history of economics after the Second World War might have been very different. Then again, if only Keynes had made some attempt to explain what he meant by 'moral science', rather than in a throw-away reference in the *General Theory*, then perhaps he might have prevented the headlong mad dash into quantificationism and econometrics in the 1960s and '70s. If only.

At the outset Keynes found Tinbergen's method 'unintelligible' 'hocus' (XIV: 289) on the grounds which he had advanced at length in the *Treatise on Probability* and in the *General Theory*: his use of statistical data was attempting to explain economic material which was not homogenous over time; it was concerned with forces which were not wholly measurable; and it sought to analyse forces as if they were atomic, rather than organic. Tinbergen was, as he explained to Tyler, endeavouring to establish linear independent relationships between factors which were essentially inter-dependent (XIV: 286). Tinbergen assumes that the future is a 'function of past statistics' rather than, as Keynes argues in the *General Theory*, to do with the expectations of and confidence about the future (XIV: 287). His analysis makes no allowance for non-numerical factors such as 'inventions, politics, labour troubles, wars, earthquakes, financial crises' (ibid.). This disengagement from reality is made worse by the claim that statistical analysis was objective, when statistics were inevitably the product of selection and 'cooking'. As he wryly commented in his 1940 reply to Tinbergen in the *Economic Journal*:

> It will be remembered that the seventy translators of the Septuagint were shut up in the seventy separate rooms with the Hebrew text and brought out with them, when they emerged, seventy identical translations. Would the same miracle be vouchsafed if seventy multiple correlations were shut up with the same statistical material? And anyhow, I suppose, if each had a different economist perched on his *a priori*, that would make a difference to the outcome. (XIV: 319–20)

Contemporary with Keynes's observations on Tinbergen were his comments to Harrod on the attempts being made by Schultz *et al.* to make economics into a 'pseudo-natural science'. The subject was, he argued, 'a branch of logic' which required (as Harrod put it) 'vigilant observation of the actual working of our system' and the constant improvement in the choice of models. This is what Tinbergen did not comprehend.

> Economics is a way of thinking in terms of models joined to the art of choosing models which are relevant to the contemporary world. It is compelled to do this, because, unlike the typical natural sciences, the material to which it is applied is, in too many respects, not homogenous through time. The object of the model is to segregate the semi-permanent or relatively constant factors from those which are transitory or fluctuating so as to develop a logical way of thinking about the latter, and of understanding the time sequences to which they give rise in particular cases. Good economists are scarce because the gift of using 'vigilant observation' to choose good models, although it does not require a highly specialized intellectual technique, appears to be a very rare one ... economics is essentially a moral science and not a natural science. That is to say, it employs introspection and judgments of value. (XIV: 296–7)

Several points may be noted about this important passage. First, that one of the defining characteristics of economics is 'vigilant observation'. Like the alchemist, the economist must be ever awake lest the vessel break: Newton, we can recall, when practising the art slept very little (Westfall, 1994: 141). Keynes demands the same of the economist; he must remain ever vigilant to make sure that an out-of-date model does not crack under the pressure of explaining the actual workings of the economic system. Second, the aim is to model reality in such a way that we can sort out the constant factors, so as to facilitate – as he argued in the *General Theory* – a way of thinking which can address the transitory and fluctuating. Third, this way of thinking about the non-constant elements involves introspection, that is to say an examination of thoughts, feelings, mental processes and values. Economics was a way of thinking, and too great a reliance on mathematical, empirical methods could result in the destruction of intuition, insight and understanding. Quantification could lead to obfuscation, that is to a neat, precise model which is of no use in dealing with a real world. These points are brought out more clearly in a subsequent letter to Harrod. It is, he writes on the 16th July 1938, important to investigate economic problems (such as the multiplier) with the use of statistics. He says this, of course, as someone who passionately believed in the need for economic debate to have recourse to more and better statistics. But, statistical analysis can be misleading and we must be conscious of its limitations.

> In chemistry and physics and other natural sciences the object of the experiment is to fill in the actual values of the various quantities and factors appearing in an equation or a formula. In economics that is not the case, and to convert a model into a quantitative formula is to destroy its usefulness as an instrument of thought ... the art of thinking in terms of models is a difficult – largely because it is an unaccustomed – practice. The pseudo-analogy with the physical sciences leads directly counter to the habit of mind which is most important for an economist to acquire. I also want to emphasize strongly the point about economics being a moral science. I mentioned before that it deals with introspection and with values. I might have added that it deals with motives, expectations, psychological uncertainties. One has to be constantly on guard against treating the material as constant and homogenous. (XIV: 299–300)

Why? Well, in order to explain this point Keynes refers to the central myth of Newtonian science: the falling apple. The economist has to take into account the mind in the machine.

> It is though the fall of the apple to the ground depended on the apple's motives, and whether it is worth falling to the ground, and whether the ground wanted the apple to fall, and on the mistaken calculations on the part of the apple as to how far it was from the centre of the earth. (XIV: 300)

This analogy strikes at the core (if I may be excused the pun) of Keynes's approach developed in the *General Theory*: like the alchemists, he sees the economic system composed of elements which have spirit or mind, they are not inanimate, lifeless cogs and wheels. The economic system is composed of mind as well as matter, spirit as well as body. Empiricism, mathematics, and reason are such inadequate instruments for understanding the inconstant, mercurial forces of human motivation, uncertainty, expectation, instrospection and values. The economist's great task is to be constantly adjusting models, correcting judgments, and seeking an 'intimate and messy acquaintance with the facts to which his model has to be applied' (XIV: 300). This is why Keynes is so annoyed by Tinbergen's 'charlatanism' (XIV: 305): he just cannot appreciate the fact that he is claiming far too much, when he ought to be claiming so very little for the mathematical approach.

In a review of Tinbergen's *A Method and Its Application to Investment Activity,* published in the *Economic Journal* in September 1939, Keynes sets out a lengthy rebuttal of Tinbergen's attempt to use statistical testing to examine theories of the business cycle. A number of his arguments bear upon the interpretation we have developed in our discussion thus far. Keynes emphasizes, for example, that economic relationships are not all linear, and measurable. He criticizes him for discounting political, psychological and social factors, the impact of government policy, the progress of technology, and the state of expectations. If followed Tinbergen's path would lead us back to Ricardo's world which is a long way from the messy reality detailed in the *General Theory.* It is a Euclidean world in which all lines are straight; it is the world of Laplace where we can know the probability of all things; it is not Newton's vegetable, alchemical world, but a Cartesian machine, where apples mindlessly fall; it is world of atomic parts, and not organic wholes.

> What happens if the phenomenon under investigation itself reacts on the factors by which we are explaining it? ... In practice Professor Tinbergen seems to be entirely indifferent whether or not his basic factors are independent of one another. ... In plain terms, it is evident that if what is really the same factor is appearing in several places under various disguises, a free choice of coefficients can lead to strange results. It becomes like those puzzles for children where you write down your age, multiply, add this and that, subtract something else, and eventually end up with the Beast in Revelation. (XIV: 310)

As in the children's game where we mechanically follow a set of rules, we can quickly arrive in a mental cul-de-sac of our own making. Linear thinking, for example, means:

> that the quantitative effect of any causal factor on the phenomenon under investigation is directly proportional to the factor's own magnitude ... But it is a very drastic and usually improbable postulate to suppose that all economic forces are of this character, producing independent changes in the phenomena under investigation which are directly proportional to the changes themselves; indeed this is ridiculous. (XIV: 312)

This is economic Newtonianism gone mad indeed, reminiscent as it is of Newton's laws: 'if a force acts on a body the acceleration it produces is proportional to the size of the force'. The point is that linearity is out of place in the analysis of material which does not conform to straight lines of causality. Economics has to deal with a reality in which lines do not fit in with Euclidean geometry and Newton's laws: it is complex and lacking in uniformity (XIV: 316). This is not to say that Tinbergen's methods are inappropriate for relatively simple problems, but it is of no use in the context of a problem as 'enormously *complex* as the business cycle' (XIV: 317). But, he concludes, (in the reply to Tinbergen in March 1940), if he wishes to practice the black magic and alchemy, so be it: he will be in the good company of Newton, Boyle and Locke!

The *General Theory* describes a world of 'psychic' forces composed of complex and volatile motivations, expectations and psychological uncertainties. Keynes no doubt feared that having vanquished the mechanistic Newtonianism of Ricardian economics, the likes of Tinbergen would seek to promote yet another form of mechanical thinking. His fears were well founded. As Keynes's revolution advanced, Tinbergen's rough beast slouched behind cluching its brand of 'black magic' and 'alchemy' (sic). Like the fake adepts of old who promised to turn lead into gold the econometricians were to find a welcome in a post-war world eager to seize the illusion of control which the new mechanicals promised. Meanwhile, in the years before the start of the war his theories were to influence the younger generation of economists and permeate official thinking in Britain and the US and several other countries. As the country moved inexorably towards rearmament and the preparation for war, Keynes was vocal as ever in urging that public opinion and policy makers should seize the opportunities for experimentation which the global conflagration provided.

5. War and the transmutation of capitalism

The alchemists understood the return to chaos as an essential part of the opus. It was the stage of the *nigredo* and *mortificatio*, which was then followed by the 'purgatorial fire' and the *albedo*. The spirit of chaos is indispensible to the work ...'. (Jung, 1970: 253)

War ... is a basic feature of coniunctio symbolism. It signifies the activated conflict between opposites which is an inevitable prelude to their union. (Edinger, 1990: 79)

Faust. And so I quickly worked out plans,
resolving to obtain a precious satisfaction:
to bar the shore to the imperious sea,
narrow the limits of the ocean's great expanse,
and force the waters back into themselves.
I've worked out every step within my mind:
this is what I want, what you must help me do!
A distant sound of drums and martial music is heard ...
Mephistopheles. That should be easy! Do you hear the distant drums?
Faust. War once again! Bad news for all who're sensible!
Mephistopheles. With war or peace, what's sensible
is to derive advantage from it.
You wait and watch for the right moments.
This is your opportunity. Now. Faustus, seize it!
(Goethe, 1994: 10 227–239)

The grand experiment has begun. If it works, if expenditure on armaments really does cure unemployment, I predict that we shall never go back all the way to the old state of affairs. If we can cure unemployment for the wasted purpose of armaments, we can cure it for the productive purpose of peace. Good may come of evil. (Keynes, XXI: 532)

Keynes's experimental method was that of an alchemist, rather than a scientist: he used his reason and intuition to bring about a transformation of the capitalist system through changing the way in which people thought about the 'economic problem'. This took place in two interrelated realms: public and professional. In the former realm it meant that he had to be committed to 'regulating the fire, mixing, adding, and above all waiting for the right reactions in the vessel' (Gilchrist, 1991: 54) of public opinion. In the sphere of professional experimentation it involved the same diligence in persuading his fellow economists: the most consummate product of this 'circus' process was the *General Theory*. However, the alchemist's great work was not completed until the war provided him with the ultimate laboratory: the realm of policy making in government. His method (*solve et coagula*) remained ever constant: dialogue, discussion, persuasion and using every opportunity to stoke the fires so as to promote change in the *vas hermeticum* of war. As in alchemy Vulcan's sword requires the help of Mars if the philosophical egg is to yield a new and redeemed creation (Haeffner, 1994: 82). With the outbreak of war Keynes was to be involved in the practical details of applying his ideas to the economic problems of the day. After the publication of the *General Theory* Keynes's health was to deteriorate and in 1937 he suffered the first of his heart attacks. He was therefore reluctant to take on too many responsibilities, but on the principle that if you want something done ask a busy man, Keynes was drawn into a work load which would have presented the fittest of men with a treacherous number of demands. Keynes devoted the closing years of his life to creating the preconditions for new possibilities even at the cost of his failing health.

The first issue which caught his attention was, typically, one of finance: how was the war to be paid for? Keynes's plan which involved financing through a compulsory savings scheme, met with the kind of criticisms that were later put forward (1944) in Hayek's *Road to Serfdom*: war-time planning would lead to a new totalitarianism in the peace. To which he responded:

> No criticism could be more misdirected. In a totalitarian state the problem of the distribution of sacrifice does not exist ... That is one of the advantages of war ... It is only in a free community that the task of government is complicated by the claims of social justice. In a slave state production is the only problem. The poor and the old and the infant must take their chance; and no system lends itself better to the provision of special privileges to the governing classes. (IX: 377)

His aim in putting forward a way of planning 'how to pay for the war' was to adapt a 'distributive system of a free community to the limitations of war' by keeping in mind three objectives:

> the provison of an increased reward as an incentive and recognition of increased effort and risk, to which free men unlike slaves are entitled; the maximum freedom of choice to each individual how he will use that part of his income which he is at liberty to spend, a freedom which properly belongs to independent personalities but not to units of a totalitarian ant-heap; and the mitigation of the necessary sacrifice for those least able to bear it, a use of valuable resources which a ruthless power avoids. (IX: 377)

Keynes saw the war as a time which was full of opportunity to change and transform economic policy and the role of the state. The chaos, blackness and destruction of war offered the prospect of a better world. It was a period for tremendous experimentation during which the state could learn to regulate spending saving, investment and consumption. Thus in his plan to pay for the war through a savings scheme Keynes insisted that he was not simply proposing an expedient, so much as:

> seizing an opportunity, where the need is obvious and overwhelming, to introduce a principle of policy which may come to be thought as marking the line of division between the totalitarian and free economy. For if the community's aggregate rate of spending can be regulated, the way in which personal incomes are spent and the means by which demand is satisfied can be safely left free and individual. Just as in the war the regulation of aggregate spending is only the way to avoid the destruction of choice and initiative, whether by consumers or by producers, through the complex tyranny of all-round rationing, so in peace it is only through the application of this principle which will provide the environment in which the choice and initiative of the individual can be safely left free. This is the one kind of compulsion of which the effect is to enlarge liberty. Those who, entangled in the old unserviceable maxims, fail to see this further-reaching objective have not grasped, to speak American, the big idea. (XXII: 123–4)

He developed this theme of seizing the opportunities of war in an article for the American journal *The New Republic* later on in July of 1940 ('The United States and the Keynes Plan'). He argues that his prescription for using the war to enhance democracy and economic progress was akin to rules of the road which prevent cars getting in one another's way without changing the destination of the vehicles or the volume of traffic (XXII: 145). The war economy could therefore be more wholesome than the profits 'orgy', 'gambling' and wage and price inflation which characterized the First World War and its aftermath. The Second World War, however, did not have to 'carry the seeds of later chaos' like the first. It could, on the contrary, provide the laboratory for 'grand experiments' to discover the mysteries of what forces shape output, consumption and employment (XXII: 154). War-time experiments might thereby confound the belief that democracies could not be wise and sensible and free of the 'poison of popular politics' (XXII: 155). The war had opened up new possibilities of civilization and individualism. But, to realise the potential of war we have to:

> Escape from the *invalidism* of the Left which has eaten up the wisdom and inner strength of many good causes. The old guard on the Right, on their side, must surely recognize, if any reason or any prudence is theirs, that the existing system is palpably disabled, that the idea of its continuing to function unmodified with half the world in dissolution is just sclerotic. Let them learn from the experience of Great Britain and of Europe that there has been a rottenness at the heart of our society, and do not suppose that America is healthy. (XXII:155)

The putrefaction of the old capitalist order was giving way to a new kind of civilization and Keynes saw himself as having a role to play in advancing this death–birth process in every way he could. In the September of 1940 he put his ideas on the possibilities of war to radio audiences in Britain, the Empire, America and Latin America. He urged his listeners to be of good cheer and to:

> stop thinking that after the war we shall have to lower our standards of life. I see no likelihood of that. On the contrary, I hope that we shall have learnt some things about central controls, and about the capacity of the country to produce which will prevent us from ever lapsing into our pre-war economic morass. There is no reason why most people should not look forward to higher standards of life after the war than they have ever enjoyed yet ... we have the capacity to replace what is lost by something much better. Some of the major glories of London date from the Great Fire. London will, I should hope, rise from the present mess handsomer and healthier than before. (XXII: 241–2)

It is as if he envisaged the fires of destruction giving birth to a new age: cities could be purged of their ugliness and the economy could be extricated from the mess of the past: blackening (*nigredo*) would be followed by whitening (*albedo*). This alchemical optimism that evil could produce good was in stark contrast to the pessimism we find in Hayek's *Road to Serfdom* which forecast that the effects of war-time planning would take us back to a new dark age. In a Treasury memo on war damage (July 1940), for example, Keynes was highly critical of the pessimistic predictions of the damage war would bring. Echoing some of his arguments in the *Treatise on Probability* and the *General Theory* Keynes notes that: 'It is characteristic of human nature to overestimate unfamiliar, unpredictable and personally catastrophic risks' (XXII: 435), and yet he points out that, as he wrote in *The Economic Consequences of the Peace*, forecasts of the damage wrought by war were overexaggerated. He thought that it was 'most unlikely that the war damage will be greater than what three or four years' normal saving can make good' (XXII: 443). Even in the midst of the war, therefore, Keynes continued to act on the 'optimistic hypothesis' (IX: xviii).

Paying for the war also raised other possibilities: how could the budgetary process be used to manage the economy as a whole? Keynes's ideas and concepts were adopted in the 1941 budget which established for the first time a method of calculating national income, saving, investment and consumption. Furthermore, throughout the discussions on budgetary policy Keynes (and his apostles) continually stressed the importance of relating financial matters to issues of social justice and need to prevent the return of mass unemployment after the war. Keynes was to give his support and encouragement to the introduction of a social welfare system (the Beveridge Report) and the development of policies designed to secure full employment (the 1944 white paper on employment). In all of this Keynes was forthright in his demand for the state to improve the collection, organization and use of social and economic data. Indeed, one of the most important effects of the war was that it brought about a transformation in the use of statistics. As he noted in 1944 with regard to the report of the steering committee on full employment:

> Theoretical economic analysis has now reached a point where it is fit to be applied. Its application only awaits the collection of detailed facts which the economist, unlike the scientist, cannot collect in a laboratory ... The authors of the Report would, I think, have written with more confidence about their plans for the future and in a spirit of more buoyant hope, if they fully appreciated what knowledge is capable of doing in making the future different from the past. (XXVII: 371)

His enthusiasm for making sure that 'the future was different to the past' also extended (in 1941) to taking on the chairmanship of the forerunner of the British Arts Council, CEMA: the Committee for the Encouragement of Music and the Arts. Despite the massive pressures on him Keynes took on this post and was wholly committed to using the committee to foster the 'arts of life' and civilize society. That he gave so much of his time and energy to getting more money for the arts and shaping its policies is testament enough to his belief that the war presented opportunities to change and improve and enhance the quality of life for all. The arts were by no means considered by Keynes to be a somewhat irrelevant or a marginal aspect of policy making even during (and especially) a war. By accepting the chairmanship of the committee Keynes was demonstrating how vital it was to defend society against the spread of a utilitarian mentality. As an economist he realized that the government had to concern itself with beauty, as well as costs, benefits and utility. Sadly, of course, unlike his views of full employment, Keynes's ideas on the need for beauty was not to be a feature of post-war reconstruction, whose hallmarks were so often to be those of functionality and utility.

In addition to the problems of internal war finance, post-war employment and the arts, Keynes's mind was soon directed towards the issue of international monetary reform: a matter with which had long been concerned. (See, for example, *A Tract on Monetary Reform* IV: 141–60; *A Treatise on Money* VI: 346–67; and 'The Means to Prosperity', IX: 355–66.) In the November of 1940 Keynes received a request from the Ministry of Information to help in countering German propaganda on a new economic order. The episode was to lead eventually to the Bretton Woods agreement which laid the basis for the post-war international monetary system. The German minister of Foreign Affairs and President of the Reichbank, Dr Walther Funk had put forward plans for a German 'New Order'. This new order would be based upon a monetary system whose core would be the German mark (the 'Funk Mark' as it became known). Keynes was requested to provide a counter argument for this plan, however, he replied saying that the notion of establishing a stable monetary system was a rather good idea and that he was not the one to put the case for *laissez-faire* in the relationship between currencies. He thought Funk's plan was excellent, and argued that instead of attacking the scheme, it should be the *bona fides* of the Germans which ought to be the main target of counter-propaganda. From this time onwards Keynes was to devote a large part of his life to bringing to birth a scheme which would have the advantages of a stable monetary system on the lines first suggested by Funk, but under the leadership of democratic countries. In a widely distributed and discussed document Keynes outlined his ideas in the December of 1940.

Keynes argued that the great mistake of 1919 was that it neglected the question of economic reconstruction, and if the same error was not to be repeated the government ought to give attention to the economic arrangements for the post-war period. At a domestic level this meant that attention had to be given to social welfare policies, unemployment and the prevention of starvation. However, the international context must not be forgotten. The post-war recovery would be gravely undermined by the return to the wild fluctuations of currencies which had characterized the 1920s and 1930s. The German scheme had merit, he argued, because it showed the way forward to the end of the chaos of *laissez-faire* in international currency arrangements. However, for such a new order to be brought about it had to be built on international foundations, and not simply on a European basis. The German plan would be one which worked to the advantage of German industry whilst the 'satellite and tributary states (would) be compelled to confine themselves to the kinds of production which suit the convenience of Germany' (XXV: 13). The challenge for Britain was to promote 'an international economic system, capable of translating the technical possibilities of production into actual plenty and maintaining the whole population in a continuous fruitful activity'. This would not be an easy task, but a new order under British leadership would offer a far more attractive prospect than one dominated by German interests as Britain would seek:

> no particular advantage but only that each member of the European family shall realise its own character and perfect its own gifts in liberty of conscience and person. We cannot perform miracles. But we have learnt the lesson of the interregnum between the wars; and we know that no escape can be found from the curse which has been lying on Europe except by creating and preserving economic health in every country. (XXV: 14–15)

Keynes's ideas stimulated discussion in London and Washington and in the summer of 1941 he put forward more detailed plans for a post-war currency union. His argument began with the problem of equilibrium in the balance of payments between countries. The imbalances between different countries had given rise to impoverishment and social discontent over the centuries with only a few brief respites in the age of Elizabeth and Victoria. However, he argued, it is now evident that:

> to suppose that there exists some smoothly functioning automatic mechanism of adjustment which preserves equilibrium if only we trust to the methods of *laissez-faire* is a doctrinaire delusion which disregards the lessons of historical experience without having behind it the support of sound theory ... So far from currency *laissez-faire* having promoted the international division of labour, which is the avowed goal of *laissez-faire*, it has been a fruitful source of all those clumsy hindrances to trade which suffering communities have devised in their perplexity. (XXV: 21–2)

The war gave us a new opportunity to break with the chaos of currency volatility and competitive bouts of deflation and the erection of tariffs, preferences and subsidies and frame a new world order. This required boldness and ambition and a fundamental break with international *laissez-faire* in money and trade. We could no longer allow capital to move around the world to the advantage of the wealth-owning classes and bringing disorganization and uncertainty to business and trade.

> the post-war world must not be content with patchwork. For this is the key problem of our post-war prosperity. If we can solve it, the rest will follow without insuperable difficulty. If we fail, our best hopes of finally abolishing economic want and of providing continuous good employment as a high standard of life will be lost to us. A vast disappointment, social disorders and finally a repudiation of our ill-judged commitments will be the result. (XXV: 26–7)

Although the final details of clearing union were to deeply disappoint Keynes, the Bretton Woods agreement realised Keynes's belief that war could release the spirit of cooperation and trust between nations. The war was thus pregnant with possibilities and when the work was done Keynes described the achievement by using an appropriate metaphor in his speech at the inaugural meeting of the International Monetary Fund and the Bank:

> The gestation has been long; the lusty twins are seriously overdue; they will have put on, I hope, as a result, a weight and a strength which will do credit to their mixed and collective parentage ... What gifts and blessings are likely to be most servicable to the twins, whom (rightly or wrongly) we have decided to call Master Fund and Miss Bank? (XXVI: 215)

Although the twins were not quite the children Keynes had wanted, he was optimistic that they could be the progenitors of a new order – even though some of the fairy gifts were to prove more of a curse than a blessing. At least they were born, however, whereas another plan to stabilize the prices of commodites remained little more than a twinkle in his eye (XXVII: 105–99).

The feeling for the possibilities of war-time was expressed in layman's terms in his talk on the financial aspects of planning for the BBC in the spring of 1942 entitled 'How Much does Finance Matter?' Keynes argues that, contrary to what many might think, there will be enough money to implement the plans for the post-war period: 'where the money for reconstruction is to come from can be solved, and therefore should be solved' (XXVII: 266). Indeed, the technical problems will, he predicted, be far 'easier to handle' after the war than before. Lower interest rates and fuller employment combined with the transformation in public opinion towards the role of state controls meant that the end of the war offered a much brighter prospect for change than was manifested in 1919. In regulating the economy to control inflation and unemployment the state will be in the position of moving forward with 'large and bold schemes' (XXVII: 268) for house building, planning the use of 'lakes and moors, fell and mountains, the downs and woodlands' and re-building London. Out of the ashes a new metropolis could arise:

> There is heaps of room, enough and more than enough, in a re-planned London. We could get all the accommodation we need if a third of the present built-up area was cleared altogether and left cleared. The blitz has uncovered St Paul's to the eyes of this generation. To leave it so will cost nothing to the community as a whole. To build may be costly. Let us offset that expense by *not* building. (XXVII: 269–70)

He was also delighted that the BBC had successfully brought good music to a growing public and had stimulated and raised public taste (XXVIII: 361; 369). And, to the end of his life he railed against the lack of concert halls and other public builidings which could serve to enrich the cultural life of the nation. Keynes hoped that the Arts Council would have a major role to play in post-war reconstruction and that the arts would no longer be seen as an expensive luxury, but an absolute necessity in a civilized society. Writing in 1945, in his capacity as Chairman of the Arts Council, he expressed the hope that:

> The re-building of the community and of our common life must proceed in due proportion between one thing and another … the theatre and the concert-hall and the gallery will be a living element in everyone's upbringing, and regular attendance at the theatre and at concerts a part of organised education … How satisfactory it would be if different parts of this country would learn to develop something different from their neighbours and characteristic of themselves … Let every part

of Merry England be merry in its own way. Death to Hollywood. (XXVIII: 370–71)

The latter comment regarding Hollywood got him into a little trouble, but it does serve to make the point that Keynes wanted to see a diverse, *culturally* affluent society, and he passionately believed that it was the responsibility of the state to promote this diversity. It also reflects upon his growing fears about the influence of American values and culture on the post-war world. He was deeply dismayed at the American attitude towards British economic problems and the fact that the US administration and Congress tended to think in purely monetary and commercial terms, rather than from the point of view of morality or comradeship. America, he thought, was a 'business country' in which it is a 'moral duty and not a self-regarding act to make any money which the traffic will bear and the law allow' (XXIV: 547–8). As the negotiations with America over the loan and lend lease had demonstrated, money came first, and the kind of moral standards which Keynes held dear, a long way second. This predominance of business and monetary values did not bode well for the future, hence in his comments on Hollywood he was giving vent to his unease about the impact of American mass culture and its adherence to *laissez-faire* capitalism. His remarks on the threat of American culture underlined what he had said about the importance of 'homespun' manufacture in his 1933 Dublin lecture.

Keynes's argument, therefore, was that the good society should not be one in which 'economic' and 'utilitarian' values were allowed to predominate. The love of money was essentially sterile and unproductive. Puritanical utilitarian approaches to government were the *real* enemy of civilization. For this world of art galleries and theatres to come about it required the use of the money instinct. Culture did not (and never will) come cheap. Only through economic growth could there be cultural growth and the fullest realization of human potential. In his 1942 BBC talk on financing planning Keynes offers the prospect of the terrible ugliness and horror of war giving way to beauty and human enrichment.

I should like to see that the war memorials of this tragic struggle take the shape of an enrichment of the civic life of every great centre of population. Why should we not set aside, let us say, £50 millions a year for the next twenty years to add in every substantial city of the realm the dignity of an ancient university or European capital to our local schools and their surroundings, to our local government and its offices, and above all, perhaps, to provide a local centre of refreshment and entertainment with an ample theatre, a concert hall, a dance hall, a gallery ... Assuredly we can afford this and much more. Anything we can actually *do* we can afford. Once done, it is *there* ... We are immeasurably richer than our predecessors. It is not evident that some form of sophistry, some fallacy, governs our collective action if we are forced to be so much meaner than they in the embellishments of life? (XXVII: 270)

Such a New Jerusalem (sic) was possible with planning and deliberation. The vain folly of unused and unhappy idleness of the pre-war era was no longer the fate of mankind.

This profoundly optimistic approach to the possibilities of war at a time when life was grim and full of uncertainty and fear is evident in his speeches in the House of Lords. In his draft speech on the Beveridge report, for example, he concludes:

> The future will be what we choose to make it. If we approach it with cringing and timidity, we shall get what we deserve. If we march on with confidence and vigour the facts will respond ... Moreover, to make a bogey of the economic problems is, in my judgment, grievously to misunderstand the nature of the tasks ahead of us. Looking beyond to the immediate post-war period, when our economic difficulties will be genuine and must take precedence over all else – perhaps for the last time – the economic problems of the day (that) perplex us, will not lie in solving the problems of an era of material abundance nor those of an era of poverty. It is not any fear of failure of physical productivity to provide an adequate material standard of life that fills me with foreboding. The real problems of the future are first of all the maintenance of peace, of international co-operation and amity, and beyond that the profound moral and social problem of how to organise material abundance to yield up the fruits of the good life. These are the heroic tasks of the future. (XXVII: 260–1)

By 1944 Keynes had achieved so much both on the world stage, and on the domestic front. His ideas now formed an accepted framework within which economic policy was being conducted. His mood is one of having completed a grand task to reform opinion. In response to criticisms that he had betrayed his early beliefs and principles in being one of the main architects of the Bretton Woods agreement Keynes replied in the May of 1944:

> I hope your Lordships will trust me not to have turned my back on all I have fought. To establish these three principles which I have just stated has been my main task for the last twenty years. Sometimes alone in popular articles in the press, in pamphlets, in dozens of letters to *The Times,* in textbooks, in enormous and obscure treatises, I have spent my strength to persuade my countrymen and the world at large to change their traditional doctrines and, by taking better thought, to remove the curse of unemployment. Was it not I, when many of today's iconoclasts were still worshippers of the Calf, who wrote that 'Gold is a barbarous relic'? Am I so faithless, so forgetful, so senile that, at the very moment of triumph of these ideas when, with gathering momentum, governments, parliaments, banks, the press, the public and even economists, have at last accepted these new doctrines, I go off to help forge new chains to hold us fast in the old dungeon? (XXVI: 16–17)

This attack on Keynes as paving the way to a new totalitarianism had been voiced most clearly in Hayek's *The Road to Serfdom* which had been published in the March of 1944. Keynes found time to read it during an Atlantic voyage and responded with a private letter to Hayek at the end of June that year. More than any other single book *The Road to Serfdom* was the text which served to provide the intellectual underpinning for the Keynesian counter-revolution in the 1970s and 1980s. It was the inspiration behind the setting-up of perhaps the most influential of British think tanks the IEA (The Institute of Economic Affairs). Keynes's response to the book is not a well developed treatise and without relating the letter to his approach as a whole, and in particular to the arguments for planning he advanced during the war, it appears a rather inadequate response to Hayek's book.

He begins by saying that it is a 'grand book' which says what needs to be said about the threat of totalitarian societies. At a moral and a philosophical level Keynes is 'virtually' in complete agreement with Hayek. Indeed, he argues that he not only agrees with his arguments, but is in 'deeply moved agreement'. His comments on Russia in the mid-twenties amply illustrate Keynes's hatred of totalitarianism in all its forms. In the preface to the German edition of the *General Theory* Keynes had conceded that the theory contained in the book 'is much more easily adapted to the conditions of a totalitarian state, than is the theory of the production and distribution of a given output produced under conditions of free competition and a large measure of *laissez-faire*' (GT: xxvi). He also acknowledged that the totalitarian systems had solved the problem of unemployment, but at the costs to freedom and efficiency (GT: 381). He differs with Hayek, however, on the practical and economic aspects and consequences of his book, rather than its moral philosophy. Given the optimistic view which Keynes had about the post-war period (and which was proved far more accurate than the dismal forecasts from the prophets of doom) he begins his critique by taking Hayek to task for deprecating the view that there was 'plenty just around the corner'. Secondly, he disagrees with Hayek as to the intractability or difficulty of solving the 'economic problem' and of giving the economic problem far too much emphasis. The kind of sacrifices of individual liberty which Hayek believes planning inherently involves is, from Keynes's point of view, simply not *necessary*. Hayek sees planning as demanding sacrifices whereas Keynes's view is that the economic problems are not so difficult as he makes them out to be and so talk of 'sacrifices' is 'increasingly unnecessary'. This argument is then followed by two significant points of agreement which puts his later main criticism into context. To begin with Keynes wholeheartedly endorses Hayek's emphasis on the importance of the profit motive. Indeed, he says that he would have liked this to have been a much bigger section of the book. Hayek argues that socialist societies disparage activities involving economic risk, and he continues:

> We cannot blame our young men when they prefer the safe, salaried position to the risk of enterprise after they have heard from their earliest youth the former described as the superior, more unselfish and disinterested occupation. The younger generation of to-day has grown up in a world in which in school and press the spirit of commercial enterprise has been represented as disreputable and the making of profit as immoral ... as a result of anti-capitalist propaganda values have already altered far in advance of the change in institutions which has taken place in this country. The question is whether by changing our institutions to satisfy the new demands, we shall not unwittingly destroy values which we still rate higher. (Hayek, 1944: 97)

Planning should not, from Keynes's standpoint, lead to a society in which risk taking is discouraged – far from it. Keynes was firmly in support of enterprise, and saw no harm in speculation provided it did not replace it as the primary business motivation. The main difference between Hayek and Keynes is not about the profit motive, and the importance of risk, but what conditions can best provide the environment in which the 'spirit' can be released and be made most productive. Planning cannot be a substitute for risk taking, but the state can seek to create an environment in which the creative 'animal spirits' of capitalism are liberated. Keynes, like Hayek, is passionately concerned with the question of liberty, hence his second point of agreement on 'the moral issue'. Keynes considered the last paragraph of page 156 to be 'extraordinarily good and fundamental' (XXVII: 386) since Hayek maintains that:

> What our generation is in danger of forgetting is not only that morals are of necessity a phenomenon of individual conduct, but also that they can exist only in the sphere in which the individual is free to decide for himself and called upon voluntarily to sacrifice personal advantage to the observance of a moral rule. Outside the sphere of individual responsibility there is neither goodness nor badness, neither opportunity for moral merit nor the chance of proving one's conviction by sacrificing one's desires to what one thinks right. Only where we ourselves are responsible for our own interests and are free to sacrifice them, has our decision moral value. (Hayek, 1944: 156)

Keynes fully endorses this, but goes on to say that he cannot accept what his book gives us by way of 'practical guidance': what he finds most objectionable is his sheer extremism. Hayek, with his relentless logic, read the experience of war-time planning as posing a threat to democracy and paving a road to serfdom which would bring Britain to a situation akin to that of Stalin's Russia and Hitler's Germany. For Keynes, Hayek is a victim of linear thinking: like Tinbergen he assumes that the future is an extrapolation of present trends, rather than of human expectations. He is making the assumption which had been examined in the *Treatise on Probability* and the *General Theory*: he was allowing the present to enter into the future and assuming that the future will resemble the past. Keynes is quite prepared to agree with him that planning does indeed bring with it such dangers. However, Hayek is, in Keynes's sense, not using his common sense. What was taking place in Britain was *very* different to that which takes place in totalitarian societies. It did not follow that war-time planning would destroy democracy, and from Keynes's point of view without it democracy would face very grave dangers. Hayek simply did not understand that planning required common purpose and justice if it were to serve democratic ends rather than pervert and subvert them. This point is made by Keynes in 'How to pay for the War' which, when read in the context of his letter to Hayek, provides a coherent defence of a democratic directiveness informed by common sense, consent and social justice.

A society which sets out to formulate a 'deliberate plan' has to ensure that social and economic justice and respect for individual freedom of choice, belief, expression and enterprise is an integral part of the exercise of weighing and considering options (IX: 390). Democratic planning takes place in conditions in which (in the language of the *Treatise on Probability*) there is an increasing weight of argument. Choices must be decided with due regard for 'public psychology, social justice and administrative convenience' (IX: 413). He made this clear in May 1943 in discussing the plans for a clearing union when he argued that:

> The economic structure of the post-war world cannot be built in secret. Mrs Sidney Webb ... once defined democracy to me as a form of government the hallmark of which was that it aimed to secure 'the consciousness of consent'. So in the new democracy of nations which after this war will come into existence, heaven helping, to conduct with amity and good sense the common concerns of mankind the instrumentalities we set up must first win for themselves a general consciousness of consent. (XXV: 269)

Planning in a democracy will be necessary at times, especially in conditions of war, and Keynes believed that it was plain common sense that planning which was motivated by considerations of what the public think and feel, by a sense of justice, and by what it is practical to do was fundamentally diffferent to that of a totalitarian society. Hayek seems blind to the facts of the real world, and thus although Keynes agrees with his arguments at many points he naturally cannot accept that all forms of planning – or deliberateness – are the same or that they lead down the same road. The *probability* was that if a society did not exercise a democratic deliberateness then democracy itself might fail and end up in the condition which Hayek rightly castigates. However, public psychology, social justice and administrative convenience cannot be settled in an abstract way. Indeed, it is this very abstract way of thinking which poses the greatest threat to civilization as it had been so plainly manifested in the theory and practice of fascism and communism. *The Road to Serfdom* is applying to politics the same kind of perverse logic which Keynes had earlier disparaged in Hayek's economics: an over-extended chain of abstract reasoning which ends up in an unreal world (XIII: 252). Keynes was proved right. Britain did *not* emerge from the war as a totalitarian society, but one which had brought a practical common sense to bear upon the massive problems which confronted it. In the general election of 1945 people voted for more of the same, and rejected the nonsense of Churchill's argument that a vote for Mr Attlee was a vote for a Hitler incarnate. They voted for social justice and a society which was fairer and more deliberate in its policy making. For Keynes the state in a democratic society has a moral purpose in pursuing justice. This pursuit of justice is what distinguishes the good society from those under the tyranny of dictators or money. His thoughts on how to pay for the war are therefore underpinned by a concept of the good society which includes the Platonic virtues of courage (IX: 373) and public wisdom and restraint (IX: 275–7) as well as justice. These virtues would not spring naturally from a society in which markets, money, and self-interest were unrestrained by directive intelligence. Balance and equilibrium required that society plan in accordance with the ideals of truth, justice, beauty, courage, wisdom, temperance and a love of knowledge (argument). For Keynes these ideas were as real and vital a dimension of human progress as the rule of law. Planning was desirable and indeed necessary in societies in which such virtues were widely shared. And, in such cases planning was perfectly 'safe' and would be unlikely to lead to the kind of dismal fate which Hayek gloomily predicted. Keynes's point is that planning in the hands of those who wish to use the state as an end in itself, rather than as a means to provide the conditions for a society in which individuals are free to determine their own choices and make their own decisions, is just as dangerous as Hayek suggests. Keynes is arguing for a 'moderate' planning in which the state acts to attain a balance of forces and motives. Maintaining such an extreme position that all planning is bad, and that only *laissez-faire* capitalism can provide the conditions for the rule of law, may well open the way for those who hold the 'exact opposite' view (XXVII: 387) on the importance of individualism and freedom under the law.

Hayek is thinking in terms of dualistic and incommensurate opposites: 'planning' and 'democracy'. However Keynes's alchemy finds this way of thinking unhelpful and something downright dangerous. Hayek sees planning and democracy as extreme opposites: they are the sun and moon of the social universe. However Keynes the alchemist is searching for a way of uniting what are in abstract Hayekian terms, 'extremes'.

> You admit here and there that it is a question of knowing where to draw the line. You agree that the line has to be drawn somewhere, and that the logical extreme is

not possible. But you give us no guidance whatever as to where to draw it. In a sense this is shirking the practical issue. It is true that you and I would probably draw it in different places. I should guess that according to my ideas you greatly underestimate the practicability of the middle course. But as soon as you admit that the extreme is possible, and that the line has to be drawn, you are on your own argument, done for, since you are trying to persuade us that as soon as one moves an inch in the planned direction you are necessarily launched on the slippery path which will lead you in due course over the precipice. (XXVII: 386–7)

Keynes realized that the great *coniunctio* of planning and democracy requires us to travel on without our books and theories if we are to attain the uniting of the spirit of capitalism with the new body of liberal democracy as it was emerging from the chaos and darkness of the Second World War. Books of abstract principles and theories will be of no use to us: as he had learnt from his study of Burke as a young man, politics was about expediency and pragmatism, and thinking in terms of absolutes was the quickest road to disaster. The transformation which was now urgently needed required us, like the adepts in search of the philosophers' stone, to rend our books and rely on intuition and feelings (Jung, 1968: 482; Fabricius, 1994: 117). Reason is wholly inadequate to the task of squaring circles. The way is not to be found in books, but in individuals who think and feel free from self-interest and greed, who have moral sensitivity and a sense of truth, beauty, and justice. As the alchemists understood, intuition and experimentation, and not abstract reasoning and books, could bring about transmutation.

> I should say that what we want is not no planning, or even less planning, indeed I should say that we almost certainly want more. But the planning should take place in a community in which as many people as possible, both leaders and followers, wholly share your own moral position. Moderate planning will be safe if those carrying it out are rightly orientated in their own minds and hearts to the moral issue. (XXVII: 387)

Planning did carry risks, but Keynes believed that the alternative posed far more risk to the future of the values which *The Road to Serfdom* expounded.

> What we need, therefore, in my opinion, is not a change in our economic pro-grammes, which would only lead in practice to disillusion with the results of your philosophy; but perhaps even the contrary, namely an enlargement of them. Your greatest danger ahead is the probable practical failure of the application of your philosophy in the US in a fairly extreme form. No, what we need is the restoration of right moral thinking – a return to proper moral values in our social philosophy. (XXVII: 387)

Planning, therefore, was not really the issue, but the morality of the community engaged in planning: 'Dangerous acts can be done safely in a community which thinks and feels rightly, which would be the road to hell if they were executed by those who think and feel wrongly' (XXVII: 387–8).

This difference between Keynes and Hayek on the role of planning in a democratic society makes a good deal more sense when we understand the direction from which both men are coming. For Hayek capitalism is to be understood as a system in which markets and the rule of law are best able to provide for individual freedom and economic efficiency. Keynes does not disagree with this. However, whereas Hayek sees self-interest as the primary force in economics, Keynes's ideas about capitalism and the role of self-interest are more in line with what Marshall sets out in the _Principles_. For Marshall the fundamental characteristic of industrial civilization was what he termed 'deliberateness', rather than competition or selfishness. This involved notions such as 'independence', and 'choosing one's own course', 'self-reliance' and a 'deliberation and yet promptness of choice and judgment'. Industrial society possessed a 'habit of forecasting the future and of shaping one's course with reference to distant aims'. This deliberateness comprises elements of competition and selfishness, but it also involves a trend towards the 'direction of cooperation', 'collective ownership and collective action' (Marshall, 1947: 5). Keynes, too, saw modern industrial civilization as essentially powered by _deliberateness_, rather than by the notion of 'self-interest' which underpinned Benthamism and _laissez-faire_ economics. The key theme which emerges in Keynes after the First World War is that this capacity for deliberateness has to be improved if individualism were to survive. What had to be found was a new wisdom which could show how society could (as he put it in 1925) '_deliberately_' control and direct economic forces 'in the interests of social justice and social stability' (IX: 305). The _General Theory_ was his most complete statement of what that wisdom looked like in theory. As he notes at the close of the _General Theory_, this will involve planning. But this planning is quite in keeping with the essential 'deliberateness' of industrialism and the freedom afforded by individualism. Unlike Hayek, Keynes saw the conflict between 'democracy' and 'planning' as a problem to be worked out using a Newtonian combination of intuition and experimentation rather than Cartesian philosophy. As was the case for Marshall, Keynes saw capitalism as having a propensity for cooperation and collective action as well as for competition and self-interest. He argues, for example, that banking policy on the rate of interest will be insufficient to determine the optimal level of investment and that full employment will require a 'somewhat comprehensive socialization of investment' which will encompass 'all manner of compromises and of devices by which public authority will co-operate with private initiative' (GT: 378). Again, in the field of international trade, competitive struggle does not have to predominate: it is possible for a system of cooperation and 'mutual advantage' to evolve so as to ensure that we do not simply shift the unemployment problems from one country to another. Countries can be good 'neighbours' (GT: 382–3).

With the dragon of *laissez-faire* economics slain in the war, the new spirit of capitalism could be set free. The old attitudes, beliefs and ideas have withered and died. Capitalism is perfected and reborn. This sense of Keynes having squared the circle comes across in some of his last pronouncements on the changes which had come about by the close of the war. In a speech in the House of Lords in December 1945, on the subject of the Bretton Woods and Washington agreements he notes, for example, that the:

> outstanding characteristic of the plans is that they represent the first elaborate and comprehensive attempt to combine the advantages of freedom of commerce with safeguards against the disastrous consequences of a *laissez-faire* system which pays no direct regard to the preservation of equilibrium and merely relies on the eventual working out of blind forces. Here is an attempt to use what we have learned from modern experience and modern analysis, not to defeat, but to implement the wisdom of Adam Smith ... We are attempting a great step torwards the goal of international economic order amidst national diversities of policies. It is not easy to have patience with those who pretend that some of us, who were early in the field to attack and denounce the false premises and false conclusions of unrestricted *laissez-faire* and in particular manifestations in the former gold standard and other currency and commercial doctrines which mistake private licence for public liberty, are now spending their later years in the service of the State to walk backwards and resurrect and re-erect the idols which they played some part in throwing out of the market place. The work of destruction has been accomplished, and the site has been cleared for a new structure. (XXIV: 621–2)

Later in an article published after his death in the *Economic Journal* Keynes gives us an almost religious description of the prospects for the future.

> In the long run more fundamental forces may be at work, if all goes well, tending towards equilibrium, the significance of which may ultimately transcend ephemeral statistics. I find myself moved, not for the first time, to remind contemporary economists that the classical teaching embodied some permanent truths of great significance, which we are liable to-day to overlook because we associate them with other doctrines which we cannot accept without much qualification. There are in these matters deep undercurrents at work, natural forces, one can call them, or even the invisible hand, which are operating towards equilibrium. If it were not so, we could not have got on even so well as we have for many decades. (XXVII: 444)

Keynes's great work was not therefore labouring against the 'natural forces' which operate in the 'undercurrents' of economic life, but was essentially a quest for another 'medicine' (sic) to complement that which had been discovered by the old adepts of the economic arts. He did not come to 'defeat' the old 'wisdom', but to perfect it. The 'classical medicine' will not work effectively without human intervention and controls (especially in the areas of exchange and trade). The achievement of the new international order set out at Bretton Woods and Washington was that it was built on the 'marriage' (sic) of 'necessary expedients to the *wholesome* long-run doctrine' (XXVII: 445). In this regard we find an echo of the new physics. Keynes ultimately sees his theory as complementary to the Newtonian economics of Adam Smith: there was a unity in the apparent contradictions and polarities. We can only wonder what Keynes might have said to Niels Bohr, the proponent of complementarity in quantum theory (Bohr, 1947: 60) had he lived long enough to attend the Newton celebrations. Although mutually exclusive – like wave and particle physics – Keynesian and classical economics are, it appears, both necessary for a complete understanding of the 'deep undercurrents' and 'natural forces' operating in economic equilibrium, even if they cannot be *logically* combined into a single picture or framework.

It is perhaps fitting, therefore, that in one of his last publications – along with his essay on Newton – Keynes should display so much of the alchemical mental apparatus which seemed to inform his life and work. The *Economic Journal* article is replete with imagery and metaphors which are highly suggestive of the alchemical quest: here we find natural forces, the Midas touch, 'medicine', 'marriage', 'conjunctions' 'wholesomeness', and the wisdom of the ancients. And in the closing paragraph a vision of decay giving way to a bright new future:

> No one can be certain of anything in this age of flux and change. Decaying standards of life at a time when our command over the production of material satisfactions is the greatest ever, and a diminishing scope for individual decision and choice at a time when more than before we should be able to afford these satisfactions, are sufficient to indicate an underlying contradiction in every department of our economy. No plans will work for certain in such an epoch. But if they palpably fail, then, of course, we and everyone else will try something different. Meanwhile for us the best policy is to act on the optimistic hypothesis until it has been proved wrong. We shall do well not to fear the future too much. ... We shall run more risk of jeopardizing the future if we are influenced by indefinite fears based on trying to look ahead further than any one can see. (XXVII: 445–6)

The alchemist in Keynes ultimately believed that wholeness was possible: he had none of the puritan's fatalism or subjection to providence. A right analysis, and a slow process of change, could bring about new possibilities. We did not have to take the way the world worked as a fixed mechanical process. There was a better system which was waiting to be released from the old base one. He believed in ideas and experiments which, if carried out with *good will* and in the light of experience, could make a better world. Keynes brought back magic into a world which had undergone generations of disenchantment crushed by the juggernaut of rational self-interest and the heavy weight of crude mechanical ideas of the economy. Keynesian economics taught us that we were no longer helpless in the face of the dark forces which brought so much human misery. Although we could not transmute human nature, Keynes believed that we could transmute capitalism in such a way as to create the conditions in which more people would have the opportunity to realise a fuller and more complete humanity once individualism was purged of its defects. However, underlying this optimism Keynes had a growing sense of foreboding that although good had vanquished evil, and had given birth to new possibilities, there were still malign spirits abroad, and they dwelt in the land of the free and the home of the brave. In the closing months of his life Keynes's fears about the post-war settlement began to echo his feelings about the Versailles Treaty. Significantly, when resigning in 1919 he wrote to Lloyd George saying that 'The battle is lost. I leave the twins to gloat over the devastation of Europe' (cited in Harrod, 1966: 253). At the Savannah conference in March 1946 Keynes uses the same metaphor to describe his fears about the future for Master Fund and Miss Bank when he hoped that there were no malicious fairies around to curse the young babes thus:

> You two brats shall grow up politicians; your every thought and act shall have an arrière-pensée; everything you determine shall not be for its own sake or on its merits but because of something else. If this should happen, then the best that could befall – and that is how it might turn out – would be for the children to fall into an eternal slumber, never to waken or be heard again in the courts and markets of Mankind. (XXVI: 216–7)

By this time he had become profoundly disillusioned with American policy and that of his own government. He returned from the US a sick man, who despite his illness, continued with his daily task of persuasion. As always Keynes, although unhappy about the state of affairs, did not give way to a sense of despondency and hopelessness. Until the last he busied himself with issues of the moment and as is evident from his last official writings, he had no intention of giving up on domestic or international economic policy. Perhaps, as James Meade and others believed, Keynes might have resigned from the Treasury, as in 1919, and resumed his role as Cassandra (Moggridge, 1992: 822). Reading his papers for 1945–6 such an outcome would have not been improbable. He had done as much as he could as an insider, and had he lived another ten years who can doubt but that his energy would have given rise to (at least) another half a dozen volumes to add to the collected works.

However, it is unlikely that later writings would have added much more to our understanding of what Keynes believed. As his great war work amply shows, Keynes was a philosopher of possibility. Bringing this possibility to birth, however, was not a matter of idle theorizing or speculative abstract economics. Keynes believed in total attention to the apparatus of policy making. Like the old alchemists, his job required him to be always in the heat and fumes of the policy process. He was ever watchful and paid the closest attention to making sure that the furnace never went out. He was not an academic 'theorist' or scientist in this sense, because he endeavoured to act upon the world so as to shape it according to what he believed was required. This meant that he would vary his policy recommendations to suit the conditions and problems of the time. His theories were 'eggs' which could incubate this potentiality and could demonstrate how to transform an imperfect economic world. Keynes's aim was to show how, working with the knowledge of natural forces, mankind can make this world more wholesome. Everything is possible if we act on the optimistic hypothesis and seek to release the potentialities of human reason and intuition. This did not mean that policy making should be unrealistic. Throughout the war Keynes was not infrequently to point out the need for realism in what could be achieved (in social welfare or full employment, for example); however, the ever present danger is that policy makers can become unable to act, to do, and to decide. Policy making involved the courage to take risks and experiment in ideas and plans and the creation of a policy making process which allowed for critical thinking, cooperation and trust. Perhaps, however, more than anything else, the war confirmed what had been apparent to him in the 1920s and 1930s, that in destruction, decay, and depression there was always a speck of philosophical gold: crises and disasters were full of opportunities for rebirth, renewal and reform. Given our lack of knowledge, and the uncertainty of existence it required a great many mental and moral qualities – including intelligence, imagination and intuition – to release the good from the powers of the bad. The record of human history sadly shows that such qualities are invariably in short supply, and that 'rare birds' like Keynes are unique events. All the more reason, at a time when we are more pessimistic than ever about the possibilities of human progress, for us to listen more carefully to what Keynes had to say and think about his contemporary relevance.

6.   Out of the ashes: Keynes's policy science

All things on earth have been given into the hands of man.
And they are given into his hands in order that he may bring them to the highest development ... Nothing created is beyond man's fathoming. And everything has been created to the end that man may not remain idle ... For though iron is iron, it is not itself a plowshare or a carpenters's ax. Although corn means bread, it is not ready to be consumed as bread. So it is with all products ... Let us not be idlers or dreamers, but always at work ... The proper way resides in work and action, in doing and producing.
(Paracelsus, 1988: 108, 111)

Workmen, up from your beds! Up, every man,
and make my bold designs reality!
Take up your tools! To work with spade and shovel –
what's been marked off must be completed now!
(Goethe, *Faust*, 1994: 290)

Chastened, together,
we try once more,
Ain't that so ...?
(Michael Tippett, *The Icebreak*)

The Keynesian age now seems a distant memory to be told by the old as a tale to the young gathered by the camp fires at the twilight of the twentieth century. Some who tell the tale recall the marvels done in his name, others how Keynes was the father of all our discontents and others (including the present author) that it was never really a Keynesian age at all. It may well be that, as Beenstock predicts, in 2036 Keynes's *General Theory* will be 'lost in the oblivion of history' (Beenstock, 1986: 135). However, as even his most severe critics argue, Keynes remains one of the greatest economists of all time (Friedman, 1986: 47) and it is therefore more likely that his theories will continue to be used and abused long into the future. Varieties of 'New Keynesians' and 'Post Keynesians' labour at the task of making Keynes's economics more relevant to present economic conditions. However, as a political scientist I believe that Keynes's continuing relevance may well be found less in his economics as such, but in terms of his contribution to showing us how to think about knowledge, uncertainty, change and policy making in a monetary society. In other words, that Keynes's ideas have much to offer as a way of thinking about policy making, even if we are less certain as to what his economics can provide by way of prescriptions for economic management.

Keynes's economics is a way of thinking about problems and their remedies in an uncertain world. We are confronted in the *General Theory* with a seemingly hopeless prospect of making decisions in situations in which we often have very little or no information; and wherein we are subjected to volatile forces which can so easily bring about an increase in human misery, falling confidence and an inability to act. It is a world in which human beings will readily seek to maintain a sense of security by holding on to their money wealth rather than create productive forms of enterprise. Keynes shows how the problems of uncertainty in the modern world have been made worse by the changes which have taken place in the values and institutional arrangements of capitalist societies which mean that the economic system can no longer attain the automatic balance of market forces as classical economic mechanics believed. Keynes's economics is imbued with Newtonian dualism: science and alchemy. It shows that policy makers inhabit a world which contains both immutable forces which in the long run tend towards a form of equilibrium, but at the same time this equilibrium is punctuated by periods when the forces do not balance out and human reason, imagination and action are needed to give direction. As a policy science, therefore, Keynes's economics turns our attention to the problems of *risk, uncertainty* and *ignorance* and the issue of how best to manage human affairs so as to ensure that decision making and action are informed by intelligence and good judgment. Faced with the dark forces of time and ignorance, however, Keynes does not accept the nihilism of doing nothing. Ideas matter because human thought shapes and gives meaning to the world: the future can be what we, as a community, choose to make it. Keynes shows us that we cannot know the future as it is infinitely uncertain, but we can know the values which give the future its meaning. A prominent 'Post-Keynesian', Paul Davidson, has expressed this in alchemical terms when he argues that, contrary to the neoclassical view of a certain 'immutable' external reality, Keynes's economics is based upon an uncertain, transmutable reality in which some aspects of the economic future are *created* by human action and enterprise. In the Newtonian realm of immutable economic laws human beings have little capacity to change the future: policy makers can only make things worse if they seek to interfere in predictable and predetermined market forces. However, in the alchemical realm – for which the *General Theory* and its subsequent clarifications is still the best guide – the world is a very uncertain and volatile place. It is a world which works in part in accordance with Newtonian economic postulates, but not in the *whole* and at all times and in all conditions. Information in this alchemical ('nonergodic') realm is imperfect and probability is inadequate for many decisions, however, as Davidson argues:

> For important economic decisions involving investment, the accumulation of wealth and finance ... agents are dealing with an uncertain, nonprobablistic creative economic external reality in which today's human actions can create a new and different future reality. Transmutable reality implies the possibility that there is a permanent, positive role for government in designing policies and institutions to provide results preferable to those that would be generated by competitive markets in a nonergodic environment. Through institutional and policy changes society can intelligently control and improve the performance of the economy in which we live compared to what would occur under a laissez-faire, competitive market system operating in a transmutable economic universe. (Davidson, 1995: 111)

Keynes's economics is therefore an optimistic way of thinking about the world. Confronted by the consequences of uncertainty and our lack of knowledge it remains convinced of the possibilities and potentialities of human reason in the face of the unreasonableness of human nature and the uncertainty of existence. Keynes's emphasis on ignorance, the limits of human knowledge and calculations, the role of 'whim, sentiment and chance' (GT: 163), uncertainty, indeterminancy, and the discursive notion of probability implies that his economics lends itself to a post-modern reading (Amariglio and Ruccio, 1995). But perhaps the designation of post-modern is less appropriate than that of 'pre-modern'. Keynes's economics, whilst sharing something of the 'nihilism' of post-modernism, faces in quite the opposite direction. Keynes's quest was for knowledge, but not *certain* knowledge of the 'modernist' variety. It was a quest in the footsteps of Newton, and not Descartes. Keynes's alchemy was a fusion of the scientific square and the personal circle (Klamer, 1995: 320), a combination of intuition and rationality. In this regard, Keynes may be read as a post-modern 'text', but Keynes's belief, that knowledge can be used to overcome the 'dark forces of time and ignorance', when considered in the context of his adherence to a Moorean view of the good suggests that Keynes's economics might be more at home in the Cambridge of the 1690s rather than the 1990s. There is a contradiction or paradox at the heart of Keynes: how can an economics constructed out of the assertion that we can know very little, that we often times simply do not know, arrive at a way of thinking which believes in the vital role of a directive intelligence in managing economic forces? Alan Coddington was essentially right in arguing that the logic of Keynesian principles leads towards an inescapable nihilism (Coddington, 1976; 1982; 1983): but the alchemist would not see a problem in a paradox such as the economics of uncertainty forming the foundation of a belief in economic management. The alchemist inhabited a world of contradictions and opposites: of such material were the dreams of philosophical stones compounded. And here we have the essence of Keynes's pre-modernism, for contradictions were not to be resolved at what may be described as a theoretical level, but in the mind and actions of those economists with the wings of eagles (Marshall) and butterflies (Malthus): the 'rare birds' who themselves embodied the working out of contradictions and the combining of opposites. Salvation came not from science (Midgley, 1992), but from the magus: a hero from the magical realm of intuition and introspection rather than a 'hero' of knowledge from the age of the enlightenment (Lyotard, 1984: xxiv). Hence, Keynes argues, from the *Treatise on Probability* onwards, that we know so very little *but* was able to see the role which human intuition and intelligence can play in responding to and shaping an uncertain and changing world. In all the situations to which Keynes applied his philosophy we always see the mind of someone who believed that clear thinking can make a better world. Human beings do *not* have to be victims of their own failings or of forces outside their control. In the case of the love of money, for example, he believed that it was necessary and possible to organize society so that other values could operate on human affairs. Mankind did *not* have to be a slave to base instincts formed out of the experience of potty training. Uncertainty and ignorance did not mean that we could not be clear about our values and ends or that we were incapable of making good judgments about the future, nor that the future was beyond our control. His essay on Bonar Law, for example, expresses much of what he thought about the dangers of policy making which addressed only the surface level of problems. Bonar Law is described as having a 'distrust' of 'any intellectual process which proceeds from more than one or two steps ahead, or any emotional enthusiasm which grasped at an intangible object' (IX: 33). Politics for this type of personality was little more than a game of chess which was played by just concentrating on those few moves which could be forseen.

> on the assumption that the pieces visible on the board constituted the whole premises of the argument, that any attempt to look far ahead was too hypothetical and difficult to be worth while, and that one was playing the game *in vacuo*, with no ulterior purpose except to make the right moves in that particular game. (IX: 34)

Policy makers with his mentality have a 'distrust of intellectualist probings into unrealized possibilities' which may lead to a perilous combination of 'great caution and pessimism about the chances of the immediate situation with a considerable recklessness about what may happen eventually' (IX: 35). Policy making had to be pragmatic and unprincipled (in a Burkean sense) because the world was uncertain and changing, and our knowledge is so very inadequate, but it also had to be open to the 'unrealized possibilities' and wary of conventional, or ruling opinion. As in the case of the 1919 peace settlement, when decision making is driven by some of the baser human motivations, decent common sense goes out the window and men give themselves up to 'passion and greed' and become blind to the real facts and their self-interest (II: xxxv).

The factors which were at work in 1919 seemed to Keynes to be operating twenty years on as he makes clear in a piece commenting on the international crisis in 1938:

> Our troubles are of our own making and our errors were obvious at the time when we made them ... But we are suffering today from the worst of all diseases, the paralysis of will. Nothing can be more dangerous than that. We have become incapable of constructive policy or decisive action. We are without conviction, without foresight, without a resolute will to protect what we care for ... Our strength is great, but our statesmen have lost the capacity to appear formidable. It is in that loss that our greatest danger lies. Our power to win a war may depend on increased armaments. But our power to avoid a war depends much more on our recovering that capacity to appear formidable, which is a quality of will and demeanour. (XXVIII: 103–4)

Action needs certain qualities of mind and a keen sense of 'good and evil and between right and wrong' (XXVIII: 104). If we do not have a clear grasp of our ideas and values and fail to formulate judgments when confronted by the turbulance of events and the haunting fears of insecurity and blind ignorance, policy makers are *more likely* to become paralysed and incapable of action to overcome the problems and evils which beset us. Events march on 'uninfluenced and unaffected by the cerebrations of statesmen' (II: 3). It is because human decision making takes place in the context of uncertainty, ignorance and volatility that Keynes argues we have to be open to those other aspects of human intelligence which are not purely rational and which have no place in the mechanistic paradigm. In analysing and in seeking to improve decision making, therefore, we must give close consideration to the role of human intuition and imagination. The danger Keynes identified was that in complex and volatile circumstances when we simply cannot know what will happen, or what the consequences of our actions will be, human beings will have recourse to falling back on conventional wisdom, mass or group opinions, assumptions about the future being like the past, or may choose to ignore the potential of sudden and unexpected change. Above all, human beings may labour under the Benthamite illusion that we know or that we can always calculate costs, benefits, risks and probabilities. But, says Keynes, this is a very dubious basis on which to make decisions: the world is not a machine, but an organic, unstable and unknowable place. Given these facts of real life, intuition and imagination are absolutely vital if we are to be able to exercise any influence on shaping the future so that it embodies the values which we wish to promote. The problem is that intuitive and imaginative capacities vary considerably between human beings. People like Newton, who could operate on both the rational and extra-rational levels, are extremely rare birds.

Keynes's economics bridged the chasm between values and public policy which had widened in the modern era. His great achievement, therefore, was, as Fitzgibbons argues, to reconnect values and policy in a way that had not been done since the the pre-modern era.

> Aristotle based politics on ethics, but the moderns base politics on the raw facts of political struggle. The arguments can be put in terms of Plato's myth about giants who tear up hard lumps of fact and hurl them at the gods. When the modern era began the giants declared they had won the battle, and that heaven had disappeared. Moore declared that the battle was a standoff, that the gods still had high heaven although they could not help the earth. Keynes concluded that good ideas and values conquer over material forces, that the gods could win both heaven and earth. (Later he was to qualify this conclusion.) (Fitzgibbons, 1988: 47)

True, policymakers cannot know about what will happen in the world, but they can know about how they think and feel. It is this clarification of inner mental states which constitutes the essence of Keynes's approach to policy making. The more we cannot know about the real world the more do we risk becoming blind to what is happening, or are victims of optical illusions, or fatalism.

> We need by an effort of mind to elucidate our own feelings ... In the field of action reformers will not be successful until they can steadily pursue a clear and definite object with their intellects and their feelings in tune ... We need a new set of convictions which spring naturally from a candid examination of our own inner feelings in relation to the outside facts. (IX: 294)

In an irreligious age the state had to take up a new responsibility to ease the sense of insecurity which was an inevitable condition of human existence. Religion – whether Christianity or Marxism – could reduce uncertainty by proclaiming a faith in a new heaven or a new earth. In an irreligious world we had to find another moral system – a new set of convictions – which might serve to control the love of money which was at the bottom of so many human problems and which also held the key to releasing human potential. Keynes's belief was that this new moral science was to be found in the alchemy of economics. In this belief he was to be proven tragically wrong. If there is any hope it must be in the recasting of economics to take account of the moral, psychological and other dimensions of economic and social life. Perhaps, just perhaps, the alchemists of modern econometrics will eventually be regarded as simply the latest in a long line of fraudulent purveyors of algebra. The present author has to confess that he sees little sign that economists have much interest in the task of making economics into the kind of moral science we find in Marshall or Keynes. The job of formulating a new moral science that deals with human instrospection, values and instincts, and which does not overemphasize the economic problem may very well fall to non-economists and to those outside the halls of academe. In the case of academics this direction may be found in the writings of scholars such as Robert Lane and Amitai Etzioni whose work has shown the way forward to creating an interdisciplinary approach to economics which is as enlightening as it is inspiring. Etzioni's *The Moral Dimension* (1988) and Lane's *The Market Experience* (1991) for example offer an exciting prospect of an economics which addresses moral issues in the context of sociology, psychology, political science and other disciplines.

Keynes, of course, was always prepared to investigate 'non-academic' ideas, theories and 'cranks' in order to find out if human intuition had discovered or confirmed truths overlooked by scholars. He was also very interested in understanding the psychology of the businessman and financial markets. The 'alchemist' Marcel Labordère and Oswald Falk, for example, both had a considerable impact on Keynes's economic thinking. With this in mind, and in the spirit of Keynes, the arguments of George Soros may have more relevance for stimulating new ideas than those of respected academics. Soros is one of the most succesful investors of recent times. In 1993 his fund had assets of over $6 billion dollars and he is most famous for having broke the bank of England and forcing the British government to abandon its membership of the EMS in 1992. Significantly from the standpoint of the present author, Soros's book is entitled *The Alchemy of Finance* – a volume written out of a fancy to provide the equivalent of the *General Theory* for the 1980s. Soros argues that the greatest error of social science was to seek to imitate the natural sciences. His theory is predicated on the idea that alchemy provides a more satisfactory basis for social science – as well as for making money.

> Social scientists have gone to great lengths trying to maintain the unity of method but with remarkably little success. Their endeavors have yielded little more than a parody of natural science. In a sense, the attempt to impose the methods of natural science on social phenomena is comparable to the efforts of alchemists who sought to apply the methods of magic to the field of natural science. But while the failure of the alchemists was well-nigh total, social scientists have managed to make a considerable impact on their subject matter. Situations which have thinking participants may be impervious to the methods of natural science, but they are susceptible to the methods of alchemy. The thinking of participants, exactly because it is not governed by reality, is easily influenced by theories. In the field of natural phenomena, scientific method is effective only when its theories are valid; but in social political and economic matters, theories can be effective without being valid. Whereas alchemy has failed as natural science, social science can succeed as alchemy. Scientific method seeks to understand things as they are,

while alchemy seeks to bring about a desired state of affairs ... Social phenomena are different [from natural phenomena]: they have thinking participants. Events do not obey laws that operate independently of what everybody thinks. On the contrary, the participants' thinking is an integral part of the subject matter. This creates an opening for alchemy that was absent in the sphere of natural science. Operational success can be achieved without attaining scientific knowledge. (Soros, 1994: 38–303)

Financiers, he suggests, exist in an essentially alchemical sphere, and Soros argues that social science ought to accept that it too inhabits the same realm wherein beliefs about reality alter and change that reality. Social science, therefore, has much to learn from the old alchemists and the 'New Physics'. Society is not a machine driven by blind forces, but is a product of mental states and human interaction. The role of social science is not simply to observe the machine, but to shape values, promote reform and explore possibilities and alternatives. From Keynes's point of view the economist did not describe and explain economic conditions and problems: theories were part of the interplay between the real world and human beings. Keynesian alchemy is (like the Royal Art) about participating in the object of study. Systems observed in conditions of human knowledge – however incomplete – are not machines, but a set of organic relationships. Theory and practice are interconnected in ways which are non-analysable, and non-causal, but are nevertheless real even though they can be only fully understood intuitively, rather than through rational calculation. Because of the organic nature of existence human consciousness – opinions, knowledge, feelings, facts and theories – can and do alter and transform the world inside our heads and the world outside our front door. Thus the worse fate that can befall modern civilization is to allow the rude mechanicals and technicians to legitimate the situation in which policy makers are deemed to be powerless in the face of a supposedly atomistic reality in which there are no alternatives and no possibilities. The problem that Keynes identified is that human beings can so easily become blinded to the possibilities of things by a 'way of thinking' which is mechanical and linear rather than organic and open to complexity. This is why mathematics is so very dangerous: it can give the illusion of knowledge, certainty and control, when in reality we have far less knowledge than we suppose, we are subject to considerable uncertainty, and we delude ourselves if we think we can control a system which is inherently unstable. Mechanical thinking tends towards thinking in terms of parts rather than wholes. Consider, for example, a situation in which we use one measurement of performance (a performance indicator) upon which to base decisions about the whole of an institution. In measuring a part we may very well fail to appreciate how a given organization works as a whole. Mathematical knowledge of this kind may mislead us into thinking about a problem in a manner which distorts rather than illuminates. An initial assumption may lead inexorably to an erroneous conclusion at the end of a straight line: the shortest distance between two mistakes. Mathematical and mechanical reasoning carries with it the risk that we may be freezing our perceptions into a fixed, inflexible set of conventional wisdoms which serve us ill when the world does not conform to our mental geometry. Hence Keynes suggests in the *General Theory* that we often need to think in terms of a non-Euclidean geometry for a world which *does* have curved surfaces. In economics and politics mechanism and linearity are endemic because of money. Money, as Marshall argues, is useful to students of society because it is a convenient measure. Money is a store of value and a means of exchange, but it is also a way of thinking about the world: it constitutes a way of transacting exchange, but also of transacting and mediating reality. Money can provide a way of measuring and expressing value and consequently it can construct an image of the world which is knowable in a mathematical sense, but nevertheless is the projection of a monetary illusion. Money can therefore blind decision makers and induce a state of myopia: we may end up seeing no further than the accountant's financial data. In such circumstances we are visted by the Midas curse: money has become the totality of what we see and touch. The existence of a monetary society means that we have to be constantly alive to the dangers of mechanism and linearity and open to the potentiality of what cannot be measured, calculated or predicted. The over-emphasis on calculation as the basis for decision can lead to a shortsightedness in thinking only of costs and benefits and monetary gain (short-termism), but a remarkable and totally misplaced confidence in our ability to forecast the long term. Making judgments in money terms can lead to a preoccupation with the present in the face of an uncertain future, whilst the belief in economic modelling can induce a sense of certainty about a future which is far too complex to be modelled with any real certainty. This situation is made more complex by the fact that these ideas about the future enter into the future itself by the decisions we make predicated on our supposed knowledge of the future. A given policy can therefore have consequences far into the future and serve to constrain choices long after the decision was made in the context of a set of misguided assumptions predicated on ideas and perceptions formed in the past. As his own work demonstrated, policy is difficult to change because of the way in which it comes to embody a framework of ideas that were formed in the past and the past is invariably a more secure and certain country than the future. However, when policy making is structured by the idea that a given framework is the outcome of something like scientific knowledge then the problem of change is all the more problematic as the weight of evidence in favour of an alternative policy may be slow in persuading decision makers to think differently.

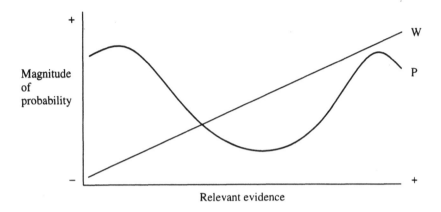

Figure 6.1   The weight of evidence

Thus an important aspect of a Keynesian approach to policy making is contained in the *Treatise on Probability* and in chapter 12 of the *General Theory*: the relationship between the weight of evidence, probability and confidence (we have illustrated this in Figure 6.1). Keynes postulated that increasing relevant evidence serves to increase the weight of argument (W), although it may serve to diminish or augment the magnitude of probability (P). Increasing evidence may, over time, increase or diminish the probability that a given action may be all for the good or bad; however, as more knowledge becomes available which is relevant to a given problem, the growing weight of evidence means that we feel more confident about what we believe to be true or the probable outcome. From this point of view we cannot know what the future will hold, *but we can be confident about the possibilities of the future.* We cannot have certain knowledge, *but we can have a sense of confidence about the rationality of our beliefs and opinions.* Policy making in a rational sociey should not be predicated on the illusion of certain knowledge, but on the reality of ignorance and uncertainty. It is the 'W' line in Figure 6.1 – the line of increasing weight of evidence – which actually demarcates the liberal from the totalitarian society feared by Hayek. The liberal society is one in which policy makers are actively seeking to increase the sum of relevant evidence upon which it can formulate judgments. Keynes's economics reminds us of the limitations of rational decision making predicated on information gathering and improving the knowledge base. Increasing weight of argument may well result in conflicting data such that we are confronted by 'six of one and half a dozen of the other'. In the *Treatise on Probability* Keynes gives an example of this kind of dilemma involving the decision to take an umbrella on a walk when the 'barometer is high, but the clouds are black' (TP: 32). In such situations we can only fall back upon our intuition and 'animal spirits' – otherwise we stand there 'uming' and 'ahing' unable to make up our minds and *do* something. More and more information may not be much of a help in enabling us to make and implement decisions. Indeed, getting additional data may simply be a cunning device to avoid and justify not doing anything. Furthermore, increasing weight of argument may give us a feeling of increasing ignorance: after all the evidence we may conclude that we know less at the end than we did at the start. Sometimes, therefore, decision making is less to do with acting on knowledge, so much as putting our ignorance to one side and getting on with it. For Keynes the entrepreneur was a special kind of decision making animal who had the confidence to act out of ignorance, as opposed to the sort of human being who refuses to act because of a knowledge of their own ignorance. If a society is to become wealthy in real terms, rather than in money terms, the state has the responsibility to formulate policies to create an institutional environment in which investment and risk taking takes place in spite of ignorance, not because of knowledge. A society which has little confidence in its future will be unlikely to promote the entrepreneurial culture in which risk taking is encouraged and in which long term investment can lay the basis of a creative and productive economy.

This takes us to the question of how policy making should proceed so as to create a society which is able to plan and act out of ignorance. To begin with Keynes would argue that a society has to be clear about its values, and what it considers the good society to be. A community has to think and feel correctly, as he told Hayek: public opinion has to be formed, enlightened and expressed. We might think of this in terms of mental experiments, that is to say, a community has to be open to debate and active in thinking about its future. This involves an interplay of 'inside' and 'outside' opinion, but also of academic and non-academic claims to knowledge. Keynes did not believe in the university as an ivory tower disengaged from the real world. He regarded them as institutions which had a central role in and *responsibility* for promoting informed and *critical* public debate. In addition to mental experimentation Keynes also argued for social experimentation as ways of learning about what kind of institutional arrangements should be developed for combatting time and ignorance. Policy making in a liberal society called for an experimental approach to human problems, so that the community could get a better understanding of its values, intuitions and feelings. On an economic level this means that we should experiment with institutional forms in such a way that we can learn from little errors rather than suffer from big mistakes. Thus the aim of public policy should be to create economic, social and political institutions which can best promote an increase in argumentative knowledge and confidence necessary for human beings to realize their individual and collective potential. This involves the organization of argument so as to cultivate a society which, although not possessed of certainty, is better able to evaluate policy propositions, or theories about problems (see, for example, Fischer and Forrester, 1993). A society which actively seeks to increase the weight of arguments may not feel more knowledgeable, but it will feel more confident about investing – time, energy, physical and human resources, and money – in the future. It will see the future as less determined by past statistical trends (XIV: 287), and more as something which is formed in the here and now by the state of confidence and expectations. A society which lacks self-confidence may be compared to an individual who lacks self-confidence. Such a society will, for example, be risk averse; timid about change; will have a propensity to fall back on convention; will be afraid of the future; will more likely be a victim of circumstances and events; will feel insecure; will prefer to dwell in the past; and it will probably be rather inward looking and self-focused. Although Keynes was critical about the use of statistics and mathematical ways of thinking he was a great advocate of organizing knowledge so that it could improve decision making. In our own time this issue of organizing knowledge to create the confidence necessary for a risk-taking, investment-orientated democratic society needs to be given a high priority in the political and research agenda. Above all, this means that we should address the design of institutional arrangements which are appropriate to decision making in the context of risk, ignorance and uncertainty in a monetary society. From the perspective of Keynes's economics this means that experiments in institutional design must involve arriving at a mix of organizational forms (markets, hierarchies and networks) which can best promote the trust and cooperation necessary for the enhancement of human creativity in a world where we simply do not know, and where increasing knowledge may make us less confident, more uncertain and more confused, but yet we are constrained to make decisions and act. This mix will vary over time and over different kinds of problems. However, whatever the mix, managing in an uncertain world will involve the use of a deliberative, directive intelligence: in other words planning. On the face of it the idea of planning in conditions of uncertainty is something of a contradiction. Given that, as Keynes argues, we cannot know, how can we plan? Keynes's response to Hayek was that we can safely plan when (as a community) we think and feel correctly. Planning in this sense involves the creation of a society which is open to informed and critical debate. In this kind of society planning is about exploring the possibilities of the future in the light of increasing weight of argument. Keynes envisaged a society in which the weight of evidence was not static, but increasing. Hayek's notion of planning was very different: a condition in which the state laid claim to know and scientifically direct the economy and society to a defined goal or purpose. Keynes's idea of planning was the complete opposite of this. Planning in a liberal society should be planning without purpose: planning without great leaps forward, and without science. Thus, in thinking about the future we must ensure that decision making is informed by imagination and intuition and in which mathematical, psuedo scientific ways of thinking do not distort our perception by creating the delusion of control and certainty. What follows from this is that forecasting should not be regarded as wholly quantitative an activity, but must aim to incorporate a good deal of qualitative, or creative imagination. Forecasting has to be concerned with clarifying what could or ought to be, rather than what might or will be. Forecasting free of mathematical obfuscation should be a way less of predicting the future, so much as part of the process wherein we configure or project its possibilities. Planning in the Keynesian sense is therefore a form of learning cycle, rather than a linear project of defining ends and means predicated on a calculation of costs and benefits. The goal in planning is ultimately to generate new ways of thinking: it should not serve to entrench a view of the world, but work so as to challenge conventional wisdom, the dominant paradigms and the prevailing orthodoxies. (It is, in Argyris and Schön's sense (1978), a double-loop, rather than single-loop process.) Another factor to consider is that, as the *Treatise on Probability* argues, in thinking about possibilities we have to think in terms of wholes, rather than parts. Planning has to be mindful of the organic nature of existence. As Keynes showed in the *General Theory*, the economy has to be understood as a set of relationships which interact and change one another and small changes in one part of the system can have massive consequences for another, seemingly unrelated, part of the economy as a whole. In this regard Keynes's economics has much in common wth the ideas of Bohm (1980), Prigogine and Stengers (1984), Capra (1983) and others in stressing the need for thinking in terms of: wholes and systems; escaping from mechanical, linear and atomistic analogies; appreciating that the world is unpredictable and unstable. Like the old alchemists, proponents of the new science are keenly aware of the relationship between chaos, instability and transformation. For Keynes the uncertainty and instability of the world did not lead him to the view that human beings were powerless. Keynes's message is it does not follow that because we cannot know, we cannot act or do. Human beings are not merely helpless parts of the whole. We are not doomed to reacting to natural forces and laws. For Keynes we are active participants in shaping and creating the future, and if we are to take part in this construction of possible realities we have to abandon mechanistic, linear ways of looking and things and make use of our intuitive and imaginative faculties in exercising reason and logic. In short, planning must be an alchemical enterprise: it must seek to transmute values and realize their potentialities (see Table 6.1).

Table 6.1   Planning as science and planning as alchemy

Planning as science	Planning as alchemy
Predicated on knowledge and certainty, regularity and stability. Views planning in Mannheimian terms: the harnessing of systematized knowledge.	Predicated on ignorance and uncertainty, unpredictability and flux. Views planning in Habermasian terms: as an exercise in argument and communicative rationality.
Sees planning as to do with control and increasing certainty.	Sees planning as a form of experimentation to increase confidence.
Organizational preference for hierarchy and state.	Preference for a pluralistic mix of organizational forms.
Predominant role of mathematics and calculation.	Aware of the limits of calculation. Recognizes the vital role of intuition and imagination.
Benthamite in inspiration. Believes in measurement of costs and benefits.	Anti-Benthamite. Regards measurement of costs and benefits with profound suspicion.
Aims to pick winners.	Aims to promote risk and enterprise.
Thinks about big change. Aims at being rationally comprehensive.	Thinks about the problem of moral risk of big change. Based on the need for logical incrementalism.
Is preoccupied with economic growth.	Is concerned with the arts of life: quality, rather than quantity.
Has an objectivist/positivist view of knowledge.	Sees knowledge as active in transforming reality and the way people think and feel.
Tends towards mechanistic, linear and atomistic thinking.	Seeks organic and non-linear ways of thinking.
Views the future as predictable.	Views the future as shapable.
Sees planning as managing interests.	Sees planning as persuasion: transmuting values and changing ideas about the future.

The economics of Marshall, Mill and Keynes was a social science which was infused with a belief in the need for mankind to be active in shaping the future. This involved understanding trends, but also in clarifying human expectations about the future and illuminating the possibilities of the future contained in the present. Hence, for example, Marshall (1947: 782) urged his readers to use their imagination and make 'playful excursions' (sic) into utopias very different from the real world (in Marshall's case economic chivalry) so as to illuminate problems and solutions. In modern day terms this may involve the enlargement of decision making so as to encompass the possibilities of forms of *communicative rationality* on the lines first expounded by a contemporary of Keynes, the great American political scientist Harold Lasswell and which has been developed in more recent years in the work of policy analysts influenced by Habermas and other critical theorists (see Parsons, 1995). This would also place *uncertainty* and *ignorance* back at the centre of attention for both scholars and policy makers. The social sciences *qua* policy sciences may therefore be viewed in the light of Keynes's economics as tools for *imagining* and realizing the possibilities of a money economy. In practice policy sciences should serve as a kind of interface between the probable and the possible. That is, they should be concerned to facilitate *dialogue* and *conversation* and with the promotion of knowledge about social, economic and political life, but also with the promotion of a society in which human beings feel more *confident* about the possibilities of argument and persuasion. If all this sounds hopelessly idealistic and totally impractical we should again pay heed to Keynes's (and Marshall's) belief that social scientists have much to learn from the study of the ordinary business of life and how business men and women think. In respect of planning, therefore, academics might turn their attention away from the rather futile debate about planning as it was framed by Hayek and look at how business plans in conditions of uncertainty and turbulence. One method which approximates closely to an approach which is conversational or alchemical is *scenario planning* as advocated by Pierre Wack (1985a, 1985b) and Kees van der Heijden (1996) and used by many successful large corporations. A Keynesian policy making process, aiming at increasing confidence, rather than certainty, should be alive to the possibilities of strategic planning on 'conversational' lines as a new institutional and societal method of decision making and future shaping. Such ideas, it seems to the present author, have considerable implications for redesigning policy analysis as less of a pseudo-scientific control exercise, than one which is about learning, participation and cooperative dialogue as a way of thinking about forecasting and planning (on this point see: de Leon, 1992; Churchman, 1971; and Fischer, 1995).

The future is not a given or distant reality – 'out there' – but something which we must strive to make. The fact that we cannot know what the future holds can lead to what Keynes saw as the Buridan syndrome: paralysis of individual and collective will to act in the face of the need to decide (XXIX: 294). Keynes saw time and uncertainty as the central problems of human existence. They required that mankind display a preparedness for risk, exterprise, boldness, imagination, and intelligence. The greatest of evils was the view propagated by the Ricardos of this word which sees human beings as powerless in the face of a great mechanical universe driven by blind forces which we can know, but not perfect. Malthus did not accept this dismal science: and neither did J.S. Mill, Marshall or Keynes. The future is in our heads and because it exists in the minds of human beings, rather than out there waiting for us, it is in our hands to make, mend, mould and mar. Progress, as Marshall argued, resides in the development of a capacity for 'forecasting the future and preparing for the next step', and of acquiring a greater 'telescopic' power of 'realizing the future' and making choices about the present and future clearer (Marshall, 1947: 248; 680). As McKenna and Zannoni maintain, the interaction of wholes and parts in Keynes suggests that:

> the future depends on the meaning human beings create, and meaning is the result of individual choice in the context of social interaction. Because meaning is potentially limitless, the future, particularly the more distant future, is also limitless. It is not the case that the far distant future is sometimes more knowable than at other times. It is always simply unknowable. What does change, rather, is the meaning people attach to this fact, and hence the manner in which people's behaviour responds to this uncertainty. (McKenna and Zannoni, 1993: 403)

We should therefore beware of falling into the Benthamite trap of assuming that rational calculation is the best way to make decisions: intuition and imagination have the most crucial part to play. Keynes would have been dismayed, for example, at the way in which the Benthamite calculation of costs and benefits and its translation into 'New Public Sector Management' has come to set the agenda for so much of governmental reform over the past decade. The current obsession with performance measurement, indicators, business culture and 'sound finance' in the public sector must inevitably ill serve the attainment of those values and ends which cannot be measured, or whose benefit resists calculation. Against this belief in quantification and the over-valuation of 'economic' aspects of decision making, Keynesianism stresses the importance of balancing the demands of economy, efficiency and 'value for money', against those of ethics, aesthetics and the arts of life. The most pernicious aspect of modern public sector management is the way in which the production of 'facts' and dubious figures relating to governmental performance and service delivery is the illusion which it creates of a world which can be rendered *more* knowable and *more* certain. Keynes's whole point is that this Benthamite approach to the human condition is dangerous because it constructs a world which is too concrete and *unreal,* and which distorts and imprisons our understanding of a real world which is infinitely more complex. To base a theory of government on the predicate that (as public choice theorists argue) human beings are simply motivated by self-interest is, as Marshall demonstrated long ago, foolish, as it is wrong. There are more things in the human heart than are dreamt of by the Benthamites of the ancient or modern variety: needs and wants which encompass benevolence, love, trust, cooperation, community, companionship, justice, and beauty. If we are to 'reinvent' and repair democratic governance after the damage done by the belief in 'the market', then an appreciation of these values must assume the leading position in the research and governmental agenda.

In the end, where Keynesianism failed was in assuming that merely adjusting the economic macro factors would be enough. Hence, the most important lessons to be learnt from Keynes's economics is how to think about economic progress. No area of Keynesian economic policy has been so badly understood as the issue of growth. Keynes did not envisage progress in purely economic terms. Indeed, solving the economic problem was merely the first stage of progressing to a more balanced world in which the passion for money would have cooled. What Keynes wanted to see was a world in which more and more people were capable of pursuing truth, beauty, love, human relationships and knowledge, rather than ever increasing consumer goods to feed an insatiable desire for superiority (IX: 326) and a feeling of security. Here the contrast with Weber's argument in *The Protestant Ethic* is telling. Weber believed that the puritan inheritance was an iron cage from which he saw no escape. He recounts how Goethe's Faust sought redemption through renunciation and in the realization that the 'age of full and beautiful humanity … can no more be repeated in the course of our development than can the flower of the Athenian culture of antiquity' (Weber, 1976: 181). Modern capitalism, woven as it is from the threads of protestant ethics, cannot easily throw aside the 'light cloak' of caring about external goods as did the puritan saints. Fate had decreed, said Weber, that the 'cloak should become an iron cage' (Weber, 1976: 181). And, in conclusion, Weber confessed that he was at a loss to know who would remain locked in this cage, or what prophets might arise to offer the promise of freedom. Perhaps it was Keynes's ultimate conceit or naivety that he believed that more and more people would be able to get out of the iron cage and that he had found a way to transform the iron bars into a doorway of possibility which would owe less to Goethian striving than to Cambridge economic alchemy.

As I noted in the preface to this book, coming as I did to the *General Theory* via Marshall and the *Essays on Persuasion*, I could never understand how economists and policy makers had arrived at the notion of economic growth which was so all pervasive in the so called Keynesian era. As far as the issue of the relation of economics to human progress is concerned, Keynes was very much in line with the ideas of Ruskin, Marshall and J.S. Mill, and if we do not appreciate this we end up in a terrible muddle in theoretical and policy terms. Keynes, like Mill, was trying to find a way to resolve the conflict between socialism and capitalism. He was concerned with how government intervention can be used to extend human individualism and freedom. Mill's economics encompassed a vision of human beings who were capable of higher pleasures, cooperation and the pursuit of justice. However, where Keynes departs from Mill is on the question of means, rather than ends. For Mill (as for Marshall) the way to realize the kind of world which is sketched out in the essay on 'The Economic Possibilities for our Grandchildren' was through shaping human nature and character – the social science of 'ethology', as Mill terms it in his *A System of Logic* (1898). It was, of course, this branch of economic alchemy to which Marshall himself belonged. Marshall begins by making it clear that economics was not simply about money, self-interest and competition. The main characteristic of modern society, he insisted, is 'deliberateness', rather than selfishness (Marshall, 1947: 6). Economic freedom involved factors other than selfishness, such as: 'a certain independence and habit of choosing one's course for oneself, a self-reliance; a deliberation and yet a promptness of choice and judgment, and a habit of forecasting the future and of shaping one's course with reference to distant aims' (Marshall, 1947: 5). In seeking to study men in the 'ordinary business of life' the economist uses money as a way of measuring motives, but money is a very inadequate measure because there are so many motives which do not have a money value, and therefore cannot be measured. Even so, Marshall regards these motives as being important and are not to be disregarded by the economist. In making this point Marshall is at pains to stress that this means that economics, although it is focused on money as a measure of motive, is far more in keeping with the 'splendid teachings of Carlyle and Ruskin on the right aims of human endeavour and the right uses of wealth' (Marshall, 1947: 22) than is commonly supposed by its critics who believe it to be solely preoccupied with individual self-interest.

Central to Marshall's approach is the view that economics, as the study of the ordinary business of life, involves the analysis of human desires and wants. These desires and wants are composed of the pursuit of gain and self-interest, as well as other altruistic motivations. The progess of civilization is seen by Marshall as a process which involves the growth in the quantity and the *quality* of wants. There is, he thinks, a hierarchy of human wants which economic advances make possible for a wider and larger number of people to enjoy. Progress as such consisted in moving from basic human wants to the desire for higher wants such as the 'pursuit of science, literature and art for their own sake', and towards a world in which: 'Leisure is used less and less as an opportunity for mere stagnation'. In such conditions human beings experience a 'growing desire' for those *activities* which satisfy the higher wants, rather than 'indulge any sensuous craving' of lower desires (Marshall, 1947: 88–9). In other words, human wants are subject to the laws of diminishing utility and returns. The lower desires need to be balanced by the pursuit of higher wants: progress was definitely not about new material consumption, but the promotion of more 'activities'. As Marshall expressed it: 'In a healthy state new activities pioneer the way for new wants' (Marshall, 1947: 89). Human progress was not therefore something which could be *measured* as it involved far too many motives and wants which were not measurable in money terms. 'Growth' was fundamentally an ethical, rather than a material, process. Modern society made attaining a balance between the satisfaction of higher (lasting) and lower (temporary) desires more possible for more people. It made possible improvements in the 'quality and tone' of life (Marshall, 1947: 13). Economic influences on human character he compares with religion on the very first page of the *Principles*. It is, he argues, as a Christian who had lost his faith, economics which has by far the most important role in shaping human 'quality and tone'. Poverty, discussed on the second page of the book, is an evil because it means that human beings are degraded by conditions of life which 'tend to deaden the higher faculties' (Marshall, 1947: 2). Real poverty is mental and spiritual, rather than physical, just as real wealth is not to be found in the futile pursuit of consumption (lower wants) but in activities which are creative and enrich the human character. Economic prosperity was consequently the product of an 'infinte variety of motives; many of which have no direct connection with the pusuit of national wealth' (Marshall, 1947: 247). Amongst these were the moral, religious, intellectual and artistic faculties of mankind and these also needed to be fostered and cultivated if a society was to become 'wealthier'.

It is these kind of ideas which are behind what Keynes has to say about wants and human possibilities. Keynes, as is evident in his essay on 'The Economic Possibilities for our Grandchildren', envisaged that it was not too far fetched to suggest that we would reach a point wherein the 'economic problem' could be solved. By this he means that the 'lower' wants can be provided for all. Once this stage has been reached, then society can turn its attention to the real problems of human progress which involve the higher wants. These will not be of a kind which are driven by or measured in terms of money. As for Marshall, the issue becomes one of how we use leisure, rather than work to satisfy our desires for material goods whose utility will inevitably decline. In this 'post-economic' world Keynes believed that there was a possibility of greater human freedom: a liberty which was without a monetary purposiveness for many (but not all), and which had the potential for developing individuals who were more open to truth, beauty, love and friendship. This notion of progress is, as Marshall observed of his own position, very close to Ruskin and Morris and an extremely long way removed from the growth obsession which characterized the Keynesian era. Read in the context of Marshall and with his Moorean faith in mind, it becomes apparent that a more accurate account of Keynes's attitude towards 'growth' and human progress shows him to have far more in common with the ideas of Arendt, Schumacher and Tawney than the theories and policies which framed political debate throughout the 1960s and 1970s. In this regard it is particularly important for us to understand the place of the arts in Keynes's political economy. For Keynes progress was to be found in the arts of life, rather than in material consumption. It was to be found in more beautiful buildings, parks, and other public spaces and in a wider appreciation of painting, architecture, books, music, theatre and dance. The aim of economics was to increase wealth in the sense which we find it in Ruskin's *Unto This Last*: it was a vision which incorporated aesthetic and ethical considerations. Although Keynes disagreed with Marshall about what these considerations should be, he was in full agreement with his argument that 'the development of the artistic faculties of the people is in itself an aim of the very highest importance' (Marshall, 1947: 213). Art and economic development might appear rather odd bedfellows, but Keynes considered that they were two apparent opposites which had to be brought together. If we are to fully grasp Keynes's economics we must give far greater prominence to his aesthetics and ethics. Economic growth could enrich the individual by providing more opportunity for creative activities – for some that might mean in 'work' – but given the nature of the iron cage of industrial production it was unlikely that a large number of people would be in such a position to find work (for money wages) 'rewarding' in a deeper sense. Of course, Keynes understood that employment endowed human beings with a sense of purpose, security and self esteem, but he was of the view that our grandchildren would find a fuller life in developing the *arts of life*, rather than 'work'. He believed that when properly managed capitalism was more likely to provide employment, and generate the enterprise and investment necessary for realizing human possibility than any other kind of economic system. The affluent society had the potential to establish the preconditions for a society in which the more fundamental problems of human existence could occupy centre stage. However, the prospects for this brave new world for our grandchildren was tied inextricably with the problem of money and money values. Keynes's economics (like Simmel's sociology) argues for money to be regarded as a primary focus of policy and social analysis. Keynes began and largely remained, as an economist preoccupied with the problem of money. After the publication of *A Treatise on Money* he came to realize the need for a more *general* theory which took other factors into account, but the issue of money remained the main intellectual concern until his death. He had taught Marshall's theories of money and although he departed from the classical theory, he did not abandon Marshall's moral views about money. Money served as a bridge in time. It joined past, present and future and was used as a means of managing uncertainty. Keynes was a keen student of ancient money and he knew well enough that the money problem had existed since the dawn of civilization. The history and myths surrounding money, as well as the injunctions of religion, illustrated the essential dualism of lucre. Although he had a distaste for money, he also believed that it had the potential for increasing good, as well as feeding evil. Thus Keynes did not share Shaw's Wagnerian sense of doom, or the view that the love of money would inevitably lead to a *Götterdämmerung* for capitalism, out of whose destruction would be born a new age free from the curse of Rhinegold. As long as man was man the problems of money and insecurity would exist and therefore the aim of public policy ought to be geared towards finding values and institutional arrangements which could make the most productive use of money. Above all else, a society should not allow money values to predominate: the curse visted upon Midas stood as a warning to societies which did not keep the love of money under control. Hence, his view was that the most dangerous of doctrines to be loosed upon the earth was Benthamism. Money was, as Marshall had argued, important to the economist because it provided a convenient measure of human motivation. However, as Marshall was at pains to point out, there were *many* other human motives which could not be reduced to money values. For Keynes Bentham was a guilty man because he had propagated the view that all manner of human motives could be calculated and known when in reality a very small aspect of human behaviour could be subjected to a cost and benefit analysis.

In practical terms Keynes's philosophy of money suggests that it is the responsibility of policy makers to ensure that the money motive does not become the dominating criteria by which decisions are made. Money is a very inadequate measure of so much of human life that it is nonsensical immorality to think that it can serve as the basis of a universal calculus. Money was the prime material of human civilization and if mankind is to progress human beings have to learn how to use money to enlarge human freedom and creativity. Money could not be left to itself and the love of money had to be constantly watched lest it escape its bounds and in its volatile state bring tyranny, destruction and death. He believed that the filthy stuff could be used for the greater good. It was the duty of the modern state to devise policies which could serve to control and regulate money and articulate values which stressed money less and beauty, human relations, truth, love and justice more. Money for Keynes was a protean force which required long-term strategies to maintain equilibrium and release its potential for creativity and life. And yet, of course, in practice Keynesianism was quite the opposite of what Keynes actually argued and inevitably short term fiscal policies and the neglect of monetary stability proved a potent and disastrous mixture. Monetary forces, as other economic forces, are ultimately the constructions of the human mind. Thus whereas for the economic Newtonians money had to be left alone since markets could not be bucked (as the political economists argued) or abolished (as Marxists believed), Keynes held that *ideas* about a monetary economy enter into the realities of our situation. Hence, as the *General Theory* concludes, in the end, ideas change the world for good or ill. The future can be whatever we want it to be, for as Keynes said, when attacking the folly and wickedness of another age dominated by the power of 'tightly buttoned' bankers and politicians preaching the nostrums of a dismal science of self interest:

> we are not tottering to our graves. We are healthy children. We need the breath of life. There is nothing to be afraid of. On the contrary. The future holds in store for us far more wealth and economic freedom and possibilities of personal life than the past has ever afforded. There is no reason why we should not feel ourselves free to be bold, to be open, to experiment, to take action, to try the possibilities of things. (IX: 125)

Bibliography

Amariglio, J. and D.F. Ruccio (1995), 'Keynes, postmodernism, uncertainty', in S. Dow and J. Hillard (eds), *Keynes, Knowledge and Uncertainty*, Aldershot: Edward Elgar.

Amis, M. (1984), *Money, a Suicide Note,* London: Random House.

Argyris C. and D.A. Schön (1978), *Organisational Learning: A Theory of Action Perspective,* Reading, Mass.: Addison-Wesley.

Atkins, S. (1994), 'Goethe's Faust', in Goethe, *The Collected Works*, Volume 2, Princeton, New Jersey: Princeton University Press.

Beenstock, M. (1986), 'The General Theory, Secular Stagnation and the World Economy', in J. Burton (ed.), *Keynes's* General Theory *Fifty Years on: its relevance and irrelevance to modern times*, London: IEA.

Bohm, D. (1951), *Quantum Theory,* New York: Prentice-Hall.

Bohm, D. (1980), *Wholeness and the Implicate Order*, London: Routledge.

Bohr, N. (1947), 'Newton's Principles and Modern Atomic Mechanics', in *The Royal Society, Newton Tercentenary Celebrations*, Cambridge: Cambridge University Press.

Bronowski, J. (1977), *The Ascent of Man,* London: BBC Books.

Capra, F. (1983), *The Tao of Physics: An Exploration of the Parallels Between Modern Physics and Eastern Mysticism*, London: Flamingo.

Churchman, C.W. (1971), *The Design of Inquiry Systems*, New York: Basic Books.

Carabelli, A.M. (1988), *On Keynes's Method,* London: Macmillan.

Coddington, A. (1976), 'Keynesian Economics: The Search for First Principles', *Journal of Economics Literature*, **14**, 1258–73.

Coddington, A. (1982), 'Deficit Foresight: A Troublesome Theme in Keynesian Economics', *American Economic Review*, **72**, 480–87

Coddington, A. (1983), *Keynesian Economics: The Search for First Principles,* London: Allen and Unwin.

Daly, H. and J. Cobb, (1990), *For the Common Good: Redirecting the Economy towards Community, Environment and a Sustainable Future,* London: Green Print.

Dardi, M. and M. Gallegati (1992), 'Alfred Marshall on Speculation', *History of Political Economy*, **24,** 591–94.

Davidson, P. (1995), 'Uncertainty in Economics' in S. Dow and J. Hillard (eds), *Keynes, Knowledge and Uncertainty*, Aldershot: Edward Elgar.

de Leon, P. (1992), 'The democratization of the policy sciences' *Public Administration Review*, **52**, 125–29.

de Rola, S.K. (1992), *Alchemy: The Secret Art*, London: Thames and Hudson.

Dewey, J. (1927), *The Public and its Problems*, New York: Holt.

Dobbs, B.J.T. (1975), *The Foundations of Newton's Alchemy or the Hunting of Greene Lyon*, Cambridge: Cambridge University Press.

Donnington, R. (1974), *Wagner's 'Ring' and its Symbols: the Music and the Myth*, London: Faber.

Douglas, M. (1995),*Purity and Danger: An analysis of the concepts of pollution and taboo*, London: Routledge.

Dow, A. and S.C. Dow (1985), 'Animal Spirits and Rationality', in T. Lawson and M. Pesaran (eds), *Keynes' Economics: Methodological Issues*, London: Croom Helm.

Dow, S.C. (1985),. *Macroeconomic Thought: A Methodological Approach*, Oxford: Blackwell.

Dow, S.C. (1990), 'Beyond Dualism', *Cambridge Journal of Economics*, **14**, 143–57.

Edinger, E.F. (1990), *Goethe's Faust: Notes for a Jungian Commentary*, Toronto: Inner City Books.

Etzioni, A. (1988), *The Moral Dimension: Towards a New Economics*, New York: The Free Press.

Etzioni, A. (1993), *The Spirit of Community*, New York: Touchstone Books.

Fabricius, J. (1994), *Alchemy: The Medieval Alchemists and their Royal Art*, London: Diamond Books.

Ferenczi, S. (1926), *Further Contributions to the Theory and Techniques of Psychoanalysis*, London: Knopf.

Ferenczi, S. (1956), *Sex in Psychoanalysis*, New York: Dover.

Figala, K., J. Harrison and U. Petzold (1992), 'De scriptoribus chemicis: sources for the establishment of Isaac Newton's alchemical library', in P.M. Harman and A.E. Shapiro (eds), *The Investigation of Difficult Things: Essays on Newton and the history of the exact sciences in honour of D.T. Whiteside*, Cambridge: Cambridge University Press.

Firth, R. (1970), 'Reason and Unreason in Human Beliefs' in Max Marwick (ed.), *Witchcraft and Sorcery*, Harmondsworth: Penguin.

Fischer, F. (1995), *Evaluating Public Policy*, Chicago: Nelson-Hall.

Fischer, F. and J. Forrester (eds) (1993), *The Argumentative Turn in Policy Analysis and Planning*, London: UCL Press.

Fitzgibbons, A. (1988), *Keynes's Vision: A New Political Economy*, Oxford: Clarendon.

Fitzgibbons, A. (1991), 'The significance of Keynes's idealism', in B.W.

Bateman and J.B. Davis (eds), *Keynes and Philosophy: Essays on the Origin of Keynes' Thought*, Aldershot: Edward Elgar.

Frankel, S.H. (1977), *Money: Two Philosophies. The Conflict of Trust and Authority*, Oxford: Blackwell.

Frazer, J.G. (1995), *The Golden Bough: A study in magic and ritual*, London: Macmillan.

Freud, S. (1908), 'Character and Anal Eroticism', in vol. 7, Penguin Freud Library, Harmondsworth: Penguin.

Freud, S. (1974), *Introductory Lectures on Psychoanalysis*, vol. 12, Penguin Freud Library, Harmondsworth: Penguin.

Freud, S. (1977), *On Sexuality*, vol. 7, Penguin Freud Library, Harmondsworth: Penguin.

Freud, S. (1985), *Art and Literature*, vol. 14, Penguin Freud Library, Harmondsworth: Penguin.

Friedman A.J. and C.C. Donley (1985), *Einstein as Myth and Muse*, Cambridge: Cambridge University Press.

Friedman, M. (1986), 'Keynes's Political Legacy', in J. Burton (ed.), *Keynes' General Theory Fifty Years on: its relevance and irrelevance to modern times*, London: IEA.

Furnham, A. and A. Lewis (1986), *The Economic Mind: The Social Psychology of Economic Behaviour*, London: Wheatsheaf Books.

Gay, P. (1988), *Freud, A Life For Our Times,* London: Dent.

Gilchrist, C. (1991), *The Elements of Alchemy*, Longmead, Shaftesbury, Dorset: Element Books.

Goethe, J.W. (1994), *Faust*, edited and translated by Stuart Atkins, New Jersey: Princeton University Press.

Gray, R. (1952), *Goethe The Alchemist*, Cambridge: Cambridge University Press.

Gray, R. (1967), *Goethe: A Critical Introduction*, Cambridge: Cambridge University Press.

Griffiths, P. (1985), 'Modern Times', in S. Sadie and A. Latham (eds), *The Cambridge Music Guide*, Cambridge: Cambridge University Press.

Haeffner, M. (1994), *Dictionary of Alchemy*, London: Aquarian.

Hansen, A.H. (1953), *A Guide to Keynes*, New York: McGraw Hill.

Hardie, J. (1980), 'The Practical Magician: A Review of J.M. Keynes, "The Collected Writings", Vol XXV', *Times Literary Supplement*, 20 June, 1980, p. 689

Harrod, R.F. (1966), *The Life of John Maynard Keynes,* London: Macmillan.

Hayek, F.A. (1944), *The Road to Serfdom*, London: George Routledge and Sons.

Hayek, F.A. (1978), *New Studies in Philosophy, Politics, Economics and the History of Ideas,* Chicago: University of Chicago Press.

Helburn, S. (1991), 'Burke and Keynes', in B.W. Bateman and J.B. Davis (eds), *Keynes and Philosophy: Essays on the Origin of Keynes's Thought*, Aldershot: Edward Elgar.

Hendry, D (1993), *Econometrics: Science or Alchemy?* Oxford: Blackwell.

Hession, C.H. (1984), *John Maynard Keynes: A personal biography of the man who revolutionized capitalism and the way we live*, New York: Macmillan.

Hill, P. and R. Keynes (eds) (1989), *Lydia and Maynard: The letters of John Maynard Keynes and Lydia Lopokova*, New York: Scribners.

Hindle, M. (1992), 'Introduction', in Mary Shelley, *Frankenstein*, Harmondsworth: Penguin Books.

Hirsch, F. (1977), *Social Limits to Growth*, London: Routledge and Kegan Paul.

Holmyard, E.J. (1957), *Alchemy*, New York: Dover.

Hudson, W.H. (1918), *Long Ago and Far Away: a history of my early life*, London: J.M. Dent and Sons.

Hume, D. (1975), *Enquiries Concerning Human Understanding and Concerning the Principles of Morals*, Oxford: Clarendon Press.

Jacobi, J. (1988), 'Paracelsus: his life and work', in Paracelsus.

Jeans, J. (1981), *Physics and Philosophy*, New York: Dover.

Jung, C.G. (1968), *Psychology and Alchemy* (Vol. 12, Collected Works), London: Routledge.

Jung, C.G. (1970), *Mysterium Coniuctionis* (Vol. 14, Collected Works), London: Routledge.

Kerr, C. (1969), *Marshall, Marx and Modern Times*, Cambridge: Cambridge University Press.

Keynes, J.M. (1971–89), *The Collected Writings*, Vols 1 to 30, Macmillan and Cambridge University Press for the Royal Economic Society, London.

I, *Indian Currency and Finance.*

II, *The Economic Consequences of the Peace.*

III, *A Revision of the Treaty.*

IV, *A Tract on Monetary Reform.*

V, *A Treatise on Money: I The Pure Theory of Money.*

VI, *A Treatise on Money: II The Applied Theory of Money.*

VII, *The General Theory of Employment Interest and Money.*

VIII, *A Treatise on Probability.*

IX, *Essays in Persuasion.*

X, *Essays in Biography.*

XI, *Economic Articles and Correspondence (academic).*

XII, *Economic Articles and Correspondence (investment and editorial).*

XIII, *The General Theory and After: Part I, Preparation.*

XIV, *The General Theory and After: Part II, Defence and Development.*

XV, *Activities 1906–14: India and Cambridge.*

XVI *Activities 1914–19: The Treasury and Versailles.*

XVII, *Activities 1920–2 : Treaty Revision and Reconstruction.*

XVIII, *Activities 1922–32: The End of Reparations.*

XIX, *Activities 1922–9: The Return to Gold and Industrial Policy.*

XX, *Activities 1929–31: Rethinking Employment and Unemployment Policies.*

XXI, *Activities 1931–9: World Crises and Policies in Britain and America.*

XXII, *Activities 1939–45: Internal War Finance.*

XXIII, *Activities 1940–3: External War Finance.*

XXIV, *Activities 1944–6: Transition to Peace.*

XXV, *Activities 1940–4: Shaping the Post-War World: The Clearing Union.*

XXVI, *Activities 1944–6: Shaping The Post-War World: Bretton Woods and Reparations.*

XXVII, *Actitivies 1940–6 Shaping the Post-War World: Employment and Commodities.*

XXVIII, *Social Political and Literary Writings.*

XXIX, *The General Theory and After: A Supplement to Vols XIII and XIV.*

XXX, *Index and Bibliography.*

Keynes, M. (ed.) (1975), *Essays on John Maynard Keynes*, Cambridge: Cambridge University Press.

Klamer, A. (1995), 'The conception of modernism in economics: Samuelson, Keynes and Harrod', in S. Dow and J. Hillard (eds), *Keynes, Knowledge and Uncertainty*, Aldershot: Edward Elgar.

Koyré, A. (1965), *Newtonian Studies*, Pheonix Book: University of Chicago Press.

Lane, R.E. (1991), *The Market Experience*, Cambridge: Cambridge University Press.

Lasswell, H.D. (1951), 'The policy orientation', in D. Lerner and H.D. Lasswell (eds), *The Policy Sciences,* Stanford: Stanford University Press.

Lindblom, C.A. (1990), *Inquiry and Change: the troubled attempt to understand and shape society,* New Haven: Yale University Press.

Locke, J. (1995), *An Essay Concerning Human Understanding,* edited and abridged by J.W. Yolton, London: Everyman, Dent.

Lyotard, J.F. (1984), *The Postmodern Condition: A Report on Knowledge,* Minneapolis: University of Minnesota Press.

Malthus, T.R. (1958), *Essay on the Principle of Population*, Two Vols, London: Dent, Everyman.

Malthus, T.R. (1968), *Principles of Political Economy*, New York: Augustus Kelley.

Marshall, A. (1885), *The Present Position of Economics*, London: Macmillan.

Marshall, A. (1919), *Industry and Trade,* London: Macmillan.

Marshall, A. (1923), 'The Future of the Working Classes', in Pigou (ed.) (1956), *Memorials of Alfred Marshall*, New York: Kelley and Millman.

Marshall, A. (1926), *Official Papers of Alfred Marshall*, London: Macmillan.

Marshall, A. (1947), *Principles of Economics*, London: Macmillan.

Marshall, A. (1964), *Elements of Economics*, London: Macmillan.

Marx, K. (1970), *Selected Writings on Sociology and Social Philosophy*, edited by T.B. Bottomore and M. Rubel, Harmondsworth: Penguin.

McKenna, E.J. and D.C. Zannoni (1993), 'Philosophical foundations of Post-Keynesian Economics', *Journal of Post Keynesian Economics,* **15,** 395–407.

Midgley, M. (1992), *Science as Salvation: A Modern Myth and its Meaning,* London: Routledge.

Mill, J.S. (1898), *A System of Logic*, London: Longmans Green.

Mill, J.S. (1924), *Autobiography*, New York: Columbia University Press.

Mini, P.V. (1991), *Keynes, Bloomsbury and The General Theory*, London: Macmillan.

Mini, P.V. (1994), *John Maynard Keynes: a study in the psychology of original work*, London: Macmillan.

Moggridge, D.E. (1988), 'Foreward', in A.M. Carabelli, *On Keynes's Method*, London: Macmillan.

Moggridge, D.E. (1992), *Maynard Keynes: An Economist's Biography*, London: Routledge.

Moore, G.E. (1903), *Principia Ethica*, Cambridge: Cambridge University Press.

Munby, A.N.L. (1951), 'The Keynes Collection of the Works of Sir Isaac Newton at Kings College, Cambridge, *Notes and Records of the Royal Society of London*, Vol. 10, 1950–51, pp. 40–50.

Munby, A.N.L. (1975), 'The book collector', in M. Keynes (ed.), *Essays on John Maynard Keynes*, Cambridge: Cambridge University Press.

Nataf, A. (1994), *The Dictionary of the Occult*, Ware: Wordsworth Books.

Needham, J. (1971), *The Refiner's Fire; the enigma of alchemy in east and west*. Second J.D. Bernal Lecture, University of London: Birkbeck College.

O'Donnell, R.M. (1989), *Keynes: Philosophy, Economics and Politics*, London: Routledge.

Paracelsus (1988), *Selected Writings* (edited by Jolande Jacobi), Bollingen Series XXVIII, Princeton, New Jersey: Princeton University Press.

Parsons, W. (1983), 'Keynes and the politics of ideas', *History of Political Thought,* **4**(2): 367–92.

Parsons, W. (1985), 'Was Keynes Kuhnian: Keynes and the idea of theoretical revolutions', *British Journal of Political Science,* **15**: 451–71.

Parsons, W. (1995), *Public Policy: The Theory and Practice of Policy Analysis*, Aldershot: Edward Elgar.

Pigou, A.C. (1936), 'Mr Keynes's *General Theory of Employment Interest and Money, Economica*, III (May).

Prigigone, I. and G. Nicolis (1989), *Exploring Complexity*, New York: Freeman.

Prigigone, I. and I. Stengers (1984), *Order Out of Chaos: Man's New Dialogue with Nature*, London: Heinemann.

Raphael, A. (1965), *Goethe and the Philosophers' Stone: symbolical patterns in 'The Parable' and the Second Part of 'Faust'*, London: Routledge and Kegan Paul.

Reisman, D. (1986), *The Economics of Alfred Marshall*, London: Macmillan.

Robertson, D.N. (1931), 'Mr Keynes's Theory of Money', *Economic Journal*, September 1931, pp. 395–411.

Robinson, J.V. (1937), *Introduction to the Theory of Employment*, London: Macmillan.

Robinson, J.V. (1969), *The Accumulation of Capital*, London: Macmillan.

Rondinelli, D. (1993), *Development Projects as Experiments: an adaptive approach to development administration*, London: Routledge.

Royal Society, The (1947), *Newton Tercentenary Celebrations, 15–19 July 1947*, The Royal Society, Cambridge: Cambridge University Press.

Ruskin, J. (1907), *Unto This Last*, London: George Routledge and Sons.

Russell, B. (1970), *An Outline of Philosophy*, London: Unwin.

Russell, B. (1994), *An ABC of Relativity*, London: Routledge.

Rymes, T.K. (1989), *Keynes's Lectures 1932–35: Notes of A Representative Student*, London: Macmillan.

Schwartz-Salant, N. (ed.) (1995), *C.G. Jung on Alchemy*, London: Routledge.

Shackle, G.L.S. (1972), *Epistemics and Economics*, Cambridge: Cambridge University Press.

Shaw, G.B. (1923), *The Perfect Wagnerite*, London: Constable.

Shaw, G.B. (1985), *Last Plays*, Harmondsworth: Penguin.

Shell, M. (1978), *The Economy of Literature*, Baltimore: The John Hopkins University Press.

Silberer, H. (1971), *Hidden Symbolism of Alchemy and the Occult Arts*, New York: Dover.

Simmel, G. (1990), *The Philosophy of Money* (edited by D. Frisby and translated by T. Bottomore and D. Frisby), second edition, London: Routledge.

Skidelsky, R. (1975), 'The Reception of the Keynesian Revolution', in M. Keynes (ed.), *Essays on John Maynard Keynes*, Cambridge: Cambridge University Press.

Skidelsky, R. (1983), *John Maynard Keynes: Hopes Betrayed, 1883–1920*, London: Macmillan.

Skidelsky, R. (1992), *John Maynard Keynes: The Economist as Saviour,* London: Macmillan.

Soros, G. (1994), *The Alchemy of Finance: Reading the Mind of the Market,* New York: John Wiley and Sons.

Spargo, P.E. (1992), 'Sotheby's Keynes and Yahuda – the 1936 sale of Newton's manuscripts', in P.M. Harman and A.E. Shapiro (eds), *The Investigation of Difficult Things: Essays on Newton and the history of the exact sciences in honour of D.T. Whiteside,* Cambridge: Cambridge University Press.

Spencer, S. (1971), *Space, Time and Structure in the Modern Novel,* New York: New York University Press.

Stewart, M. (1967), *Keynes and After,* Harmondsworth: Penguin.

Thomas, K. (1973), *Religion and the Decline in Magic,* Harmondsworth: Penguin.

Tippett, M. (1995), 'The Mask of Time', in Meirion Bowen (ed.) *Tippett on Music,* Oxford: Oxford University Press.

van der Heijden, K. (1996), *Scenarios: The Art of Strategic Conversation,* Chichester: John Wiley.

von Franz, M.-L. (1990), 'Science and the unconscious', in C.G. Jung (ed.), *Man and his Symbols,* Harmondsworth: Arkana, Penguin.

Wack, P. (1985a), 'Scenarios, uncharted waters ahead', *Harvard Business Review,* Sep–Oct 1985, 73–90.

Wack, P. (1985b), 'Scenarios, shooting the rapids', *Harvard Business Review,* Nov–Dec 1985, 131–142.

Weber, M. (1976), *The Protestant Ethic and the Spirit of Capitalism,* translated by Talcott Parsons, London: Allen and Unwin.

Westfall, R.S. (1972), 'Newton and the Hermetic Tradition', in A.G. Debus (ed.), *Science, Medicine and Society,* London: Heinemann.

Westfall, R.S. (1975), 'The role of Alchemy in Newton's Career', in M.L Righini Bonelli and W.R. Shea (eds), *Reason, Experiment and Mysticism,* London: Macmillan.

Westfall, R.S. (1980), *Never at Rest: a biography of Isaac Newton,* Cambridge: Cambridge University Press.

Westfall, R.S. (1984), 'Newton and Alchemy', in B. Vickers (ed.), *Occult and Scientific Mentalities in the Renaissance,* Cambridge: Cambridge University Press.

Westfall, R.S. (1994), *The Life of Isaac Newton,* Cambridge: Cambridge University Press.

Winch, D. (1970), 'Introduction', in D. Winch (ed.), *J.S. Mill, Principles of Political Economy,* Harmondsworth: Penguin.

Winch, D. (1987), *Malthus,* Oxford: Oxford University Press.

Winslow, E.G. (1986), 'Keynes and Freud: Psychoanalysis and Keynes's

Account of the Animal Spirits of Capitalism', *Social Research*, Winter, 549–78.

Winslow, E.G. (1989), 'John Maynard Keynes's Poetical Economy', *Journal of Psychohistory,* Fall, 179–94.

Winslow, E.G. (1990), 'Bloomsbury, Freud and Vulgar Passions', *Social Research*, Winter, 785–819.

Wood, J.C. (ed.) (1983), *John Maynard Keynes: Critical Assessments*, 4 Vols, London: Croom Helm.

Yolton, J.W. (1993), *A Locke Dictionary*, Oxford: Blackwell.

Index

Printed by Printforce, United Kingdom